W9-AUJ-547

ROSEWOOD
CONFIDENTIAL

THE UNOFFICIAL COMPANION TO

Pretty Little Liars

Liv Spencer

ECW Press

Copyright © Liv Spencer, 2012

Published by ECW Press
2120 Queen Street East, Suite 200, Toronto, Ontario, Canada M4E 1E2
416-694-3348 / info@ecwpress.com

All rights reserved. No part of this publication may be reproduced, stored in a retrieval system, or transmitted in any form by any process — electronic, mechanical, photocopying, recording, or otherwise — without the prior written permission of the copyright owners and ECW Press. The scanning, uploading, and distribution of this book via the Internet or via any other means without the permission of the publisher is illegal and punishable by law. Please purchase only authorized electronic editions, and do not participate in or encourage electronic piracy of copyrighted materials. Your support of the author's rights is appreciated.

Library and Archives Canada Cataloguing in Publication

Spencer, Liv
Rosewood confidential : the unofficial companion to Pretty little liars / Liv Spencer.

ISBN 978-1-77041-095-4
also issued as 978-1-77090-217-6 (PDF) and 978-1-77090-218-3 (ePub)

1. Pretty little liars (Television program). 2. Television actors and actresses—United States—Biography. 3. Shepard, Sara, 1977- Pretty little liars. I. Title.

PN1992.77.P645S64 2012   791.45'72   C2011-906984-9

Cover design: Rachel Ironstone
Interior design and typesetting: Melissa Kaita

Thanks to Jennifer Knoch and Crissy Calhoun — you're always better off with a really good lie. xoxo Liv

Second printing, July 2012 at United Graphics Incorporated in the United States.

Images Copyright: *Front cover photos:* Kristian Dowling/PictureGroup; *back cover photo:* © Roberto A. Sanchez/iStockPhoto.com. Interior photos: Scott Gries/PictureGroup: 29; Evan Agostini/PictureGroup: 33; Dave Proctor/startraksphoto.com: 36; Michael Simon/startraksphoto.com: 39; Tony DiMaio/ startraksphoto.com: 43, 46, 49, 72, 102; Sara De Boer/startraksphoto.com: 56; Greg Weir: 62, 132, 176, 184, 197; MPI26/Mediapunch Inc.: 68; MPI24/MediaPunch Inc.: 82; MPI20/MediaPunch Inc.: 88; Scott Kirkland/PictureGroup: 111; Vince Bucci/PictureGroup: 118; Amanda Schwab/Startraksphoto.com: 123; Kristian Dowling/PictureGroup: 140, 258; MPI01/MediaPunch Inc.: 144; Albert Michael/startraksphoto. com: 148; Kurt Thomas Hunt: 158; John Salangsang/Shooting Star: 165; Adam Rose/ABC Family via Getty Images: 171; Kyle Rover/startraksphoto.com: 194; Frank Micelotta/Fox/PictureGroup: 206; Alex Berliner/abimages via AP Images: 220; James Colburn: 229; Michael Williams/startraksphoto.com: 234; Gregg DeGuire/PictureGroup: 240; Sthanlee B. Mirador/Shooting Star: 248. *Photo section:* Eike Schroter/ ABC Family via Getty Images: 1; MPI01/MediaPunch Inc.: 2; MPI20/MediaPunch Inc.: 3; MPI21/ MediaPunch Inc.: 4; Bruce Birmelin/ABC Family via Getty Images: 5; Adam Rose/ABC Family via Getty Images: 6; MPI26/MediaPunch Inc.: 7; Charley Gallay/WireImage: 8.

The publication of *Rosewood Confidential* has been generously supported by the Government of Ontario through the Ontario Book Publishing Tax Credit. We also acknowledge the financial support of the Government of Canada through the Canada Book Fund for our publishing activities. The marketing of this book was made possible with the support of the Ontario Media Development Corporation.

Canadä

Contents

Season 2

Introduction

A seemingly perfect small town, four beautiful former besties with heavy secrets, and a sassy, all-knowing text message from beyond the grave. With a hook like that, *Pretty Little Liars* was already a hot property when it made the leap to the small screen, with legions of dedicated fans thanks to Sara Shepard's best-selling book series. Executive producer I. Marlene King and her team did what many fans would have thought impossible: they improved upon the original, and in the process created a runaway success that attracted an audience well beyond the core teen demographic.

There's a lot to love in *Pretty Little Liars*, as its devoted fanbase attests, with our record-breaking tweets, passionate shippers, and constant speculation on the show's central mysteries. But the reason we relate to it goes deeper, beyond the fashion, suspense, or the mischievous glee that comes from adding "bitches" to the end of any sentence. Even with its surreal storylines and impeccably polished cast, *Pretty Little Liars* gets its emotional core from very real experiences.

While not many of us have been bullied by someone posing as a dead friend, we have been bullied, we have lost friends, we've kept secrets, we've felt isolated and insecure. *PLL* go-to director Norman Buckley explained it well, noting that even at its most dramatic, the show is still realistic: "I think it's about those feelings of anxiety and lack of self-worth and the pain of trying to define yourself in adolescence. And it's that sense of anxiety that something bad is going to happen. . . . I think that's where *Pretty Little Liars* so magnificently clicks into the teenage zeitgeist: in this day and age, I'm sure every teenager out there is feeling that sense."

This companion guide celebrates everything that makes *PLL* must-watch TV. I begin with background on Sara Shepard, her book series, and ABC Family's adaptation, and then share the stories of the cast members who made *PLL*'s beloved characters their own.

Each episode of seasons 1 and 2 gets a detailed analysis of some of the major themes, character developments, and noteworthy events, followed by these categories:

HIGHLIGHT Whether it's an epic kiss, a tear-jerking scene, a great one-liner, or a big reveal, this is the moment you'll want to talk or tweet about immediately.

EXTRA CREDIT For all the Spencers out there who want an A+ in *Pretty Little Liars*, here you'll find explanations of references and details worth noticing.

SLIP UPS Nobody's perfect, not even in Rosewood. This category outlines inconsistencies and goofs.

BACK TO THE BOOKS Want to know where the small screen adaptation departs from Sara Shepard's novels? You'll find the comparison between *PLL*-verses here.

PLL IRL The fictional world of Rosewood is left behind, and here you'll find interesting details, stories, and reactions from the cast and crew about making the show.

Qs & A Track the mysteries of *PLL* here with questions and clues about Ali's death, A, and the hooded, glove-wearing saboteur that I've nicknamed the Gloved Wonder.

Make sure you watch (or rewatch!) an episode *before* reading its corresponding guide — you will encounter spoilers for that episode (but not for anything that comes later). And there are plenty of exciting extras in the pages that follow, like actor biographies, in-depth explorations of literary and film references, and details on how the show is made.

And after you've read *Rosewood Confidential*, you'll have all the info to fit right in with the Pretty Little Liars — so read on, bitches.

— *L*

Building a Mystery
SARA SHEPARD'S KILLER SERIES

Before there was a mysterious text message from beyond the grave, before there were four former friends separated by secrets, before Rosewood was built and rebuilt on the Warner Brothers back lot, Sara Shepard had only a blinking cursor but she conjured a world of decadence and deception, best friends and betrayal, and created a series that would sell millions of books and become a veritable pop culture phenomenon.

Sara grew up in a family that valued the arts, and she recalled, "My mother constantly encouraged my sister and me to read, draw, write, and be creative." The author-to-be started honing her storytelling skills at a young age, tapping out tales on her father's computer by the time she was in fifth grade. Looking back, the author joked, "Of course, I would be all amped up to write chapter one . . . but would have no idea what to do with chapter two. I wasn't great at plotting back then." Though she was still a couple of decades away from being a bestselling author, Sara did have an early taste of literary success: in fifth grade she won second prize in a library contest for a short story called "Quizzles."

The budding author continued to write throughout high school, where she showed such promise that her English teacher told her she could skip the essay component and focus on writing fiction instead! But following her inner Spencer Hastings instead of her inner Aria Montgomery, Sara refused the offer. Looking back, the author lamented, "Like an idiot, I said *no*. I wanted to write the themes about, I don't know, *The Fountainhead*. *The Scarlet Letter*. What was *wrong* with me?"

In her undergraduate studies at New York University, Sara started out studying biology but admitted, "[I] was afraid of my teachers and fellow bio majors so I switched to English, where everyone was laid-back and happy and talked about books all day." During her college years she got to combine her love for fashion and writing when she interned at *Elle* magazine, though she didn't get to put many words to paper. Sara remembered, "Like the girls on *The Hills*, it involved a lot of folding, steaming, and basically doing the work no one else wanted to do." She found a better fit, and some actual writing and editing experience, at Time Inc.

Sara went on to real journalism work after graduating, and reporting satisfied her writerly side for a few years, until the events of 9/11 forced her to look at her life to date. "As lots of people did after September 11, I decided I was going to make the most of my time," explained the author. She decided to go back to school, enrolling in the MFA program at Brooklyn College in 2002. There she studied under celebrated writers like Michael Cunningham (winner of the Pulitzer Prize for his Virginia Woolf–inspired novel, *The Hours*).

Spending her days honing her skills, writing, rewriting, and workshopping, Sara decided she might be ready for some paid work. Her sister worked at Alloy, a company that originates creative properties that cross platforms like *Gossip Girl*, *The Vampire Diaries*, *Sisterhood of the Traveling Pants*, and now, *Pretty Little Liars*. So, to get her foot in the door there, our ambitious author crashed the company Christmas party! This holiday caper paid off, and Sara started doing freelance work for Alloy. One of her earliest projects was ghostwriting the Samurai Girl books, a six-novel YA series about a girl who is married into the Yakuza (the

Japanese Mafia) and must train as a samurai to protect the people she loves. In 2008, the books were adapted into a miniseries for ABC Family, but by that point Sara was already hard at work on a series of her own that would later become the network's hottest property.

With the Samurai Girl novels, Sara had proven herself to Alloy as a pen-for-hire. But when the company discovered she had grown up along the Pennsylvania Main Line (the towns along the train route out of Philadelphia) and knew a thing or two about the lives of the east coast elite, they realized they might have a good match for a new idea they'd been developing, one they described as "*Desperate Housewives* for teens."

Though the author had never seen an episode of that hit ABC series, she got the concept right away. Once she started thinking about her glossy suburban backdrop, she realized how well it would work: "Main Line Pennsylvania is full of very idyllic sights — old converted barns, beautiful green fields, gorgeous homes, a lot of old battlegrounds, and tons of venerable private schools — and I liked mixing those details in with the main characters' flawed lives. The point is that *everyone's* lives are flawed in one way or another, no matter where you live."

After meetings with editors and execs, in what Josh Bank, east coast president of Alloy, calls "intellectual potluck," Alloy had the concept, but they needed someone to bring it to life, and that's where Sara came in. She joined in the brainstorming process, fleshing out the mystery and those four little liars. They wondered, "What happens if some girls start getting weird texts?" Then the missing friend came into the picture. Sara explained, "Then I started to develop what this friend could be like and the secrets that she would have on them. It all kind of came together pretty slowly. I did think about the characters a lot right away and their secrets and things like that. As far as what the series has become, I mean, I don't think I knew from the start that it would be such a mystery with such a backstory and so much tragedy."

Turns out, Sara wasn't just revisiting her high school stomping grounds, but her high school self. Sara went back to her teen journals, noting, "I would reread them a lot and just kind of see what I was thinking and what mattered a lot." She ended up putting a bit of her teen self in each character. She says she was probably most like artsy Aria: "She's kind of not really interested in being popular and she just wants to be herself. I think at least the last couple of years of high school I was a lot like that. I identified with her with how all she really wants is just to get out of this little town and the people are all the same." (Sara is careful to specify that she didn't engage in any steamy extracurriculars, though Ezra Fitz is named after someone she went to elementary school with.) Like Spencer, she was a type-A overachiever. Like Emily, she swam on her high school team. And like Hanna, she was into fashion, and also had what she calls "eating issues," explaining that it wasn't "bulimia, and not exactly anorexia, but I certainly used food and exercise as control. It was a lonely time of my life, but as I know *so many* people go through it, I wanted to make sure one of my characters struggled with it."

Balancing a complex mystery as well as the personal stories of the four protagonists isn't easy, but with her editors' help, Sara worked out a system that worked for her. "It's definitely like putting together a puzzle," said the scribe. "I outline each book very carefully. Usually, I first think about what my aim for the book is concerning the overarching Alison DiLaurentis mystery: what we know at the beginning, and what we'll know — or think — at the end. From there, I think about the prologue, which is always a shared memory from the past, usually a scene involving Ali. Each girl takes away something a little different from the prologue, and I want to thread this through the book and use the girls' perspectives to get a little bit closer to the real truth about what happened to Ali. And then I think about the girls' front stories — often having to do with love, fractured friendships, or family troubles — and how A might use their problems to his or her best advantage. It's difficult to keep straight, but it's my favorite and most rewarding part of writing the series." Beyond that, the author's secret to success is simple: she writes every day, even when she doesn't have a deadline. Luckily for Sara, it's a labor of love: "For me, writing is something I have to do . . . if I don't, I start to get a little crazy."

The first book, *Pretty Little Liars*, was published by HarperTeen in October 2006, and the tantalizing premise and stylish neon cover caught the eye of readers and reviewers alike. *Publishers Weekly* observed, "Readers will certainly find enough drama to keep the pages turning . . . and they will no doubt have fun piecing together who and what could be behind those bizarre messages. This is clique lit with a mystery twist." *Library Journal* noted, "Shepard writes a suspenseful page-turner that will have teens thirsting for more." The second book, *Flawless*, was out just a few months later in March, and by April 2007 had climbed to #3 on the *New York Times* children's bestseller list (later books would hit the #1 spot). By August 2007, the series made it onto the series bestseller list, keeping company with Harry Potter, the Twilight saga, and other heavy hitters.

Sara's editor Farrin Jacobs gave her take on the books' astronomical success to *Publishers Weekly*: "You're watching people do something you would never do. It's fun to see something happen to them. There are a lot of consequences in these books. It's definitely 'peel back a veneer on the perfect life and look at what lurks beneath that.'"

Alloy had started the series thinking there would be four books. Then in August 2007 the series was extended to eight, and it seemed the timing would be perfect: the final book, *Wanted*, would be released in time with the debut of the TV series. But with a dedicated fanbase, 2.4 million books in print, and book sales that went up 39 percent with the success of the TV show, no one was ready to say goodbye to Rosewood, so Sara agreed to write another four books.

Thanks to the success of the TV show, which takes different directions than the books did, the author now has a new challenge: satisfying fans of the TV show who have become attached to certain characters and want to see more of them in the books. Although she does see the two worlds of *PLL* as "parallel universes" she admits she's being influenced by the show and would like to please her fans. "I've started thinking about how to incorporate some of those popular characters from the show back into the books. Unfortunately, I still haven't figured out a way to bring Toby back to life that isn't completely soap opera–ish. But Ezra is back in *Ruthless,* book 10. I never intended to bring him back, but readers demanded it!"

Though she has a hot property on her hands with *PLL,* Sara hasn't limited her writing to the murder and intrigue of Rosewood. She's published two novels for adults to date. The first, 2009's *The Visibles,* is the story of a young woman exploring family ties, both biological and emotional. *Publishers Weekly* called it "tightly constructed and captivating" and "complicated, rewarding, and full of heart." Released in October 2011, her second adult fiction offering, *Everything We Ever Wanted,* is an exploration of the ripples caused by allegations of scandal in a wealthy Pennsylvanian family. *Kirkus* called it "a fine character study on the repressed lives of the American elite."

But Sara hasn't forgotten her teen writing roots, and between her two adult books, on December 8, 2010, she released *The Lying Game,* the first in a new four-book series about twins separated at birth. The new series was also well received, with *Library Journal* declaring the first volume "a thrilling mystery with just the right doses of romance and danger," and *Publishers Weekly* praising it as "a fun and fast-moving mystery." Like *PLL, The Lying Game* was brought to the small screen by ABC Family, and it's been steadily picking up steam.

Looking ahead, Sara's finishing the third *Pretty Little Liars* cycle and the first of *The Lying Game,* and hopefully has more adult books percolating in her mind. The driven yet modest author is proud of everything she's done, but maintains, "Hopefully my greatest accomplishment is yet to come."

PRETTY LITTLE LIARS CHEAT SHEET

Pretty Little Liars (October 2006): Three years have passed since four besties were divided by the disappearance of their friend Alison. The former friends have fallen apart, but texts from an anonymous "A," who seems to know all their secrets, and the discovery of Ali's body force them back together.
A-bomb: "I'm still here, bitches. And I know everything."

Flawless (March 2007): A continues to taunt the girls, threatening to expose their secrets, and ultimately lashes out by exposing Byron's affair to Ella and luring Hanna to the Foxy dance, where her recent ex, Sean, is putting the moves on Aria. The Jenna Thing is on everyone's minds, but they decide to keep it out of the murder investigation. Spencer has Toby pegged as A, but by the end he's eliminated as a suspect.
A-bomb: "P.S. Wondering who I am, aren't you? I'm closer than you think."

Perfect (August 2007): A outs Emily to her parents, who put her in a "gay away" program. Aria is kicked out of her house and moves in with Sean, but hooks up with Ezra. Hanna's popularity has taken a downturn, but she soon has a bigger problem thanks to A. With the help of a psychologist, Spencer remembers something important — and incriminating — about the night of Ali's death.
A-bomb: "She knew too much."

Unbelievable (May 2008): Aria connects with Jenna, but can't get her to share what she knows about Ali's death. Spencer has a run-in with A that only one of them comes out of alive. The girls are ready to move on, but Emily catches a glimpse of an Ali lookalike and realizes they may never be free of her.

A-bomb: "Mirror, mirror on the wall, who's the naughtiest of them all? You told. So you're next."

Wicked (November 2008): A brand new A emerges, and Ali's murder is as unsolved as ever, with the prime suspect denying the charges. Emily questions her sexuality again. Spencer starts to question whether she's a Hastings after all. Hanna and her stepsister feud over Queen Bee status. Aria ends up in a bizarre love triangle with her mom. And a dead body disappears from the woods.

A-bomb: "Honestly, bitches . . . did you really think I'd let you off that easy? You haven't gotten nearly what you deserve. And I can't wait to give it to you. Mwah!"

Killer (June 2009): Emily has boy drama, Hanna and Kate compete for Mike Montgomery's affection, and Spencer gets hustled. Aria falls for Jason, but the girls suspect that he, along with Officer Wilden, was involved in Ali's murder. The girls have another brush with death, and Aria saves someone who looks an awful lot like Ali.

A-bomb: "One of these things doesn't belong. Figure it out quickly . . . or else."

Heartless (January 2010): Hanna gets sent to a psych clinic, Spencer learns a dark family secret, Emily lives among the Amish, and Aria gets clues about Ali's death from a psychic. The girls are rounded up by the police, suspected of conspiring to murder Ali, but they're let off thanks to the arrest of a new suspect.

A-bomb: "All those clues I've given you are right, Little Liar — just not in the way you think. But since I'm such a nice person, here's another hint. There's a major cover up taking place right under your nose . . . and someone close to you has all the answers."

Wanted (June 2010): Aria, Spencer, Hanna, and Emily meet someone whom Ali kept secret. The girls are lured to the Hastings' house in the Poconos, which is set ablaze by A with the foursome trapped inside. They escape and assume that their torment is over, but the end of the book promises another twist for senior year . . .

A-bomb: "It's all led up to this big moment. The curtain's about to go up, bitches, and the show is about to begin. Get ready to meet your maker. It won't be long now. Kisses!"

Twisted (July 2011): After a trip to Jamaica, the girls have new secrets to hide — like murder. And a new A knows what they've done. Meanwhile their senior year is fraught with trouble: Aria feuds over Noel Kahn, Hanna ends up in some naughty pictures, Emily is cast as a homewrecker, and Spencer spills secrets.

A-bomb: "You think that's all I know, bitches? It's only the tip of the iceberg . . . and I'm just getting warmed up."

Ruthless (December 2011): Spencer fears revenge from a betrayed former study buddy, Hanna plays at Capulets and Montagues, Emily betrays a friend, and Aria rekindles an old romance. A lashes out once more and threatens that she'll expose the girls' biggest secret.

A-bomb: "Hannakins: I know you guys are living out your own private Romeo and Juliet love story, but remember: Both of them die in Act V."

Pretty Little Secrets (January 2012): A special holiday flashback revisits the girls in the winter of junior year. Unaware that a new A is watching them and waiting, the liars still manage to get into trouble. Spencer wants what her sister has, yet again; Emily gets caught up with a band of naughty elves; Aria combines an impromptu wedding with some animal rights activism; and Hanna competes for the affection of her personal trainer.

A-bomb: "Buckle up, ladies. If I have anything to say about it, this New Year's will be your last."

Great Adaptations
MARLENE KING AND THE
MAKING OF *PRETTY LITTLE LIARS*

"I'm not a teen girl, I'm in my 40s, and I love the Sara Shepard books," said Marlene King, the woman who adapted *Pretty Little Liars* for ABC Family. "I think, universally, what's fun about the show is the mystery, and I don't think it matters if you're a guy or a girl and what age you are."

Before she was dreaming up A's evil plans, Marlene went to California's Pepperdine University where she earned a BA in broadcasting. After graduation, she got a part-time job to pay the bills, but her focus was on writing scripts. Three years later, a project with her writing partner Roger Kumble was optioned by Disney. The duo spent a year rewriting *Some Enchanted Evening* but it was ultimately never made. She and Kumble worked on a variety of optioned projects, navigating "development hell" but gaining invaluable experience. "That was our big learning curve on how to find our voices and be writers," explained Marlene, "and we were fortunate enough to get paid at the same time."

One of Marlene's solo projects, *Now and Then*, found its way into Demi Moore's hands; having fallen in love with it, Demi produced the film (and she acted in it). It was Marlene's big-break moment. Released in 1995 and directed by Lesli Linka Glatter (who directed the pilot and season 1 finale episodes of *PLL*), the story is about four childhood girlfriends who reunite in their mid-20s, and through flashbacks we see a particularly important summer of their lives and friendship in the '70s. Marlene said of her work with Demi, "We had a great collaboration for many years, and that was definitely a turning point in my career." Marlene's other credits include *Senior Trip* (1995) and a segment of *If These Walls Could Talk* (1996).

Around then, Marlene switched focus, from penning scripts to raising kids (though she did cowrite the 2005 Lindsay Lohan picture *Just My Luck*). When she decided to return to work, she wanted to focus on television rather than feature film work. She'd written one TV pilot for The WB (which became one half of The CW in 2006) for development exec Kate Juergens, who was now executive vice-president of series programming at ABC Family. The two met to chat and, as Marlene describes it, "we had such similar sensibilities, we were like long-lost friends. I knew we could do something together. And the next day they sent me the first *Pretty Little Liars* book."

Now a division of the Disney-ABC Television Group, ABC Family got its start as part of Pat Robertson's Christian TV empire in 1977 and grew to be The Family Channel in 1990, and changed hands from Fox to Disney in 2001. In the past, its programming was focused more on religious shows, original TV movies, and reruns of comedies, but it now boasts series like *The Secret Life of the American Teenager*, *Make It or Break It*, *Melissa & Joey*, *Switched at Birth*, *The Lying Game*, as well as the canceled but still loved *Kyle XY* and *The Nine Lives of Chloe King*.

For those unfamiliar with the relationship between producers, studios, and networks, Marlene explained that going straight to ABC Family and connecting with a particular property is unusual: "I sort of got in through the back door that way. Normally, you would meet with the producer, which was Alloy Entertainment, and then the studio [Warner Brothers] and then the network [ABC Family], but I had a meeting of the minds with the network and they hired me right off the bat and then I met with the producer and the studio and thank god we all got along."

The *Pretty Little Liars* TV adaptation had been kicking around for about five years by the time Marlene got her hands on it. It was at The CW for development — a logical home for it, considering the network's success with other Alloy Entertainment properties like *Gossip Girl* and *The Vampire Diaries*. But soon enough the producers tried their luck, and ultimately found great success, with ABC Family.

Marlene got to writing the pilot and knew she'd made the right choice: it was the perfect fit for her. "It was the first thing I'd done since I wrote *Now and Then* that I just had joy writing. I had a smile on my face the whole time I was writing that script." The only struggle came in capturing the right tone for the series, something that Marlene, the other producers, and the network met about constantly. "We probably had 50 'tone' meetings before we made the pilot. But it is what makes *Pretty Little Liars* unique unto itself. It is a little bit of mystery, it is a little bit of soap, it is a little bit of heightened reality, it is so many things rolled into one that it became original in that way."

Oliver Goldstick (*Inconceivable, Ugly Betty, Everwood*), who executive produces and writes on *PLL*, said the creators worked hard to "pay allegiance to the books." Marlene was set on keeping Sara Shepard's "formula of answering big mystery questions, but then immediately introducing another mystery on top of it." While the first episode covers the entirety of the first book, the pace slows down after that — so book fans never know when, or even if, a particular plot or character will pop up onscreen.

When it came time to cast the pilot, which filmed in Vancouver, the creators were aware that while the novels established very specific looks for each girl, finding the right actress to bring to life each character's personality trumped the question of hair color. Casting director Gayle Pillsbury worked hard to find the right four PLLs, and Marlene credits Alloy Entertainment executive producer Bob Levy with being crucial to the assembly of this winning cast: "[He] had a tremendous influence on the casting process. He spots the 'it factor' immediately."

Lucy Hale was the first of the liars cast, having just worked with Bob Levy on *Privileged*, an Alloy/CW show that lasted just one season. Next up was Troian Bellisario: "as soon as she came into the room, we knew she was Spencer! She was so smart and so gutsy. Then we cast Shay [Mitchell] and she felt so right," explained Marlene. "The hardest person to cast was the role of Hanna. Ashley Benson had been on *Eastwick* and it was canceled on a Monday night, and on Tuesday morning we had her reading for the role of Hanna."

Though Ashley and Lucy had known each other back in their early teens, the group didn't actually all convene until the first "table read" of the pilot, when the cast and key crew first gathers with their scripts to read through an episode before filming begins. Troian remembered, "It was kind of like, we hope this works, we hope this works. And then it was so easy, it was crazy." Shooting the pilot in Vancouver in November meant missing American Thanksgiving, so the cast had their own dinner in what was "really our first social time just sitting down with each other," recalled Troian. "It was so weird. I just think they did the best job casting because literally we felt like we knew each other our whole lives. Ever since that Thanksgiving dinner, the girls call me for anything. I feel like I can call them for anything." And that bond goes beyond the inner circle of the four liars. "These crew members are like our big brothers and really watch out for us," said Lucy, "and these girls, don't even get me started. I just love them to death and we're completely bonded."

Building those bonds with the *PLL* "work family" is one of the perks that keeps Marlene King working insanely long hours. "Spending this time with these people is remarkably rewarding, and becoming truly good friends is a special experience. You don't get that on movies because it's so temporary. So this is definitely the best job, and the icing on the cake is that people are watching it and enjoying it and that it's successful." As a showrunner, a regular day for Marlene is minimum 12 hours long. "It's sort of nonstop. I write and then I'm on the stage producing. I am involved with every facet of the show being made."

But why stop there? Marlene is also working on an adaptation of another beloved YA series: she was asked by Sony to rewrite the script for *City of Bones*, the first film based on the Mortal Instruments series by Cassandra Clare. "It's teen girl sensibilities but with all this great action and mythology. I read the first few books, and I was immediately thrown into this world."

After the pilot, *Pretty Little Liars* has been filmed almost entirely on the Warner Brothers back lot in Burbank (with the occasional location shoot). "We basically look and go: 'We have to have this. How can we make it work on the back lot?'" said Goldstick. "We wink sometimes at the audience because we know it's a bit coinkidinky that there's the one cop who shows up at the school three times. Hopefully the audience is somewhat forgiving of that, recognizing that it is a world where it's a town that's been created. It may not be on the map, but it's the map of our imagination." Hardcore *PLL* fans don't mind at all, because a series shot on the back lot means the chance to pass through Rosewood on a Warner Brothers studio tour. Despite the success of the show, it has a small budget, and each episode is filmed in seven days instead of the usual 14 or so. (In season 2, two episodes had to be filmed simultaneously to save costs.) For Marlene, that creates a "little show that could" feeling among the *PLL* family.

Some viewers are surprised that such an edgy show is on ABC Family, including Oliver Goldstick who watched the pilot and said to Marlene, "It's a very different Family than I thought." The network has been very supportive of the show, and the only "note" about content that the showrunners received early on was about onscreen drug use. (Maya could be identified as a marijuana smoker, but they couldn't show her being a chronic smoker like in the books.) "They sort of have a universal theme that they don't want really bad behavior to go unpunished," explained Marlene. (So watch out, A . . .) Beyond the network's potential reaction, the writers were concerned with the problem of making

Great Adaptations

PRETTY LITTLE PRECEDENTS

Sara Shepard's book series was born of the concept *"Desperate Housewives* for teens," and as the series has come to life on TV, it's clear that the women of Wisteria Lane are not the only inspiration for our little liars. As Marlene said of her show, "It's a little *Veronica Mars*, a little *Gossip Girl*. It has the darkness of *Vampire Diaries* at times. *Twin Peaks. Desperate Housewives.* And even with all of those influences, *Pretty Little Liars* has become its own original thing."

Desperate Housewives (2004–2012): Just like in the first season of this ABC evening soap, in *PLL*, four beautiful friends with very different personalities are tied together by a friend's death in a picture-perfect setting that hides secrets, lies, and crime.

Gossip Girl (2007–present): Before A, there was another all-seeing cyberbully, and her identity is one secret she'll never tell. An Alloy Entertainment property that's been a hit for The CW, the show mixes soapy fun with earnest friendship and romance drama to keep viewers hooked. Like *PLL*, *Gossip Girl* is a show that cares about how it looks — from fabulous fashion and killer hair to hiring the best cinematographers and directors in order to deliver that signature look. And before it was the theme song for *PLL*, The Pierces performed "Secret" on *Gossip Girl* in the season 1 cotillion episode "Hi, Society."

Veronica Mars (2004–2007): R.I.P., *Veronica*. A great show gone too soon, the series centered on Kristen Bell's Veronica, a girl whose beautiful and wealthy best friend was murdered. As an unofficial operative in her dad's detective agency, Veronica proves to be the sleuthiest teen ever, solving crimes each episode while uncovering the answer to season 1's big question — who killed Lilly Kane?

Twin Peaks (1990–1991): David Lynch's unforgettable series had at its heart the murder investigation of prom queen Laura Palmer, but that central mystery was only the start of a tangled web of a group of deeply deceptive girls sympathetic to the audience. "With teenage protagonists, everybody is lying," said Goldstick, "that's what's interesting. The books tapped into something organic because we're all trying on identities but at that age, it's daily. You're posing and you're praying no one's going to call you out. The A of it all is also a huge part of today's culture, where people — because of the internet and blogs — aren't taking responsibility for their actions in the same way."

The A of it all and "plain old addictive soapiness" (as the *New York Times* described the show) made *Pretty Little Liars* a hit when it premiered on June 8, 2010, helped along by a smart and aggressive marketing campaign by ABC Family. It was the highest-rated original series debut in the network's history, and

characters and intrigue. Its campy, twisted humor and haunting tone made it unclassifiable, genre-wise, and paved the way for risk taking in shows like *Pretty Little Liars*. Mature content advisory is definitely in effect.

Heathers (1989): "I just killed my best friend." "And your worst enemy." "Same difference." Before *Mean Girls*, before the word "frenemy" even existed, this movie took the clique that ruled the school and killed them off Heather by Heather. Dark and hilarious, with dialogue that people over a certain age may not be able to decipher, *Heathers* placed #5 on *Entertainment Weekly*'s list of top teen flicks, saying its "spin on cliques, teen suicide, and homosexuality still has bite."

Mean Girls (2004): Before Alison DiLaurentis ruled the girls, Regina George was the queen bee of all queen bees. The Tina Fey–penned flick has become a classic — not only for its hilarious quotable one-liners, but for its surprisingly accurate depiction of what it's like to navigate friendships as a teenage girl. The dynamics between the four little liars and Ali, as well as the fast and fun dialogue of the show, find a precedent here.

by the end of June, the 10-episode season had been bumped up to 22 episodes. The answer to how many seasons the show will last is as elusive as the real identity of A; originally conceived as five short seasons of 10 to 12 episodes each, the show's success has meant 22- to 25-episode long seasons (split in two halves to keep with ABC Family's broadcast schedule), and Marlene's original estimate of five seasons is sometimes upped to seven. Sara Shepard couldn't stop after four volumes, and as she keeps writing the series, there's more and more material for the show-runners to draw from if they want to. By the season 1 winter premiere, the show had "moved from a 'promising newcomer' to 'bona fide hit' status," according to Deadline.com, with two million more viewers tuning in. Part of that leap in viewership is credited to *Pretty Little Liars'* amazing online fandom. With the cast, directors, and creators only a tweet away, fans flock to Twitter, giving the creators instantaneous feedback on how a story line or character is landing with viewers and spreading the word about how crazily addictive and fun the show is.

A big part of what makes *Pretty Little Liars* unique is the tone (that took 50 meetings to find) — a mix of the dark and mysterious, the creepy and scary, the campy and playful, and the best friend and boyfriend drama. Of that signature tone, Marlene said, "I call it the schizophrenia of *Pretty Little Liars*. In one minute the girls are talking about murder and death and destruction and the next minute it's 'What shade of lipgloss is that?' It's just the world these girls live in that they can bounce around like that. It's their lives. They're still going to date, have guy trouble and girl trouble and parent trouble, and they still have to have fun, so we'll continue to have all those balls in the air."

The writers put a little bit of themselves in each of the girls and, as Marlene says, she puts herself in the parents' characters. Creating deep characters means there's lots to explore, but that doesn't mean Marlene will give up A's identity until she is good and ready. "I want A to remain a mystery as long as possible because it's so much fun."

Meet the Cast

Meet the Cast

TROIAN BELLISARIO AS SPENCER HASTINGS

While those who know her would say they've never met another person like Troian Bellisario, they've probably literally never met another Troian — an Etruscan name that means "woman of Troy." Troian Avery Bellisario, born October 28, 1985, in Los Angeles, was named after her great-grandma and, though she loves the name, knows she has a lifetime of mispronunciations and misspellings ahead of her. Troian's unique look comes from her mixed Italian, Serbian, French, English, and African-American background, but she and her brothers grew up in the heart of Hollywood. Her father, Donald Bellisario, is a TV producer (*NCIS*, *JAG*, *Quantum Leap*) and her mother, Deborah

Pratt, is an actress and producer. Mary-Kate and Ashley Olsen, who lived across the street from her, were her play-pals when she was five.

Growing up "on the Universal back lot," as she puts it, allowed her to be a fly on the wall, observing television and film-making and getting into some harmless mischief. "It was really fun," Troian remembers. "My brother and I stole a bunch of golf carts and drove around the set of *Jaws* when we were little. I'd watch the people behind and in front of the camera, and I knew I wanted to do what the people in front of the camera were doing."

Her first forays into acting were as a kid. Her debut was in *Last Rites* in 1988 (at age three), and she did one episode each of *Quantum Leap, Tequila and Bonetti, JAG*, and *First Monday*. On *NCIS*, Troian had a recurring character, playing sister to her real-life stepbrother Sean Murray. She also costarred in *Billboard Dad*, one of the Olsen twins' many straight-to-video comedies. With the exception of that last project, Troian's early acting experience was on sets where her father was the boss, a fact that didn't escape the youngster. "I was always aware of the nepotism. I didn't feel respect on the set. I didn't focus on what I was doing. I focused on, 'These people think I'm only here for one reason, because of my dad.' I didn't like it."

Aside from the family business, another constant in young Troian's life was her school: from kindergarten through to high school graduation, she attended Campbell Hall, a private coed day school in Hollywood. "The school was the sort of environ-ment that, when they see that someone wants to be the best, they will absolutely push you. It wasn't just getting into an Ivy League, it was how many Ivy League schools accepted you. It was becoming valedictorian of the class." Which she was. "I was applying to schools I didn't even know if I wanted to be in — except I 'should' want to be in them," recalls Troian, who earned top marks in history, math, and other subjects. But Troian stuck to her true love, acting, and attended the University of Southern

California theater program. She signed with an agent in her freshman year.

Troian shone at USC and spent one notable summer busking in New York City's subways: with another USC student, she performed the balcony scene from *Romeo and Juliet*, timed to last just one stop. Upon graduation, Troian was cast as an understudy in a Geffen Playhouse production of *Equivocation*, alongside Patrick J. Adams. "And at first I didn't want to do it," Troian recalled, "because I was like, 'Oh my gosh, an understudy.' I was worried about what it was going to be like to watch so many amazing people from backstage, and I was worried if I was going to get jealous, but it was actually the best learning experience ever. I got to see professionals working in a professional theater." She continued to perform in plays and acted in short films, and with some like-minded friends formed a theater company, the Casitas Group.

In fall 2009, she got the audition for *Pretty Little Liars*; the scene was Spencer flirting with Wren, bumming a cigarette from him outside the dinner party. "I did a great job because I never, ever in a million years, thought that they'd want someone like me. So that gave me the freedom to be like, 'Alright, I'm just gonna have fun with this because they're not looking for me; they're looking for some pretty blonde thing.' Then they called me back and I was kind of like, 'Wow!'" Troian immediately read the book series, calling it "an actor's dream to have a backstory and history and the way of thinking all mapped out for you."

Troian feels connected to Spencer: "I grew up in a very wealthy family around a very wealthy group of people. My high school was a private school where you went to an Ivy League. That's just what was expected of you and nothing less. So I grew up never being okay with a B, because a B was not good enough. And it wasn't really my parents. My parents told me, 'Put down the books, go outside, you look like death.' They were always very supportive of me. But I think it was the school I went to and the world I was born into. And I think Spencer is kind of in that. She's in this beautiful, golden cage where everybody just says, 'You have everything, so you have no excuse to trip up.'" Her empathy for her character shows in her pitch-perfect performance, and Troian is very candid about how her own experiences have helped her understand a character like Spencer Hastings. "My life has given me a lot of love for people like Spencer and for girls like I was, who really are struggling because they feel like nobody will give them the time of day or love them unless they're perfect. And that just takes time and, it feels like, somebody on the outside to come to you and say, 'What do you like? What do you want to do? Because I'll love you no matter what.'"

A passionate and thoughtful person, Troian considers the kind of role model she is, appearing on a TV show that millions of young women watch. "The struggle that I have every day is knowing that while I can be an inspiration to a lot of girls, I can also make them feel more and more distant from themselves. I sit in a makeup chair for two hours a day so I can look as good as possible for my show, but that also creates a false image for viewers to expect of themselves. I want to find a way to help girls love themselves for who they are, not what some false image on the television or the cover of a magazine is telling them they should be, because guess what — not even those girls look like that."

The hectic filming schedule doesn't give Troian and the other PLLs much downtime: "The girls and I shoot Monday through Friday, generally before sunrise until after sundown. It's a tough job. Your weekends are spent doing laundry, calling the people you love, trying to have a drink, relax, and preparing for the week. On top of that, I'm a really ambitious person with a lot of things that I want to create and do, like painting or making my own film, which I'm in the process of doing right now. That's really what changed for me: learning how to juggle and learning how to be easier on myself. I'm like Spencer at this point in my life: I get stressed out really easily, and the first thing I have to do is not let myself go down that road." Among her extracurricular projects are a short film called *Exiles* (a reimagining of *Romeo and Juliet*) and a music project with Shane Coffey under the name "Family."

Chad Lowe, who plays Byron Montgomery and has directed *PLL* episodes, sums up the ambitious and talented young actress best: "And Troian, what can you say? We're all going to work for Troian some day. We're all going to work for Troian, it's a fact."

ASHLEY BENSON AS HANNA MARIN

Born December 18, 1989, in Anaheim Hills, California, Ashley Victoria Benson has been performing since she was just two years old — singing, dancing, modeling. In fact, the flexibility to focus on her career was so important that Ashley was homeschooled for high school. "I've never been to a prom or a dance, so it's funny because we have dances on the show and I'll be like, 'Oh yay! It's my school dance!'"

Ashley's career began with dance lessons at age two, and before long she was modeling. "I did a lot of Guess ads from the time I was six to 12, and I did a ton of TV commercials. I did tons of Barbie commercials. I was with Mattel for years." Ashley loved getting to do things like ride on Thunder Mountain all day while filming an ad for Disneyland at age nine. "I just loved being on set and in front of the camera. I went to an acting class out in L.A. for, like, two years, and I started doing guest spots on shows."

It wasn't all dreamy though; classmates made fun of her and bullied her because of her success. "I was in the popular group in elementary school," remembers Ashley, "and then I started doing things in the business, and I got kicked out of my group and I was picked on every day. I was the outcast, and I would cry and I would want to skip school. So I definitely know how Hanna feels, and I've been in her shoes when I've been popular. So it's very easy to relate to Hanna when she was younger."

Her biggest education outside of school was on the set of *Days of Our Lives*. For 175 episodes, Ashley played Abigail Deveraux. Explains Ashley, "I have learned so much from being on soap operas and working with amazing actors who've been on there for like 30, 40 years. It was an honor to work with them. It's definitely given me all my background." But the relentless schedule meant little opportunity for other projects. "Soap operas are filmed year round. So, you never really get breaks. You get Christmas off, and you get certain [times] off. Usually for TV shows you get a four-month or three-month break, but for soap operas you really don't get a break."

In 2007, Ashley left *Days* behind to star in *Bring It On: In It to Win It* as "good girl" cheerleader Carson. And it was a real challenge: she had to do all her own stunts, but Ashley was up for it. "Cheering is so different from dance, because you have to be sharp and you have to be on a point, and if you move wrong then you just screw up everything. Luckily, I was on the West Coast side so you've got to have a little more flavor, which was fun, but it was definitely different." Though she'd already been on shows like *7th Heaven*, *Zoey 101*, and *The O.C.*, Ashley continued to rack up credits on shows like *Supernatural* and *CSI: Miami*, and in movies like *Fab Five: The Texas Cheerleader Scandal*, *Bart Got a Room*, in which she starred with William H. Macy, and *Christmas Cupid*, an ABC Family Original Movie with Chad Michael Murray.

She was cast as Mia Torcoletti, a regular on ABC's *Eastwick* (2009), playing the daughter of Rebecca Romijn's character. The series (which filmed on the back lot at the WB just like *Pretty Little Liars* does) only lasted 13 episodes. But that cloud had a silver lining for Ashley: as soon as the show's cancelation was announced, the producers at *Pretty Little Liars* cast her as Hanna Marin.

Ashley loves filming the flashbacks, because younger Hanna is "probably my favorite part of Hanna to play, just because she's so sensitive and so insecure and just so vulnerable. I've been there before. I've been in her shoes, where she hasn't been included, and I've definitely gone through some friends who have treated me really poorly. It was to the point where I had to get a whole new group of friends that were just like Lucas. So it's really interesting. But when I'm on set, I really just channel my character and it's kind of easy for me to drift off and be Hanna, just because I feel for her and I know what it's like. I'm really passionate about always playing into flashbacks, because there's a lot that you get to see. You know, how she was treated and what she went through." A lot of Hanna's fans relate to younger Hanna, as well: "Girls come up to me all the time and they're like, 'I've been where you've been, and I feel like I'm Hanna.' I feel like a lot of girls are really into the show because they can relate to us so much."

As much as she brings heart to Hanna, Ashley knows how to deliver a one-liner — skills perhaps picked up from her acting role models Lucille Ball and Reese Witherspoon. "The writers give [Hanna] the best one-liners, and everybody loves it. It's great to have comedy in a drama. It's so much fun, I love it."

The vivacious young star spent her season 2 hiatus filming *Spring Breakers* opposite Selena Gomez, and she can cross being a *Seventeen* and *Teen Vogue* cover girl off her bucket list. But her accomplishments and success hasn't changed who Ashley is at heart: a diehard Lakers fan (her older sister, Shaylene, is a Lakers

Girl) who adores her dog, Olive, and loves dancing around goofily with the abandon of a two-year-old. It's just that now she shares those moments via YouTube for her growing legion of fans.

LUCY HALE AS ARIA MONTGOMERY

Standing only 5'2" and wearing a size 00, the first word people often use to describe Lucy Hale is tiny (her *PLL* costar Shay Mitchell even called her a "Polly Pocket"). But despite her small size, she's a big talent, and had already recorded an album and headlined two TV series before *Pretty Little Liars*.

Of the four liars, Lucy Hale came to the show with the most acting experience, but when Lucy started in showbiz, she had her sights set on recording songs rather than being onscreen. "I grew up my whole life singing; that's what I wanted to do," she told MTV. "Acting wasn't even in the picture." Luckily for *PLL* fans, once Lucy started acting, she couldn't get enough.

Born June 14, 1989, Karen Lucille Hale grew up the youngest of three children in Memphis, Tennessee, a city steeped in music history, the perfect place to nurture her budding musical talent. There she took voice lessons and did a few gigs, performing country standards and show tunes. In 2003 she auditioned with 2,000 other kids for a spot on a new reality show *American Juniors* and eventually sang her way to the final five. The grand prize? Releasing an album together as a band, the self-titled *American Juniors*, which came out in 2004. The album fizzled and the band members went their separate ways, but Lucy looks back on her first taste of the spotlight fondly. "It was fun to be on TV with kids my age. Now that I look back, we worked so hard. Twelve hours a day with dance rehearsals and singing. It was definitely insane!"

The one-season show ended up having a huge impact on the young actress's career — it convinced her that Hollywood was where she wanted to be. When she was 15 Lucy persuaded her mom to let her come out for L.A.'s pilot season (roughly mid-January through March), where she landed a Hollywood agent, and eventually convinced her mom to pack up from Memphis so the aspiring star could explore some of the doors her reality show stint had opened up. (The rest of her family remained in Memphis.) "My mom is amazing," says Lucy. "She quit her job and got a nursing job out here. We just moved out here. We didn't think twice about it. We were really naive about the situation. We didn't know what we were getting into."

"I don't think I booked anything for a solid year, but I learned an awful lot about the industry," said the actress. The roles did trickle in eventually though, with guest spots on *Ned's Declassified School Survival Guide* (with future *PLL* actress Lindsey Shaw), *Secrets of a Small Town* (a series that didn't make it to air but also starred future gossip girl Leighton Meester), *Drake & Josh*, *The O.C.*, and *How I Met Your Mother*.

Finally, her series of one-offs came to an end when she landed the role of little sis to the *Bionic Woman* herself. Unfortunately even superpowers are no match for a writers' strike, and the 2007 series was shelved before it had even finished its first season.

Lucy kept auditioning though, and her persistence paid off with her first major movie role as Effie, little sister to Lena, in *Sisterhood of the Traveling Pants 2* (2008). A month later, she was also back on the small screen, having earned a lead role in a much-hyped CW show, *Privileged*, an adaptation of an Alloy novel, this one called *How to Teach Filthy Rich Girls*.

The TV adaptation starred Joanna García as an ambitious young journalist who gets pulled into the world of Palm Beach's elite as a tutor for twin Paris-Hiltons-to-be, Rose and Sage; Lucy played Rose, the nicer twin. But like *Bionic Woman*, *Privileged* never saw season 2, and Lucy was hunting for work yet again.

Lucy's performance on *Privileged* hadn't gone unnoticed though, and when ABC Family was casting a new teen series, the petite performer was on their minds. Lucy first auditioned for Hanna, but the casting department quickly realized they had the perfect Aria, and she was the first liar to be signed on. She was also the only one who actually matched her description in the book (with one exception: Book Aria is *tall*).

The actress resembles her character in other ways too, and Lucy points to Aria's stubborn streak as something she recognizes in herself. Plus, she told *TV Guide*, "Growing up I always felt like I was different from the girls my age because I had different interests and was thinking about different things. Aria's like that too." She sees Aria as surprisingly mature. "I've never played someone who's been so young but yet has a personality that's much older," she noted. "I remember reading the books and thinking this girl is really . . . almost like an old soul. So I definitely wanted that to come across in the show."

With a hit show on her hands that means 16-hour days on set, Lucy has never been busier. She starred in the TV movie *Sorority Wars*, did guest spots on *CSI: Miami* and *Private Practice*, and scored a role in *Scream 4*, the latest installment of the classic slasher series because one of the producers' wives was a huge *PLL* fan.

Even though she's put her music career on the back burner, she found a way to add to her acting resumé and show off her vocal talents in the modern day fairytale *A Cinderella Story: Once Upon a Song* (2011). Following in the footsteps of Hilary Duff and Selena Gomez, Lucy plays a girl who dreams of becoming a recording artist, but has to deal with the meddling of her wicked stepsister (Lucy's real-life pal Megan Park).

Despite having an acting career that's like a fairytale in itself, Lucy hasn't written off a career in song. "If I ventured out into that world, it'd be a dream come true. I took guitar a while back, and my heart wasn't in it at the time, but I'm ready to try it again. I sing in the car, at home — it's a huge part of my life, especially since I'm from Tennessee. When I'm ready for it, I'm going to dive into it 100 percent."

After three years in L.A. and numerous jobs playing other people, the actress is finally starting to figure out how just to be herself. She revealed, "Now I'm not trying to be something I'm not. I know what I believe in. I know my morals and I know what I have to offer. I am a 5'2" girl with big eyebrows and I'm fine with it."

SHAY MITCHELL AS EMILY FIELDS

Shay Mitchell could be the girl next door: she loves fashion, dancing to Beyoncé, interior design, making goofy YouTube videos with her friends, and streaming shows on Netflix. But with her lustrous dark brown locks, gorgeous almond eyes, and tall, curvaceous frame, there's no way she could be overlooked. Castmate Lucy Hale summed it up: "When Shay walks into a room, all heads turn!"

Born April 10, 1987, Canadian Shannon Ashley Mitchell had her sights set on the spotlight from an early age. She loved putting on performances for her family and started taking dance lessons at age five, and after her family moved from Toronto to Vancouver when she was 10, she attended an open casting call for a modeling agency, naturally standing out from the crowd and getting signed. In her teen years she modeled all over the world, but when she didn't fit in with the industry's size-zero standard, she resigned from the runways. "I knew I wouldn't be able to continue modeling, I enjoyed food too much!" explained Shay. "My saying is 'Everything in moderation,' but for someone who isn't naturally thin, that motto doesn't work out so well when you're trying to fit into extremely small sample sizes." She wishes that the fashion industry showcased a wider variety of body types, and that girls didn't use the Photoshopped standards of the modeling industry as their own benchmark for beauty. The former model has her own message for women everywhere: "There are always going to be people and images telling you what 'beauty' and the idea of 'perfection' is. But what I find beautiful is being unique, and there is no one else who can be a better you than *you*."

With high school completed and a stint living in Thailand and Hong Kong under her belt, Shay moved back to Toronto, where she worked as a server in a downtown restaurant, took acting classes, and nabbed herself a film agent. In 2009 she landed her first role, although it wouldn't demand too much acting ability: she played a model on groundbreaking Canadian drama *Degrassi: The Next Generation*. (Trivia bonus: her scene was with another Canuck who soon hit it big south of the border — *The Vampire Diaries*' Nina Dobrev.) Shay's next TV appearance was as a beachside babe longing for her departed man in Sean Paul's video for "Hold My Hand." A guest spot on *Rookie Blue* and a four-episode stint on Disney action adventure *Aaron Stone* followed.

As her IMDb entry got a little bit longer, Shay decided to commit to her new career by moving to L.A. She'd recently auditioned for a new TV show there, and just four days after moving to the land of glitz and glam, she found out she'd landed a lead role. "Let's just say there was screaming in my hotel room when I got the news!" said Shay. The actress had been intrigued by the project from the start. When her manager initially called her about *Pretty Little Liars* and told her the title, she exclaimed, "Stop. How cool is that title?" Shay initially auditioned for the role of Spencer, and was asked to read again for Emily, and our glam girl ended up connecting with the sweet girl next door.

Though she's certainly less of a jock than Emily Fields is, the actress soon found she had a lot in common with her Rosewoodian alter ego. A self-described girly-girl, Shay did play sports in high school, though she could be found on the basketball and volleyball courts rather than in the pool. More important, however, are the similarities in personality between her and Emily. Said Shay, "She's extremely loyal to her friends. She can keep a secret. I'm sure that if you were to tell your secret to someone, you should tell it to Emily. She's the smoother-over. She wants everything to be good, so she tries to keep the peace in her group of friends. I like that about her, and I try to do the same in my group of friends."

The actress also remembers the insecurities that come with being in high school. At the end of elementary school, Shay's friends became frenemies when they decided to join the mean girl clique. "When I first got into high school it was super tough. Girls were super jealous. They were catty and not so nice," remembered the actress. "I ended up eating my lunch in the bathroom quite a few times and/or begging my grandma, who was at our house, to pick me up early." But luckily she soon found some new pals who valued friendship over popularity. With her Filipino, Spanish, Scottish, and Irish roots, she also felt a little self-conscious among her blue-eyed, blonde-haired friends. When she was 17 she even dyed her hair blonde and got blue contacts! The rest of her social circle just couldn't relate: "When I would explain what my background was the only thing that came into their mind was, like, 'Oh, yeah. I think my nanny is Filipina.'" Looking back, she wishes she could offer advice to her younger self: "Hold your head high and be true to yourself. Uniqueness is beautiful."

This theme of self-acceptance became a crucial part of her role as Emily, who spends season 1 facing then embracing her same-sex attraction. Though some straight people shy away from gay roles, for Shay it was a non-issue. While she did do research with gay friends and family members so she could understand how it felt to come out, when it comes to Emily's lady loves, Shay thinks it's terribly straightforward. "What's the difference between a gay person and a straight person, really?" she asked. "Who you're attracted to? Who cares. I really think that the world is heading in that direction too, that they're starting to understand that love is love. Someone asked me the other day if I would play another lesbian character on TV or in a movie, and I was like, 'Uh, yes? That's not even a question.' I love Emily. I am so lucky to be playing a character as awesome as her."

Shay's sensitive, high-profile portrayal of Emily ended up being more than just acting; it became a sort of activism, especially for teens going through a similar experience. The star gets encouraging feedback all the time, and she explained, "It still humbles me every single time. . . . I still get letters all the time from girls who are closeted or just coming to terms with their sexuality, and they say that watching Emily helps them feel less alone, or that she has inspired them to come out. I can't tell you how much that means to me. I really can't."

Shay's activism extends beyond the world of Rosewood though, and she used her hiatus from filming in February 2011 to spend three weeks in Cambodia with the Somaly Mam Foundation, an organization working to thwart human slavery and sex trafficking. On her second day there she tweeted, "Meeting some of the most beautiful & strong women here. They are an inspiration to us all . . ." It's just the way fans feel about Shay Mitchell.

IAN HARDING
AS EZRA FITZ

Appropriately enough for a show about lying, Ian Harding attributes his interest in acting to being a spinner of yarns as a kid. "I always liked telling stories," he explained. "I had little action figures that my friends would simply bang together but I would always have to have a reason for the fighting. I would also tell my mom tall tales about little things that happened during the day. If I lost my jacket, it was because the dog next door who I hit with a ball last week at long last sought revenge by tearing it from my body, I fought him off, though, wielding a mighty stick . . . blah blah blah."

Born September 16, 1986, on an army base in Heidelberg, Germany, Ian moved to Virginia with his parents and older sister when he was about three. His military family was anything but militant though, and his parents gave the kids considerable freedom. Ian noted, "My parents supported my sister and me in everything we pursued, and let us make our own mistakes."

Ian only had his family as an audience until high school, when, like many boys, he followed the girls to the drama program. "I went to this high school and they had *excellent, excellent* sports teams, and these guys were all-American everything, and I wasn't that good. So I was like, 'I think I'll do this drama thing because it's coed.' I went to an all-boys school, and girls from various girls schools did it. So I was like, 'Oh yeah, women.'" But once he got started, acting became the new object of his affections. "The girls kind of took second place to the actual performing," recalled Ian.

After high school, the aspiring actor decided to take his training to the next level, enrolling at Carnegie Mellon University, a school renowned for its fine arts program. The modest performer explained, "I actually didn't know if I was any good at acting. I loved doing it, and knew I wanted to get better at it, so I figured going to college for it made the most sense." At CMU he developed his skills on the stage, something he finds immensely valuable, even though he acts mostly on camera now. Said Ian, "I think theater gives you the basics: how to break down a scene, how to get the character into you, et cetera. It's so technical, and you have to be able to reach the person in the back row, so, in terms of training, any time spent on a stage or in a theater program seems invaluable to me. Also I feel like theater helps you to respect the work, because acting, or performing in general, can be very difficult. If you don't respect it, it won't respect you."

After graduating from university Ian didn't set his sights on the stage, however. Like many young actors, he was drawn to the bright lights of Hollywood. Only a few days after graduating in May 2009, he moved to L.A. and found an apartment. His resumé was fairly short, starting with a Sheetz commercial (which you still can, and *must*, watch online) and including a bit part in the 2009 retro comedy *Adventureland*. He landed a small part in the 2010 rom-com *Love and Other Drugs*, though most of his scenes ended up on the cutting room floor (and unlike most actors, Ian admits to being grateful for this).

In fall 2009, Ian got an email from his agent about a new ABC Family show, and he went in to audition. He did approximately five auditions and callbacks, and he admitted, "I just kind of flirted with everybody that I came across." Whether it was because of his flirting or his acting or both, Ian got the part of Ezra Fitz.

Playing a high school teacher who falls in love with his student, Ian had landed a meaty, controversial part, and he praises the show's writers for depicting the relationship with heart and sensitivity. "I tread on such a thin line," explained Ian. "Because it's something that's real and honest and they've found — I venture to say — soul mates. It's such a difficult thing to describe because obviously there's a huge, huge connection and I think you root for it, because it's obvious. The only thing that's separating them is about six to seven years age difference, which is not terrible, and it's also not like I'm 40 and she's 12. So that's obviously an issue. And when I'm your teacher, that's another problem. But minus that, they're two people that love each other. So the circumstances are just not in their favor."

While he was prepared for some outcry against the pairing, the actor didn't foresee the passionate devotion the couple (a.k.a. "Ezria") would inspire in fans. While he's happy to see fans so engaged, he does worry that diehard teen devotees can't see past the specifics. He hears people say, "I wish I had a hot English teacher like that" or "I wish I had that," but cautiously advises, "That's a very specific situation. By no means am I saying, 'Go out and try to boost that grade,' if you will."

And what about Lucy Hale, the person he works with so intimately? Ian revealed, "She and I are very open with each other, and have a comfort level that's unlike any working relationship I've ever experienced. Our real-life interactions have all the trappings of a great friendship. We just happen to make out with one another for a living." He also notes that Aria's the one he probably would have gone after when he was in high school. He told *TV Guide*, "She's unique and has the whole short, brunette thing, which in high school is all I dated. I think I would've been driven to how creative and artsy and well spoken she is. Shay Mitchell's character is pretty awesome too. I just think the whole lesbian thing would've thrown a wrench into the relationship."

But even as he's getting used to being a working actor, the self-effacing Ian Harding still hasn't gotten used to his new heartthrob status. "I was in Paris at the Louvre," he recalled, "and I realized that people were paying more attention to me than to the *Mona Lisa* . . . It was a surreal moment and I actually started shaking. I had to go out and have a glass of wine."

KEEGAN ALLEN AS TOBY CAVANAUGH

What's Keegan Allen's biggest pet peeve? Being lied to. Luckily for him, he landed the role of one of the few honest people in Rosewood, Toby Cavanaugh. Born July 22, 1989, Keegan grew up in L.A. in a supportive and artsy family — his dad's an actor, his mom's an artist. He first took an interest in film in high school, but Keegan wanted to be behind the camera, not in front of it. He got into video production, camerawork, and cinematography, and he acted on stage, away from the cameras.

Before *Pretty Little Liars* came along, Keegan didn't have much experience on the set of a TV show. He'd appeared in episodes of *Big Time Rush*, *I Hate My Teenage Daughter*, and *CSI*. His first audition for *Pretty Little Liars* was for the part of Wren, which ultimately went to Julian Morris, but Keegan was asked to come back to try out for Toby. The actor played him as a "wholesome, haunted child, someone loving and authentic," and *Pretty Little Liars* had found its misunderstood outsider.

The self-described obsessive reader picked up Sara Shepard's books after he was cast and read the eight volumes in two weeks, getting totally sucked into the series like millions of other readers. "I knew a lot about Toby before we even shot the episode where my character comes in. I knew how he was portrayed in the books," explained Keegan, "and I tried to bring him to life with that, but still bring something new and authentic."

His interest in the mechanics and artistry of filmmaking continues, and Keegan's favorite part of filming *PLL* is the opportunity to "work with these amazing directors that are very creative. Our cinematographer, Dana Gonzales, is an incredible director of photography. You can tell he loves the vision of the show and he shoots it [as if it's] a movie." And speaking of mechanics, there is an unexpected side benefit of being Toby Cavanaugh. "I literally learned how to reassemble a motorcycle a million times now!"

Keegan loves his costars, calling Lucy Hale "a comedian," Shay Mitchell "just like this bright light," and crediting Ashley Benson with the ability to "make me laugh harder than anybody." Though their onscreen relationship is rather strained, Keegan has nothing but praise for Tammin Sursok: "I'm like, 'Hey, what's up, sis?' And she calls me bro. She's an amazing singer/songwriter. And she'll come in sometimes and we'll hang out in our dressing rooms and play music. She's so cool and fun. She likes to poke fun at me and she's like my big sister on set, for sure." Of Troian Bellisario, Keegan says, "She is my kind of person. Our chemistry started from the second that I met her; we were really cool with each other and we would bring each other CDs. She's just the most intellectual and really down-to-earth person. . . . We're really good friends and when we hang out it's really fun. She's my favorite person to hang out with on set and I'm around her the most. I'm really close with all of the people in the cast but I'm mostly around her for our scenes. It's always a good time with Troian." Because he's good friends with Ian Harding, Keegan is lobbying for a bromance between Toby and Ezra so the two actors can share the screen.

When he's not on set filming, the young actor likes to go skateboarding or surfing. But now that he's on a hit show, his experience has changed a little bit: "I have to be ready because sometimes people know who I am, and I'm sure it's really crazy to see Toby being a beach nerd, like, on the beach. So, there have been instances where I've been getting fan mail and getting recognized. It's really cool, but it's very different."

Besides being recognized, Keegan has developed an addiction to social networking, calling it "digital crack." "I'm on Twitter all the time now [@KeeganAllen], retweeting things and tweeting, and it's like actually the fastest way to keep up with news throughout the world. Social networking is where it's at; it's a really interesting way to connect with the fans. It's not weird, it's not awkward, you can directly connect with them and they can directly connect with you and see what you're saying. . . . I learn a lot from the girls too with social networking."

Keegan's day-to-day life has certainly been transformed since landing a role on *Pretty Little Liars*, but he feels his personality changing a little bit too. "I am very much extroverted, crazy, fun, active, and social," explains Keegan. "Then to play this character, he's kind of crept into my life now, more so than before I started the show. Now I find myself pulling a Toby here and there, being like introverted, weird, and not as social, and I feel like it is because of the show."

SASHA PIETERSE AS ALISON DILAURENTIS

Though she plays the ringleader of the pretty little liars, Sasha Embeth Pieterse insists that she isn't the one who raises all the (good-natured) trouble on the set of *Pretty Little Liars*: "Ashley pranks everyone on set. She's the prankster of us." Born February 17, 1996, just 15 when she was cast as Alison DiLaurentis, Sasha is by far the youngest of the main cast members. But in her case, youth doesn't mean inexperience: after leaving Johannesburg, South Africa, with her family, she was raised in Las Vegas by her parents, both professional dancers, and got into show business early. She appeared in commercials and modeled as a child, before beginning her acting career in earnest in 2002. At six years old, Sasha played Buffy Davis on *Family Affair*, and she won a Young Artist Award for her performance in 2003.

Since then, she's appeared in *Stargate SG-1*, *The Adventures of Sharkboy and Lavagirl in 3-D*, *Wanted*, *House*, *The Air I Breathe*, *Good Luck Chuck*, *CSI: Miami*, *Without a Trace*, *Medium*, *X-Men: First Class*, and *Geek Charming*. In the *House* episode "Autopsy," she played a girl with cancer. Just nine years old at the time, Sasha so impressed *House* star Lisa Edelstein that she counts Sasha among the top guest stars ever to appear on the long-running series. The young actress loves the variety in her career so far: "I was a cancer patient, I was bald, and then I was a Goth in one movie, so I've kind of always been all over the spectrum, which has been really entertaining for me because I get to become all these different characters." Other than her recurring part on *Family Affair*, Sasha's biggest TV experience pre-*PLL* was on *Heroes* where she played Amanda Strazzula, a girl with "pyrokinesis," the ability to make objects spontaneously combust.

Another character who likes to play with fire is Alison DiLaurentis. "What is cool about Alison is she's got so many layers and, as an actress, that's so cool as I get to sink my teeth into her as a character, 'cause there are so many aspects to her," explains Sasha. "I don't feel like I'm playing the same character every day. There's just so much to her and everything is different. It's kind of funny saying that because it's all flashbacks and you'd think a lot of them would be similar, but there's always something new and different and revealing."

Along with Ashley Benson, Bianca Lawson, and other hopefuls, Sasha originally auditioned for the role of Hanna, but the powers that be wisely saw more Ali in her. Of her character, Sasha says, "She's like Regina George [from *Mean Girls*]. She's very manipulative, but at the same time, she's got a really sweet side too. She really does care for the girls, but she kind of has them under her thumb." Sasha sees Alison's manipulative nature as a double-edged sword for the other girls: "As much as she makes them do things they don't want to do, at the same time she makes them do things they *want* to do — even if it gets a bad result. So she kind of brings out the good and the bad in them at the same time."

Sasha loves her costars, but that doesn't stop her from turning up the mean-girl vibe when the camera is rolling. "I feel bad because I totally belittle someone, and I'm just like, 'Oh I'm sorry!' but it's so much fun. She's like my guilty pleasure to play." Another challenge is playing a character so crucial to how the characters think and feel about themselves. "Each thing that Alison does in a flashback, it affects the girls in a certain way, and so not only do I have to recenter myself and figure out where in the timeline this is happening, but I also have to play the scene to how it affects them in the present. Something is either haunting them or they're remembering something good or whatever it is, it's affecting them in the present, and so also in the scene, I have to target what made them feel that way."

The fan response to Sasha's portrayal of Ali has been overwhelmingly positive, and she loves connecting to viewers on Twitter (@sashaapieterse). As she said when season 1 was airing, "Everyone's a big fan [of the show] already, which is so great to see. It just makes us feel better, I know for sure, knowing that we're doing a good job and that we're portraying the characters the way they want to see it. It means the world, because that's what we're doing, that's our job, that's what we're living for, so it's very interesting and very exciting to see all the feedback." And in the offline world, the feedback has been just as positive. Sasha's adjusting to the experience of being recognized when she goes out in Los Angeles, which is the reality for a young star on a hit show.

What's most special to Sasha is that she's able to take Sara Shepard's Alison and bring her to life. Of the original novels, Sasha said, "You can visualize everything, and I love that about it. And I love how she describes every character so immensely — it's just amazing how she does [it]. It's kind of nice just to bring Alison alive."

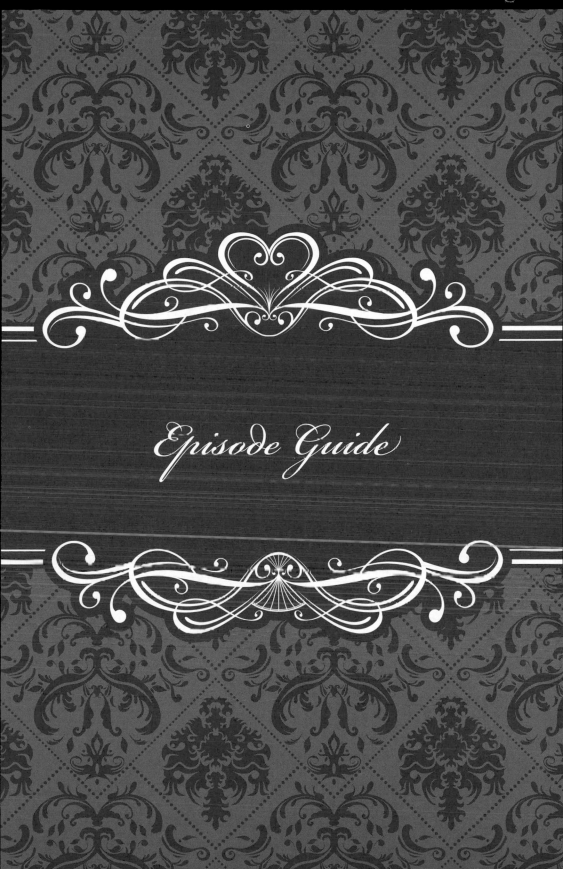

Episode Guide

Season 1

1.01 PILOT

(AIRED JUNE 8, 2010 | WRITTEN BY I. MARLENE KING | DIRECTED BY LESLI LINKA GLATTER)

Alison: "Friends share secrets. That's what keeps us close."

It was a dark and stormy night in Rosewood, Pennsylvania, when five beautiful BFFs gathered for slumber party gossip and secret drinks. And, of course, one of them disappeared. It's a scene that could kick off a horror movie, but rather than playing like a tired concept, the opening of *Pretty Little Liars* works as a conscious nod to the genre that will provide the show with many of its thrills, and it's perfectly appropriate for a night that still haunts the surviving girls.

After Alison's dramatic disappearance, we enter Rosewood by following someone who is getting reacquainted with the town. Aria's been in Iceland for a year, and though she's returning to her hometown, the place seems as strange and foreign to her as it might to us viewers. She's got more than boxes to unpack and sort through: the people who were once her best friends seem distant, and one of them (Hanna) doesn't even look or act like the same person. There are embers of the old friendship though: Aria feels comfortable enough to go to Emily (already established as the warmest of the group), and Hanna helps Spencer rethink her night's wardrobe with offhand insight into the Hastings sisters' relationship that even Spencer may have been unwilling to acknowledge. But despite their history and these small gestures, the awkwardness is definitely there. As Aria says, they are "friendly, but not friends." Though this can happen to any tightly knit group, Emily is wise enough to recognize why they've lost touch, saying to Aria, "Maybe that's what we had to do." They buried their friendships in order to bury Ali, that terrifying night, and all the secrets that didn't vanish along with their friend.

These secrets help drive the episode, give us plenty of insight into Rosewood's former A-crowd, and save the characters from looking like one-dimensional high school stereotypes. Spencer has all the marks of a good-girl overachiever, but is that because she wants what her sister has? Even with a black mark on her record, she's a little too flirty with Wren, and despite her blazers and ties, perhaps Spencer's not as straight-laced as she appears.

Hanna's given herself a very effective makeover, physically and socially. As she's trying to rewrite her place in the yearbook, she's revising her family history in order to make herself feel as invulnerable as she looks striding out of a department store with stolen designer glasses. But her teary-eyed stare when Mrs. Marin connects her shoplifting to an absent daddy, and flash-backs to Hanna squirming under Alison's thumb (aside from her hilarious cookie-eating defiance), suggest that Hanna's easy, breezy exterior is just a cover. Aria may resent her father for his secret student-teacher affair, but she's flirting with making the same mistake. Emily has that all-American style and a sweet demeanor, and she's trying to be the perfect daughter, but she's already railing against her mother's control, and Maya ignites a spark of rebellion in her that could turn into a transformative blaze. And when talking about secrets, let's not forget the mysterious Jenna Thing, the one terrible secret that all four girls share.

In Rosewood, land of polished perfection and foie gras welcome baskets, lives of great privilege come with heavy expectations: your secrets can threaten your social status, your family, and maybe even your future. As Ashley Marin succinctly sums it up, "In Rosewood you don't have room to make a mistake." But mistakes have been made, and while they should have been buried with Alison, this episode's saucy communiqués from the mysterious A are like the stuff of the horror movie opening: back from the dead.

HIGHLIGHT Though the pilot offered lots of jaw-droppers and exciting moments, nothing quite matches that first mass text from A: "I'm back, bitches. And I know everything."

EXTRA CREDIT
- Spencer's reading Harper Lee's *To Kill a Mockingbird*, a beloved Pulitzer Prize–winning novel about racism and the pursuit of justice in the American South. (For more, see page 66).

- Notice that the paper is called the *Rosewood Observer*? A fitting title for a town whose citizens are under close scrutiny.
- Spencer wears the shirt that Hanna picked out for her at the mall.

SLIP UPS The girls are headed back to school, so presumably it's early September, but the leaves have already changed color and mostly fallen off the trees. When Aria and Ali catch Mr. Montgomery in his not-so-stealthy makeout, we can't see inside the car because of the reflection of the sky and trees. How can the girls see him so clearly from the same perspective?

HOLLY MARIE COMBS
AS ELLA MONTGOMERY

New York City attracts most actors at some point in their career, but Holly Marie Combs started her career there at age seven, when she moved to the Big Apple with her young mother, an aspiring actress. Holly started with work in print ads and commercials, progressed through a few small film and television roles, and then landed her breakthrough role on the TV drama *Picket Fences* (and earned a Young Artist Award). Holly is best known for her starring role as Piper Halliwell on The WB supernatural drama *Charmed*, a part she played for eight years. When *Charmed* cast its last spell, Holly took some time off to be a mother to her three sons, feeling she'd neglected her family and friends. But before long her husband (*Charmed* crew member David Donoho) was encouraging her to go back to work. When she read the *PLL* pilot she realized it was "something that was worth leaving my kids for."

BACK TO THE BOOKS The pilot covers most of Sara Shepard's first book. The most noticeable difference is in the physical descriptions of the characters (in the books Emily has red hair and freckles, Spencer is blonde, and Hanna brunette), something that caused an uproar among book fans. Also, in the books, three years have passed since Ali's disappearance rather than just one, giving the girls more time to grow apart. Sara Shepard was pleased that the pilot kept some of the smallest details of her book, including Aria's pig puppet, Pigtunia.

PLL IRL Ali gay-baits Emily by saying that she might love Beyoncé too much: in real life the R&B superstar is Shay Mitchell's favorite artist. Aria and Ezra's steamy bathroom hook-up led to many "Did they or didn't they?" discussions among viewers. Showrunner Marlene King's mother was no exception — she thought they went all the way. Marlene was taken aback, telling her, "Mom! She's not that kind of a girl." For actors Ian Harding and Lucy Hale, shooting that bar hook-up scene was more awkward than sexy, since the two had only met briefly beforehand. Parts of the pilot were filmed in Vancouver in November, so when they had to don bikinis and pretend it was summer, the girls modeled a look bolder than one even Aria would pull from her closet — augmenting their beach look with Ugg boots, kept just out of the frame. Marlene revealed that the scene that always makes her cry is when Alison's body is found, and Aria pulls up and the liars come together.

Qs & A What is The Jenna Thing? Why has Jenna come back to Rosewood? Who was the blonde girl Spencer saw in the window across the street? Alison's body was found behind Maya's house a year after her disappearance; did she die the night she disappeared?

1.02 THE JENNA THING

(AIRED JUNE 15, 2010 | WRITTEN BY I. MARLENE KING | DIRECTED BY LIZ FRIEDLANDER)

Byron: "Sometimes telling the truth does more harm than good."

While the pilot episode focused on the girls' individual secrets and what Ali held over them — which A somehow knows all about — "The Jenna Thing" clues us in to the *major* secret that ties the girls together: they blinded Jenna when a prank on her "peeping Tom" stepbrother Toby went horribly wrong. For the past year, Aria, Spencer, Hanna, and Emily have lived their lives trying to pretend it never happened, but now that Jenna has returned to Rosewood High it's impossible to ignore their guilty feelings. Her walking stick clicking through the hallway is a constant reminder of what they've done and can't undo. Ali was clearly the ringleader the night The Jenna Thing happened, but the girls feel culpable too, not least because they failed to stand up and do the right thing: they let Toby take the blame. Aria's dad believes that telling the truth about his own misdeed might do more harm than good, and the girls embrace that sentiment. They make the decision to protect themselves rather than come clean to the police about who might have a motive to kill Alison.

In Rosewood, everything is picture-perfect, but maintaining that façade requires that people bury their secrets and pretend to be something they're not. Though the threat of being judged a "freak" like Toby Cavanaugh would usually keep the PLLs in control, they find it impossible not to give in to their emotions in "The Jenna Thing," despite the potential fallout. Spencer is an overachiever desperate to make her family proud, but it's the moment she gives in to her connection with Wren that catches her sister's notice. Aria and Mr. Fitz try to do "the right thing" and keep their distance, but, in the end, they can't deny their attraction to each other (especially when caught in a rainstorm!). In an unsettling parallel, Aria gains insight into her inappropriate relationship with her teacher when her dad opens up to her about his affair with his student. As Emily grows closer to Maya, she begins to question her identity and whether she's "normal," and the all-seeing A somehow knows exactly how to taunt her to make her feel even more insecure. Hanna mimics her mother's behavior: not only do their morning routines match, but like Ashley and the cop, Hanna tries to strengthen her relationship with Sean by putting the moves on him. Having the perfect

CHAD LOWE AS BYRON MONTGOMERY

Coming to acting in his teens, Chad Lowe followed in the footsteps of his older brother, Rob Lowe, but made a name of his own from the start. His first notable part was the title role in the short-lived 1984 sitcom *Spencer*, but the job that would put him on Hollywood's radar was his next major role, which earned him an Emmy Award; he played the HIV-positive Jesse McKenna on the drama *Life Goes On* from 1991 to 1993. Since then he's appeared on shows such as *Melrose Place*, *Popular*, *ER*, *Law & Order: Special Victims Unit*, *CSI: Miami*, *True Blood*, and *24*, as well as in feature films such as *Unfaithful*. Chad is the only *PLL* cast member who also works behind the camera: after directing episodes of shows such as *Law & Order*, *Brothers & Sisters*, and *Bones*, the actor took the helm of *PLL* for "Touched by an 'A'-ngel" and "Father Knows Best." From his position in the director's chair, he got to work with most of the cast, and he has nothing but praise for his costars, especially the four leading ladies. "They're really kind and very conscientious and work very, very hard," said Chad. "And I don't think for a minute [they] take any of this for granted."

boyfriend is an essential part of her post-Alison makeover. But the preacher's son isn't interested in getting busy, and Hanna is left feeling rejected instead of wanted.

By keeping so many secrets — and adding to the list every day — the girls are sinking deeper into trouble with their parents, boyfriends, besties, and potentially even the police. And with A promising Aria that her secrets about Fitz and about her father will lead to "hurt," she's more under the mysterious tormentor's thumb than the others. Unlike Wren who gets to make his own choices in life, the girls of Rosewood feel that even when they do exercise some free will, they have to do it secretly, hiding who they really are. But Jenna says she knew exactly who Alison was; does she know the other girls' secrets too?

HIGHLIGHT The total awkwardness of wide-eyed Aria sitting between her mom and her teacher/love interest in the dark movie theater.

The WB back lot is smaller than you think:
Emily's house is actually right next to the town's main street.

EXTRA CREDIT

- Aria's mom makes a crack about Hanna's funeral dress coming from Curvy Girl Clothing, a company that specializes in the "trendiest and sexiest" styles, perhaps a less-than-kind joke about Hanna's heftier days.
- As Ezra and Aria exchange meaningful glances in class, the word innocence can be seen on the chalkboard behind Fitz. It seems ironic, but the show's producers may have meant it sincerely, since they see this relationship as true love bogged down by circumstance.
- Mr. Fitz and the Montgomery women see *It Happened One Night*, a 1934 romantic comedy directed by Frank Capra and starring Clark Gable and Claudette Colbert as an unlikely couple who fall in love despite the obstacles in their path.
- Award-winning architect Frank Gehry designed his hat trick

CHUCK HITTINGER AS SEAN ACKARD

Though Chuck Hittinger thinks Sean is a good dude, he'd love to one day play the dark, mysterious type, like Toby Cavanaugh, his favorite character on the show. But that first time will have to wait for Chuck as *Pretty Little Liars'* preacher son Sean Ackard is proving to be a good boy. Playing Sean is already a first for the actor. He's had guest spots in *CSI: Miami*, *Without a Trace*, *90210*, *Numb3rs*, and *ER* as well as TV movies, but *Pretty Little Liars* was his first recurring role on a TV series, quickly followed by *Jonas*. Up next for Chuck is a turn in the return of the *American Pie* franchise, *American Reunion*.

chair in 1992 as part of a collection of furniture wherein each piece was named after a hockey term; he likely didn't intend it as flirty conversation fodder between a teenage girl and her sister's fiancé.

- The scene where Ezra picks up the rain-drenched Aria in his warm and dry car is an homage to "Don't Stand So Close to Me," the 1980 Police song about a student/teacher relationship.
- The original peeping Tom, who spied on Lady Godiva, was blinded as punishment.

BACK TO THE BOOKS This episode goes mostly off-book while honoring several major plot points — The Jenna Thing, Emily's feelings for Maya, Spencer and Wren's illicit smooch — as well as little details like the Hastings' Star Power game. In *Flawless*, a caught-in-the-rain Aria gets into her love interest's car . . . but it ain't Ezra's.

SLIP UPS Hanna pours herself a cup of coffee but never takes a sip. The clock in the Marins' kitchen reads 10 to 6, but it's late enough in the morning that Wilden has already held a press conference about Ali.

PLL IRL Iowa-born Bryce Johnson brings sketchy cop Darren Wilden to the screen. Bryce is best known as a high school quarterback on Ryan Murphy's pre-*Glee* series, *Popular*. The actor was popular indeed, with guest spots on over 20 TV shows and voice work for hit video games like *Call of Duty*. If *PLL* doesn't give you enough Bryce in a uniform, you can also catch him on the dark mockumentary TV show *Death Valley* as Officer Billy Pierce.

Qs & A Who was the older boy with a girlfriend that Ali was seeing the summer she died? What did Ali tell Jenna when she visited her in the hospital? Spencer sees Jenna texting with multiple devices — is she A?

1.03 TO KILL A MOCKING GIRL

(AIRED JUNE 22, 2010 | WRITTEN BY OLIVER GOLDSTICK | DIRECTED BY ELODIE KEENE)

"Heads up, BFFs. It's open season on liars and I'm hunting." — A

Starting and finishing in the wilds of Rosewood, "To Kill a Mocking Girl" is an episode of hunters and hunted, predators and prey, even though the distinction between those roles is sometimes a bit muddled. Our foursome thinks they're hunting for A, but A's first text in this episode sets the record straight: the girls' newest accessory is a big red bull's-eye.

Aside from A, the people on the prowl are mostly out for sexual trophies. In the locker room, Ben's teenage lust takes a sinister turn, as Emily fights against him and begs him to stop. It's heavy material for the third episode of a teen TV series, but important nevertheless: every two minutes someone is sexually assaulted in the U.S., and many incidents go unreported by people who are too afraid to come forth or who don't know that partners can be rapists too. Toby emerges as an unlikely hero, but does his locker room rescue confirm or challenge his peeping Tom reputation?

Hanna's insecurity turns her into a kind of sexual predator, and she's got her sights set on Sean's V-card. Though she's ripped her new look from *Teen Vogue* and cast aside "Hefty Hanna" like last season's wardrobe, she's not as bulletproof as she wants to be. And in this episode's flashbacks we start to see why Hanna's confidence is so low. Ali, her supposed best friend, is as cruel to her as an enemy would be. When Hanna tries to speak up after the fire, Alison snaps and goes right for Hanna's sore spot and then trivializes her, making her feel like an accessory, easily swapped for a new bestie. Though Hanna's seduction attempt is painful to watch, Sean's incisive insight into Hanna helps our own understanding of her, especially when he asks her why she's acting like she has something to prove. Hanna tells Mona, "It's

TO KILL A MOCKINGBIRD

"In a small town like this, what people think about you matters." Although Ashley Marin uttered those words in the pilot of *Pretty Little Liars*, they could have been pulled straight from *To Kill a Mockingbird*, Harper Lee's Pulitzer Prize–winning novel of the American South in the 1930s. The show's most frequent literary reference, the novel is narrated by Scout, a woman looking back on her childhood when she was a smart, spunky tomboy who wouldn't have taken any of Alison's mean-girl bullying.

In the first part of the novel, we follow along as our protagonist and her older brother Jem (and often, their imaginative pal Dill) occupy themselves with the stuff of childhood in Depression-era Maycombe, Georgia: make-believe, school, and getting into mischief. Their most common fixation is Boo Radley, the mysterious (and potentially violent) shut-in next door who they try to lure out at every opportunity. We also learn about the backdrop to this business of growing up: a deeply conservative, traditional town segregated racially and, to a lesser extent, economically.

Part two brings to the forefront the consequences of the townspeople's deep-seated prejudices. Scout and Jem's father, Atticus, an attorney and the moral paragon of the novel, is called upon to defend Tom Robinson, a black man accused of rape. Despite Atticus's brilliant defense and the man's obvious innocence, the all-white jury sentences Tom to death, and Jem and Scout are forced to open their eyes to life's injustices. Later, Bob Ewell, a man Atticus publicly exposed as a liar at the trial, is determined to get revenge for his humiliation. He even goes so far as to attack the children outside their home, but they are saved by an unlikely hero — Boo Radley.

This attack finds its *PLL* parallel in "To Kill a Mocking Girl" when another misunderstood outsider with a bad rep comes to save someone in need: Toby saves Emily from Ben's unwelcome advances. Marlene King (a huge *Mockingbird* fan — she even named her son Atticus) has frequently referred to Toby as the show's Boo Radley, and this episode is only the beginning of that comparison. Though Alison told the girls that Toby was a pervert who spied on them, they only have her word for it, and it may be that they'd benefit from Scout's realization that Boo was "real nice," to which Atticus responds, "Most people are, Scout, when you finally see them." In a show centered on seeing as watching and surveillance, seeing as understanding is just as important.

But sometimes it takes a dramatic event to remove the blindfold of convention from a person's eyes. In *To Kill a Mockingbird*, the children's loss of innocence was brought about by Tom's unjust conviction; in *PLL*, a sobering reality kicks in after the death of our Mocking Girl, Alison, who unlike the titular bird, is not harmless. The girls are only starting to see how much Alison influenced the way they saw themselves and others, and though they may be more open minded than their parents, they too may be guilty of following Maycombe's Judge Taylor's maxim: "People generally see what they look for, and hear what they listen for."

Atticus's unflagging compassion for others (regardless of their race, reputation, social standing, or even their ignorance) is one of the novel's most important messages, and it's hopefully one the former A-crowd will absorb with their required reading. Atticus counsels Scout, "You never really understand a person until you consider things from his point of view . . . until you climb into his skin and walk around in it," an important lesson for our girls as they start to see things free of Alison's influence.

As A draws closer and Ali's death gets more complicated with every episode, there's one more important takeaway from Harper Lee's classic: the importance of courage. And not the courage of "a man with a gun in his hand." Rather courage based on perseverance, as Atticus says, "when you know you're licked before you begin but you begin anyway, and you see it through no matter what."

not a race," and maybe she even means it, because Hanna doesn't need to have sex to prove something to other people, she needs it to prove something to herself. She sees this rite of passage not just as validation but transformation, a sign she's a woman and has left her heavy past behind.

Juxtaposed with Hanna and Sean's uncomfortable attic rendezvous, Emily and Maya's playful photo session comes off all

the better for the contrast — a clever decision for the show's first girl-on-girl kiss. While Sean and Hanna are in the dark, the photobooth is bright, lit with camera flashes, and the chemistry between the girls outstrips that of the unfortunate hetero couple. The tiny space is a bit like a closet, because that's where Emily's determined to stay, even if our stealthy photo stealer has other plans for exposure.

Toss in Ashley Marin and Detective Wilden's self-serving parlor games (who's hunting whom?), and Meredith Sorenson's shameless pursuit of Byron Montgomery, and it looks like Rosewood's been caught up in a giant game of Manhunt. But without even knowing it, our BFFs are playing the most dangerous game of all — one where A makes all the rules.

HIGHLIGHT Emily and Maya finally locking lips: an important moment for the two girls and for family programming.

EXTRA CREDIT

- Things between Melissa and Spencer are like *The Hurt Locker*, Kathyrn Bigelow's Academy Award-winning 2009 film about an elite bomb squad deployed to Iraq. It's an apt comparison for this sibling relationship, marked as it is by frequent explosions and palpable tension.
- The latest *Mockingbird* lesson on the chalkboard: "Adult Insight vs. Children's Intuition," a conflict that's as present on the pages as in the classroom. For more on *Mockingbird*, see page 66.
- Hanna used to spend her weekends alone with *Dance Dance Revolution*, an arcade and console dance game that challenges people to keep up with choreographed steps.
- Unlike Ben, Hanna stops when Sean says no, and bonus points to her for having a condom in hand.

SLIP UPS Hanna says she can't afford a weekend at a five-star hotel for a romantic getaway with Sean, but based on her wardrobe, she probably spends that much on one trip to the mall. Photobooths only take pictures four at a time, but Emily and Maya's takes seven. The first and the seventh photo both show up in the film strip. What happened to the extra middle ones? When the girls see Toby with Jenna in the school hallway, Aria is surprised and asks when Toby got back, but they saw him walk into the funeral with Jenna in the pilot.

BACK TO THE BOOKS In *Flawless*, Aria confronts Meredith and tells her to stay away from her dad. When Spencer goes to Philadelphia to see Wren in *Flawless*, the two do more than talk. Also in *Flawless*, Hanna tries to seduce Sean, and when she's rejected, she doesn't just steal Sean's car; she's drunk when she does it and Mona's along for the joyride.

PLL IRL Emily might have had a good time at the party, but Shay didn't finish shooting until 6:30 a.m.! It was a late night for all the liars, who started playing Truth or Dare and Never Have I Ever around 3 a.m. Emily's not-so-charming aggro boyfriend is brought to life by Steven Krueger, who's guest-starred on *Parenthood*, *CSI: NY*, *No Ordinary Family*, and *Madison High*. Steven loved filming this episode's fight with Toby: "We had a stunt coordinator on set the whole time and we really choreographed out the fight scene. There was blood involved and all that good stuff. . . . I have a new respect for actors that do a lot of action movies. They have to focus on the acting as well as the fighting and the stunts."

Qs & A Why is Toby back in Rosewood after being gone for a year? What did Alison have on Toby? How did Ali's bracelet end up in the middle of the forest? Is A giving them a clue? What will the Gloved Wonder do with the photos of Maya and Emily?

1.04 CAN YOU HEAR ME NOW?

(AIRED JUNE 29, 2010 | WRITTEN BY JOSEPH DAUGHERTY | DIRECTED BY NORMAN BUCKLEY)

Season 1

"It won't be that easy, bitches." — A

In a bold move, Spencer decides it's time to block all communication from A, and the other three follow suit. That act of defiance sets the tone for an episode where the girls have to choose between acting out and playing along. The balance between keeping secrets and keeping up appearances is hard to maintain, and in "Can You Hear Me Now?" we see the ugly consequence of slipping up. Saddled with the fallout from the drunken party in "To Kill a Mocking Girl," here the teen residents of Rosewood try their best to be mature beyond their years — with varying degrees of success.

Hanna tells the other PLLs that the Ackard car situation is being handled in a grown-up way, but she's quick to revert to childlike glee when she's reunited with her father, who lavishes her with the attention she so desperately craves — at first. Unfortunately for Hanna, her bubble is soon burst when she's forced to face the reality of her new family situation: her dad doesn't want her to live with him, and he introduces her to his fiancée and soon-to-be stepdaughter, the seemingly perfect Kate. Hanna feels like her efforts were for naught: she and her mom have been replaced, and her boyfriend situation is a disaster. That vulnerability makes her an easy target and A hits the spot with her song dedication.

Discussion about *To Kill a Mockingbird* continues in Mr. Fitz's class, and its themes again resonate nicely with the girls' situation. The forces that shape a person as they grow from a child into an adult — their choices, the changes they're subject to — are front of mind for the PLLs, especially Aria who feels that Ezra is treating her like a child when it comes to the subject of her parents' relationship. Because she is sensitive about the age difference between them, she reacts more immaturely than usual for her and he responds in kind. His little temper tantrum in class is totally deserving of Aria's countering flip-out at his apartment. Despite Fitz's insistence that her parents' problems aren't hers to solve, the weight of her father's secret is heavy on Aria. Just as she sees hypocrisy in Atticus's decision to cover up a crime to protect Boo Radley, Aria decides she doesn't feel comfortable lying to her mom any longer. But A beats her to the

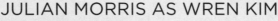

JULIAN MORRIS AS WREN KIM

Playing Melissa's beau with a roving eye is Julian David Morris, who was born January 13, 1983, in London to an accountant father and teacher mother. In his early teens, Julian formed an interest in theater, and it wasn't long until a TV director spotted him in 1996 performing at London's Anna Scher Theatre, which led to his first onscreen gig in *The Knock*. Though he bashfully describes his time working with the Royal Shakespeare

punch: will Ella fault her daughter for hiding the truth?

Partnered with the total outsider Toby Cavanaugh, Emily finds herself identifying with him. She feels like she's masquerading as an insider, conflicted about who she's supposed to be versus who she *wants* to be. Toby gives her sage advice: to be herself no matter what the "idiots" want from her. And in an act of great maturity, Emily decides to be thoughtful rather than impulsive, letting Maya know that she needs time and space to figure out who she's growing up to be, and Maya responds in kind, sweetly telling her she's willing to wait.

Til now, Spencer has been making uncharacteristically reckless decisions in an effort to measure up to the Hastings' level of perfection, even though, like Aria and Fitz, she knows her choices aren't "smart." And her actions haven't had the desired

Company as being limited to small roles, Julian did get to perform in the child parts in *Macbeth* and *Richard III* opposite actors of the highest caliber. After some parts on British TV, including a recurring role on *Fish*, Julian landed the lead in *Young Arthur* (opposite then-up-and-comer Paul Wesley). One of his first lead film roles in America was for the thriller *Cry Wolf*, which costarred Jared Padalecki (*Supernatural*) and Jon Bon Jovi. Once he'd made his breakthrough from the U.K. to the U.S. the actor picked up part after part in hit shows like *ER* and *24* and in the films *Whirlygirl*, *Donkey Punch*, *Sorority Row*, *Valkyrie*, and *Beyond*.

When Julian landed the part of Wren on *Pretty Little Liars*, the actor's schedule was already chock-full, as he was in the process of filming the ABC series *My Generation*. Luckily the two shows shared parent studios, and the actor simply hopped on a plane from Texas, where *My Generation* filmed, back to "Rosewood," a.k.a. the WB back lot. Of his character and his questionable choices, Julian thinks he's an "inherently good person": "I mean it's clear that Wren felt like he made the wrong choice. For him, Spencer was the girl. I certainly think, from how Wren feels, those emotions run deep."

effect: the Golden Orchid nomination is unwanted attention, and she's isolated from her family because of the Wren situation. But when he shows up to take responsibility with her father, he's wasted, and, like Aria does with her older beau, Spencer plays the adult in the situation by fixing him some black coffee and making sure he doesn't drive drunk.

Under the pressure of fitting in and making their parents proud, each girl is forcing herself to be someone she's not. And by keeping secrets instead of leaning on each other like true friends do, it's clear the girls' bonds of friendship are still a little rusty. When coupled with a creepy makeshift grave of roses and dirt in the Hastings' kitchen, A's cliffhanger message is deeply threatening, but A's right, in a way: growing up and deciding who they want to be *won't* be that easy.

HIGHLIGHT Hanna's perfect ability to be friendly and bitchy to Kate at the same time, commenting on her interest in "fake-looking veneers."

EXTRA CREDIT
* The episode title refers to the long-running ad campaign by Verizon Wireless, which ended in April 2011.
* A compares Ali to the Wicked Witch of the East, a character from *The Wonderful Wizard of Oz*, L. Frank Baum's classic children's tale about a group of misfits and one very lost girl, on a quest to see the wizard of the strange land of Oz. The tale was adapted into a stage play and the iconic 1939 film starring Judy Garland, which is a favorite of the *Pretty Little Liars* writers judging by the number of references to it.
* Emily and Toby share a *Twilight*-y moment in science class: Edward and Bella first got to know each other as lab partners too.
* In Ezra's apartment, he has a poster of *Effetto Notte*, the Italian title for Truffaut's 1973 film *La nuit Americaine* (known in English as *Day for Night*). The film concerns a controversial

marriage between a woman and her much-older doctor.
- The song A dedicates to Hanna is "I Don't Need You Anymore" by Jim Camacho from his album *Beachfront Defeat* (2009).
- The message scrawled on the mirror is reminiscent of the threatening messages from an all-knowing stalker in the 1997 horror flick *I Know What You Did Last Summer*. The lipstick-on-mirror message in the movie is even more terrifying: one of the characters wakes up with all her hair cut off and the word "SOON" written on her mirror.

BACK TO THE BOOKS In the book series, Hanna has already met Isabel and Kate during the Ali years, but in *Flawless* she is surprised to find them at a dinner she thought was just going to be father-daughter time. Maya tells Emily in that same book, "I'll wait for you . . . however long it takes," as TV Maya does in this episode. In *Perfect*, Fitz has similar advice for Aria about her parents' problems, "It has nothing to do with you," and she feels like he's treating her like a child.

SLIP UPS How did the PLLs block all unknown emails and texts across all their devices with just one command?

PLL IRL Roark Critchlow plays Hanna's absentee dad, Tom Marin. A TV and film veteran, Critchlow is best known for his work as Dr. Mike Horton on *Days of Our Lives*. Though he and Ashley Benson never appeared in scenes together, his *Days* character was her character's uncle. And playing a TV dad is nothing new to him: he was Jamie Lynn Spears's dad on *Zoey 101*. Playing Hanna's stepmother Isabel is Heather Mazur, a Yale and Carnegie Mellon educated actress, who has had recurring roles on TV dramas like *CSI: New York*, *Criminal Minds*, and *Medium*.

Qs & A Who was filming Spencer and Wren through the window? How did A get into Spencer's house?

1.05 REALITY BITES ME

(AIRED JULY 6, 2010 | WRITTEN BY BRYAN M. HOLDMAN | DIRECTED BY WENDEY STANZLER)

Aria: "You're the teacher. I'm the student. Remember?"

With no dramatic cliffhanger endings or big horror movie moments (potential monster in the closet aside), "Reality Bites Me" is a quiet episode, focusing for the first time on some of the show's adult storylines, though there's a lot of slippage between childlike and adult behavior.

After A's tell-all letter to Aria's mom, Byron and Ella's marriage is in serious trouble, and after a year of carrying the very adult burden of her father's secret, Aria is reduced to being a mostly powerless child (though she does try to protect her brother in a very motherly way). Often when she's frustrated with her parents, Aria runs to Ezra, who treats her like an equal. But of course, she's not his equal, as their outing with Hardy makes clear. Afterward, scared of public judgment and aware that he's crossed a critical line, Mr. Fitz explains, "In theory, we are a lot more wrong than we are right." Interestingly, Aria's rebuttal could have easily been used by her father during his recent affair: "We're here now, and it's just the two of us, and it feels good. So let's not care together." Caught up in the romance, she's blind to her own hypocrisy, forgetting that the rules are there for her own protection. With the discovery of A's text, Ezra suspects Aria of being less than the adult he wants her to be, and he tosses out his student along with her "enhanced mac and cheese." But Ezra's abrupt dismissal of Aria is a bit childish too: he's been too carried away with a passion befitting an adolescent and forgotten that Aria is one.

Spencer and Hanna also end up doing a little parenting of their parents. Ashley Marin's relationship with Hanna blurs the line between mommy and bestie, as they share shoes and leftovers and advice about boys (Momma Marin's switch from "She's cute" to "She's hateful" makes for a great casual exchange), but in this episode it's Hanna who's trying to protect her mother from the news about her father's engagement. Ashley's hurt expression reveals a chink in her Executive Mom armor. In Spencer's case, the episode starts with a gift of childhood-fave buttercreams from Daddy and a daughter who lights up at the prospect of quality time with him, but Spencer ends up teaching her father a lesson, daring him to be hypocritical about her recent plagiarism. It's also a great moment of self-awareness for Spencer, as

LESLEY FERA AS VERONICA HASTINGS, AND NOLAN NORTH AS PETER HASTINGS

Lesley Fera's resumé reads like a list of major shows of the past decade, but she's best known for her recurring parts on *24* (as Angela Nelson) and *CSI: Miami* (as Dr. Joyce Carmel). An accomplished theater performer, Lesley earned one review for *Variety* that could easily be reapplied as praise for her turn as Veronica Hastings: an "appealing amalgam of compassion, ethics, optimism, and efficiency."

Though a new face for the *Pretty Little Liars* demographic, Nolan North, as Peter Hastings, is well known as a voice actor, bringing to life some of the most famous characters in video games and animation — from Superman to the Penguin, the Prince in *Prince of Persia* to Nathan Drake in the *Uncharted* series. At the start of his career, the New Haven–born actor starred on *Port Charles*, a soap opera set in an intrigue-filled fictional city, so his stint in Rosewood, Pennsylvania, just might feel like coming home.

she realizes she can't let people become collateral damage in her drive for success.

Emily most consistently acts her age in this episode. While she defends Toby's rep in front of the other girls, she's not brave enough to be seen with him in public. She's still the good girl afraid of what other people will think, afraid of taking a chance on something outside the Rosewood-approved norm. The town's Holden Caulfield has given her some advice she really needs though, telling her, "Different's good. I like different. This town has too much of the same." Toby's interactions with Emily certainly make him seem less foreboding, he's even awkwardly cute, and his disappointed cringe when Emily blows him off shifts him in our eyes from sinister to soulful, perhaps more ally than enemy.

While most of the episodes so far have centered on A, intrigue takes a backseat this time, with a return to the kind of problems people face in normal life outside of A's sinister web. But the girls can't get too complacent, for as A warns, "You never know what's going on when your back is turned."

HIGHLIGHT Hanna's the It Girl of this episode: between her subtle support of Emily and her great one-liners, she is both heart-warming and hilarious.

EXTRA CREDIT

- The film *Reality Bites* is an iconic 1994 comedy/drama that focuses on four 20-somethings struggling with the cold, hard realities of careers (or lack thereof) and relationships (or lack thereof).
- The board in the classroom has notes about chemical bonding; appropriate as Toby and Emily explore a little weird chemistry of their own.
- The band that Toby and Emily bond over is indie rockers Circa Surprise, which formed in a Philadelphia suburb in 2004.

- Oh, Hardy, *Chitty Chitty Bang Bang* isn't Mexican porn, it's a children's novel by Ian Fleming (of James Bond fame), which was adapted into a musical in 1968. But close.
- Toby's reading *The Catcher in the Rye* by J.D. Salinger, the 1951 classic American novel about angsty outsider Holden Caulfield.
- The security guard is trying to get Lionel Richie tickets. Richie first hit the big time with American R&B/soul group the Commodores, before launching a successful solo career in the '80s with a string of hits perfect for slow dances at weddings or for brokenhearted people sobbing into their pillows.

SLIP UPS Is Mike Montgomery deaf or just dim? Aria can overhear her parents' fight from upstairs, and if he did just listen, he'd figure out what was going on in no time. Why does Jenna lean toward the elevator mirror to apply her lipstick? A mirror should be no use to her at all.

BACK TO THE BOOKS In *Unbelievable*, Spencer's parents find out she cheated before she's the Golden Orchid winner, and they encourage her to keep lying about it. She comes clean to the judges after winning, because she realizes, "Being perfect didn't mean anything if it wasn't real." Book Sean is also a part of a true-love-waits type club, and Hanna wants to go to impress him in *Flawless*.

PLL IRL The actor who plays Hardy, Fitz's buddy from college, is Patrick J. Adams, Troian Bellisario's real-life boyfriend, best known for his role on *Suits*. In a *PLL* podcast, executive producer Oliver Goldstick gave a special shout-out to the moment when Spencer realizes her dad's approval isn't worth it.

Qs & A Who was videotaping the girls? The lipstick on the mirror is Ali's signature color and its the same shade Jenna is wearing in the elevator scene ("Jungle Red" by NARS). Why is Jenna seeing a therapist? Did A somehow know that Fitz would see Aria's text messages?

1.06 THERE'S NO PLACE LIKE HOMECOMING

(AIRED JULY 13, 2010 | WRITTEN BY MAYA GOLDSMITH | DIRECTED BY NORMAN BUCKLEY)

Toby: "I've also done things that I'm not proud of. We've all got secrets, Emily."

The beloved tradition of crowning homecoming king and queen is basically a popularity contest, and — at the outset of the episode — Hanna Marin is determined to win. She's transformed herself from Hefty Hanna to Hanna 2.0, "Rosewood's It Girl," but who she is beneath the lipgloss isn't so easily denied. She tries to get back into Sean's good graces by attending his chastity group meeting, but finds she has more in common with the wisecracking, self-deprecating Lucas — a guy who Mona deems too loserly to even talk to at the homecoming dance. After a string of bitchy comments from Mona about Spencer, Aria, and Lucas, Hanna seems to finally be waking up to the fact that Mona might be funny and insecure, but she's also obsessed with social standing in a way that Hanna isn't anymore. And ultimately, the fact that she chooses her old friends and the mystery of Ali's killer over receiving the crown, never mind giving up on the boy Hefty Hanna would have died to date, means she's well on her way to becoming Hanna 3.0.

While Hanna accidentally spends most of the night with Lucas, using him for her Toby-recon mission, Emily takes Hanna's earlier advice and brings someone to homecoming who will make her happy — Toby. While Emily doesn't have romantic feelings for him (as she clearly still does for Maya), his friendship has been invaluable to her as she struggles with her identity crisis. Their connection has been a secret until this "coming out" moment, and the girls react just as Toby and Emily predicted they would. Though Aria, Spencer, and Hanna are far less concerned about social appearances than Mona is, Emily feels they are prejudiced against Toby, and the girls try desperately to prove that they're not being petty, that Toby really is a "dangerous freak."

Mona's focus isn't just on how cool or popular someone is, but on how wealthy. She dares to mock Spencer for bringing her "Cinderfella," Alex. While über-entitled Spencer is concerned about Alex spending his hard-earned money on homecoming, she at least doesn't share Mona's or Melissa's classist attitude. In an easy act of revenge, Melissa gives Alex the idea that Spence is just using him to make Daddy angry by dating "below" her class. The unfortunate A-related distractions make Melissa's story more than a little believable. Will Spencer be able to convince him otherwise when she can't tell him the truth without facing terrible consequences?

Aria faces a similar problem with Fitz: she can only tell him so much about A without betraying her oath of secrecy with her best friends. And from those friends, she's still keeping her relationship with Fitz a secret. The girls rally around Aria, trying to cheer her up in the wake of her parents' marital discord, but it's Hanna who sees what the real problem is — boy drama. She helpfully tries to get Aria out of her sweatpants-wearing rut by telling her that the guy — the Icelandic Viking boyfriend Hanna assumes she's pining over — should be forgotten. She says they're "in two completely different places," and with that, she accidentally hits on the main issue keeping Aria and Fitz apart. He echoes that sentiment in their epic hallway moment: though he assures her he could never hate her, he hates hiding their relationship, denying her normal teenage experiences like the one she was having with Sean on the dancefloor. Will his honesty about why he's been distant change their relationship, or

TORREY DEVITTO AS MELISSA HASTINGS

The actress who plays Spencer's uppity older sis couldn't be more different from her character, and she's even more accomplished (just don't tell Melissa). Born in New York, on June 8, 1984, Torrey DeVitto balances her busy acting schedule with interests in photography, volunteer work in hospices, and fundraising for charities that are close to her heart. She's also an accomplished musician like her father — Liberty DeVitto, long-time drummer for Billy Joel — and Torrey can most recently be heard as a featured violinist on Stevie Nicks' 2011 album *In Your Dreams*. Though she has diverse interests, Torrey has known she wanted to act since she was a teen. "I graduated high school early and knew that I wanted to jump right into acting. Even while I was in high school I was always auditioning for anything that came through Orlando, where I lived at the time." Onscreen, Torrey's made her mark in ABC Family's *Beautiful People*, The CW's *One Tree Hill* (where she played not-so-nice nanny Carrie) and in a number of films including horror flick *Killer Movie* (2008), which costarred her future husband Paul Wesley. The two got married in 2011, and by year's end were working together again: Torrey landed a role on *The Vampire Diaries*' third season.

Of her *PLL* character, Torrey said, "Everything has to be perfect, and [she] would rather be seething through a smile than show is her English teacher at just as unbridgeable a distance for Aria as a hottie in Reykjavík?

Toby tells Emily what we, the audience, have long known: everyone has secrets, and he and Jenna are no exception. In a jealous snit, Jenna warns Toby that as soon as Emily finds out about his secret, she'll reject him — and that prediction seems to be playing out. Toby's shame about the secret Ali knew was enough for him to take the heat for blinding Jenna in the fire, and Jenna kept her mouth shut about their illicit romance too. With Toby's file stolen and its secrets known to Hanna, Spencer, and Aria, there's no telling what the fallout will be for Emily. Is Toby just trying to be open with her about his past, or is Emily on the run from Ali's killer as the girls believe? The Gloved Wonder, bucket of paint in hand, seems to be pretty confident that the population of Rosewood just dropped by one.

you any type of negative emotion," and, fortunately, Torrey's relationship with her own two sisters is the "antithesis" of Spencer and Melissa's fraught sibling dynamic. But working with Troian Bellisario is a whole other story: "Troian is so smart and has so much to offer, and so our conversations, even between scenes, I just love talking to her. I just thought she was so talented from the second that I worked with her and met her. I love doing scenes with her, I just think she's a really amazing actress. I really lucked out." Of the cast members, she hasn't yet had the opportunity to share the small screen with, Torrey is curious about that Mr. Fitz. Explained Torrey, "The only person on the set that I've not gotten to work [with], that I think would be fun, is Ian Harding. Only because, he lives literally across the street from me. He's one of my closest friends. Although it might be interesting, he kind of cracks me up so I don't know if I'd be able to keep a straight face if I worked with him." Unfortunately for the actress, while lots of unexpected things happen in Rosewood, Melissa cracking up with laughter is unlikelier than A being kind to the PLLs.

HIGHLIGHT An episode that truly looks amazing: the girls' excellent homecoming outfits, hair, and makeup paired with the elaborately decorated school gym takes the episode to a *Gossip Girl* level of stylish.

EXTRA CREDIT
- The writers offer more love for *The Wizard of Oz* in the title's play on Dorothy's "There's no place like home" and A's message that changes the third scary thing one might come across in the woods from bears to bitches.
- Lucas loves a pop culture reference: he compares Hanna to Barbie and Shakira and himself to *Saved By the Bell*'s awkward nerdy character, Screech; his *Star Wars* comparison — Hanna leaving homecoming is like Han Solo abandoning his ship *Millennium Falcon* — goes over her head, but his penchant for watching A&E's *Hoarders* with his parents hits pay dirt.
- Toby's "scene" is listening to The Smiths in his bedroom; the English alternative band (1982–1987), fronted by Morrissey, is in heavy rotation for every brooding boy (and with good reason).
- Hanna combines her interest (fashion) with Aria's (literature) when she describes a dress as "*The Bell Jar*," Sylvia Plath's 1963 novel about a young woman's descent into depression.
- Toby suggests to Emily that they hit the retrospective of Austrian-American filmmaker Fritz Lang, best known for *Metropolis*, *M*, and his contribution to American film noir.
- When Aria is in the bean-toss booth with Ezra, she is momentarily framed by the heart-shaped hole in the spinning wheel, a visual cue to her feelings for Fitz and his for her.

BACK TO THE BOOKS Toby takes Emily to "Foxy," a charity ball, in *Flawless* and she's the one who has an insightful encounter with a fortune-teller. Spencer brings a date to Foxy that she's just using and ends up hurting him, which is how the night plays out with Alex despite TV Spencer's much better intentions. Lucas arrives on the scene in *Perfect* and, poor guy, has the hermaphrodite nickname in both PLLverses.

SLIP UPS In "Can You Hear Me Now?" Ezra says he can cook two dishes, but in the hallway at the dance he says he can make three dishes. Way to improve your culinary skills, Mr. Fitz!

PLL IRL 2AM Club plays Rosewood's homecoming; the California band formed in 2007 and got their name from their favorite bar. The homecoming dance took three days to shoot. When the PLLs were filming closeups, they changed from their towering heels into Uggs or flip flops, but the extras powered through in heels for three whole days! Hanna's outfit is a Sue Wong ostrich feather dress, though costume designer Mandi Line added the lace panel on the front. (The designer later regretted that she didn't make it shorter to show off Ashley Benson's great legs!) Aria's dress is a bit of a Frankenstein: the base is a Bebe sequined dress, with a vintage lace panel from the '40s, shoulders from an H&M T-shirt, '60s beading repurposed into a belt, and a crinoline from Polkadots & Moonbeams underneath. Spencer's dress is by Bebe, and Emily's is Jill Stuart. A stunt double was supposed to film the moment where Emily falls as Toby chases her, but Shay tripped while filming, so she accidentally ended up doing the stunt herself!

Qs & A Ali's lipstick color makes another appearance in the kiss mark on Spencer's tarot card. In Toby's file, the girls learn that he *was* in Rosewood when Ali disappeared and that Ali knew about the affair between Jenna and Toby. Spencer thinks Toby's tattoo (901 Free at Last) refers to September 1st, a.k.a. the day Ali went missing. Is she right?

DIEGO BONETA AS ALEX SANTIAGO

He's been called "the Hispanic Robert Pattinson," and while he may not have reached an R-Pattz level of superstardom yet, the talented actor and singer Diego Boneta may be well on his way. Born November 29, 1990, in Mexico City, the bilingual Diego started his career on the Mexican reality show for kids *Código F.A.M.A.,* where he sang his way to fifth place. His exposure on the show led to jobs on two children's soap operas, *Alegrijes y rebujos* and *Misión S.O.S.,* and the teen-targeted *Rebelde.* His experience doing telenovelas in Mexico not only provided good acting training, but forced him to develop a dedicated work ethic and made him 100 percent sure performing was what he wanted to do. He explains, "There are no child labor laws in Mexico. I was working 20-hour days. Fifty-three days straight. Christmas — half-day off. So when people ask me, 'Diego, are you passionate about what you do?' I just tell them, 'What 12-year-old kid would be willing to do that?'"

Eager for more acting opportunities, the performer came to the U.S., landing a lead role in *Mean Girls 2* (opposite Meaghan Martin and future *PLL* guest star Claire Holt), a recurring role on the rebooted *90210* as Javier Luna, and, of course, the part of down-to-earth country club employee Alex on *Pretty Little Liars*. The role was only supposed to last three episodes, but it became five, no doubt in part because of Diego's onscreen charm. Of his experience on *PLL*, the actor said, "It's just a great, great family. I love my character Alex. I love Spencer and Alex's relationship. I love working with Troian. It's just a real pleasure."

Even as he got his acting career off the ground, Diego was still dedicated to his music. He released his first album, *Diego*, with EMI in 2005, and his second, *Indigo*, in 2008, and is currently at work on a third. He's also caught the ear of TV producers with his songs, landing song placements on *Pretty Little Liars* and *90210*. You can catch him showcasing his singing skills as the male lead in the highly anticipated big-screen adaptation of rock musical *Rock of Ages*.

1.07 THE HOMECOMING HANGOVER

(AIRED JULY 20, 2010 | WRITTEN BY TAMAR LADDY | DIRECTED BY CHRIS GRISMER)

Officer Barry: "Everyone lies."

Riding the tail end of last week's carnival roller coaster, "The Homecoming Hangover" explores not just the consequences of the previous episode's high drama, but also sees some Rosewood residents sobering up enough to see their past actions and attitudes from another perspective.

Hanna finally gets her hands on the homecoming crown, only to find that it's a little flimsy, telling Lucas, "It always seemed so huge." She's not just talking about size, though: the crown is a symbol of all her social striving from the last year, and suddenly it's not quite living up to her expectations. Though she and Sean should be the dream couple, a fairytale king and queen, the crowns are plastic and their smiles just as phony — not to mention that her king didn't even bother to put on pants. Lucas also helps her see that other people aren't as dazzled by A-crowd status as Hanna was: he saw Alison as "straight-up evil" all along. Hanna's starting to sober up from her drunken rise to the top and sees some of the damage she might have done on her popularity bender. She realizes she doesn't have to be aloof and flawless all the time. She chooses a photo for the yearbook that shows the strain between her and Sean and, with the help of a couple LOLcats and a snowboarding turkey, sees the fun in laughing with someone she used to laugh at.

Spencer also goes "social slumming" in this episode, venturing into spaces not frequented by Rosewood's racquet-wielding elite. Though she's offended at Hanna's dig that "not everyone has a daddy with a checkbook to make the bogeyman go away" (which coming from a girl whose mom sleeps with a detective to get her off the hook is a *tad* hypocritical), after seeing the staff bitch board, Spencer realizes that her position of privilege comes with prejudice, justified or not. However, the humbled Hastings doesn't slink back to a members-only area with her tail between her legs, but swallows her pride and attempts to prove she's not defined by her wealth, setting aside her Latin textbook for some sexy Latin beats and some *definite* health code violations.

In Emily's tense bedside chats with her mom about Toby, we see the most open-minded of the foursome come up against the

BRENDAN ROBINSON AS LUCAS GOTTESMAN

Playing Rosewood's most loveable loser, Brendan Robinson found himself in a role close to his own high school experience. The actor attended a small arts high school, where he took tap dancing lessons instead of PE. It was during his teen years that he had his first film role, and though he'd been taking acting lessons since age five, it convinced him he should be Hollywood bound. He caught an agent's attention and landed a few guest spots on shows like *Cold Case* and *Miss Behave*. *Pretty Little Liars* is his biggest project to date, and he confesses that when he found out in a preconceptions of her spectacularly close-minded mother. Mrs. Fields is more concerned than any teen queen about what people think, asking Emily, "Do you have any idea what our neighbors think of him, what they're going to think of you?" A little dramatic irony underscores how out of touch Mrs. Fields is being: she asks if Toby tried to pressure Emily into anything, but of course it's golden boy Ben who put Emily in a compromising position. But don't worry, Military Momma, Toby's really the least of your worries, because Emily's ready to stop being controlled by what other people think. She tells Maya that she doesn't care if anyone sees the photos of them kissing, and announces, "I'm trying this new thing called being honest with myself."

Ultimately, that's what Spencer and Hanna are doing here too, stripping away their social armor and assumptions, and

---

Barnes & Noble that he landed the gig he wanted to jump up and down in the aisles.

Lucas is often compared to loveably geeky Seth (Adam Brody) on *The O.C.*, a show that Norman Buckley also worked on, and the director offered some advice to Brendan on playing the show's token nerd. The actor explained, "He said, 'The reason why Adam Brody was the breakout star of that show is because he never let what the characters were thinking of him affect his character.'" Brendan took the advice to heart and noted, "So when I'm preparing, I never judge the character in any way — it's not, 'Yes, Lucas is a geek.' I don't see him that way as I'm stepping into the role." The advice worked, and fans everywhere fell in love with the bighearted and direct character who helps bring out the kinder, quirkier Hanna. It's a testament to Brendan's charming portrayal, and something executive producer Oliver Goldstick wasn't prepared for: "I didn't think the audience would embrace Lucas like they did. That was really interesting. The studio called us right away and said, 'Put him in more episodes.' We said, 'Lucas, really, in this world?'" Call it revenge of the nerds.

as they skewer fruit or giggle over silly videos, viewers have to rethink their own prejudices against the girls themselves. Though their top-tier social status could make us quick to judge them, watching S and H come down to earth makes our living rooms seem not so different from those in Rosewood, PA.

HIGHLIGHT Even with Alex's stir-fry abandoned, Spencer and Alex cooked up something with sizzle, and it's great to see Spence loosen up and let her hair fly free.

EXTRA CREDIT
- Ms. Shepard is writing notes about *Madame Bovary*, Gustave Flaubert's 1856 classic novel of a bored doctor's wife trying to pass the time with affairs and extravagant living. While this could be a nod to Aria's inappropriate relationship, it could also be an inside joke: Emma Bovary is one of Sara Shepard's favorite characters.
- Lucas says Ali had snakes growing out of her head, referring to the Greek myth of Medusa, a Gorgon with a mane of snakes and gazing upon her would literally turn people to stone.
- Ezra gave Aria a copy of *Winesburg, Ohio*, the classic 1919 collection of connected short stories by Sherwood Anderson about the residents of the titular small town. Ezra's inscription to Aria is fitting, for the last story ends with a young dreamer on a train leaving town, and no doubt Anderson's final words would be appealing to Aria: "The young man's mind was carried away by his growing passion for his dreams . . . and when he aroused himself and again looked out the car window the town of Winesburg had disappeared and his life there had become but a background on which to paint the dreams of his manhood."

SLIP UPS Talking to Emily, Spencer takes her Oxford Latin Dictionary out of her locker twice. While Emily and her mom debate the innocence or guilt of Toby Cavanaugh, a *Self* magazine temporarily disappears from Emily's bed. Probably just a continuity error, but it's also symbolic of Emily's need to hide her true self from her parents. During Spencer and Alex's fruit kebabing sesh, the mix of pineapples and kiwis on his kebab changes between shots.

BACK TO THE BOOKS Sean sends Aria flowers in this episode, but in *Flawless* Aria and Sean are actually a couple for a while. It isn't Ella who leaves the Montgomery house after the affair is exposed but Byron, who moves in with mistress Meredith, in *Perfect*.

PLL IRL Of her cameo appearance in this episode, series author Sara Shepard said, "The best part was the whole world of Rosewood . . . every house, every car, every bedroom, everything was as I imagined in the books." She called being on camera "insanely exciting," and Lucy Hale is quick to praise the author's acting debut, calling her a natural. The song playing as Alex and Spencer dance in the kitchen was written and performed by Diego Boneta (who plays Alex) called "Siempre Tú." It took so long to get the shot of the file flying into the river that they ran out of papers and the props department had to start blow-drying them. (That may be why the final episode includes a wide shot where Aria is mouthing words but no sound is heard.)

Qs & A The Gloved Wonder repainted the Rosewood population sign after homecoming, but Emily is alive and well. Does that mean Toby *is* dead, or was that just a scare tactic for the viewers at home? What is the Gloved Wonder planning on doing with Jenna's file? Did Jenna poison those cookies?

1.08 PLEASE, DO TALK ABOUT ME WHEN I'M GONE

(AIRED JULY 27, 2010 | WRITTEN BY JOSEPH DOUGHERTY | DIRECTED BY ARLENE SANFORD)

*Aria: "This is still Alison's movie,
and we're just filling up the screen."*

"Never look back," Alison tells Hanna in the flashback, but this episode is all about taking a long, hard look at the past, at Ali's legacy and how she still affects the girls. As they try to work through their grief by creating a meaningful memorial to Alison, the PLLs struggle with who Ali really was and what it means to be "friends forever" when one friend is forever trapped as a 15-year-old mean girl.

In the flashback, Ali glamorizes dying young — "That's immortality, my darlings" — but beyond the horrific reality of *how* she died, there's the cold truth that an early grave means she doesn't get the chance to grow up. The girls are maturing beyond Ali's influence, using both the good and bad in her to help guide their choices, overcoming their fear of what Alison would think. The flashbacks illustrate to both the audience and the PLLs what a bully Alison could be — judgmental, bitchy, cruel, and domineering. She maintained her control by putting other people down, from Jenna and Toby and Lucas to her very best friends, making sure they're aware of their "flaws" and that she has potentially damaging info on them.

The girls find it hard to break free from Ali's influence, despite their growing self-awareness. Even Aria decides to go on the group date with Noel Kahn after remembering Ali's advice not to be "too coy" with him. Hanna pretends to be more superficial than she is in order to protect her image and her family's social status, but she's actually being a total sweetheart, selling her designer handbags to help out her mom. She knows to keep their financial trouble private, and judging by Ashley blanching when she thinks Byron knows they're hard up for cash, discretion is exactly what Hanna's mom wants from her daughter. In Rosewood, the adults are just as protective about their picture-perfect identities, walking a *very* fuzzy line between right and wrong, and always-sassy Hanna calls out Darren the Towel-Wearing Cop on his hypocrisy. She refuses to let him intimidate her, something she could never have done with Alison.

Through Jason, Spencer discovers that Alison set her up to take the fall if The Jenna Thing ever came to light: as a way of protecting herself, Ali told Jason it was *Spencer's* idea to stink-bomb Toby. That revelation and Jenna's that Alison was afraid of and "done" with Spencer could make Spencer's efforts to honor Ali feel misguided. But instead she's relentlessly protective of Alison's memory, of the persona that Ali created in her "movie" life. What the foursome says about Alison at the memorial is from the heart, even if it's not the whole awful truth. The PLLs are relieved that Jenna's speech follows suit: she says that Alison's legacy is in how she inspired people with her strength . . . but is she hiding a second meaning in those words? Ali's strength was often destructive, and she could inspire the worst in others. Is Jenna seeking retribution for what was done to her? Ali may have managed to skirt responsibility, planting misdirection that lingers even after her death, but Jenna seems to want the girls to pay for their wrongs. In the world of *Pretty Little Liars*, is justice blind?

HIGHLIGHT Spencer and Jenna's conversation in the library is an incredibly tense scene and promises future fireworks between the two strong-willed girls.

EXTRA CREDIT
- With Alison in the spotlight, A is almost entirely off duty in this episode, save for one text to Spencer.
- Noel gets tickets to Band of Horses, best known for "The Funeral" off their 2006 album *Everything All the Time* and

JANEL PARRISH AS MONA VANDERWAAL

Pretty Little Liars is known for its trademark doll-decorated covers, but Janel Parrish is probably the only actor on *PLL* who's best known for playing a doll. One glimpse at her heart-shaped face and perfectly symmetrical features and it's no surprise that Janel starred in the 2007 *Bratz* movie that brought the famous dolls to life.

Born October 20, 1988, in Oahu, Hawaii, Janel knew acting was her calling when she was just five, sitting in the audience of a touring production of *Phantom of the Opera*. It wasn't long before she was on the stage herself, having landed the role of Young Cosette in a touring production of the legendary tear-jerker musical *Les Misérables*.

After she took her bow on Broadway, Janel started looking for more acting opportunities. She got her first TV role on *Baywatch* (a show filmed in Hawaii at that point) but soon was flying back and forth to L.A. for auditions, until the actress and her mom decided to move to Hollywood when Janel was 14. After adding roles on *Zoey 101*, *The O.C.*, and *Heroes* to her resume, Janel earned a spot in the Bratz movie — her most high-profile role until *PLL*. The role also allowed her to show off her singing skills, and she recorded a song, "Rainy Day," for the soundtrack. Geffen Records even signed Janel, and she started working on an album. "I write a lot of my own music," said Janel. "A lot of it is piano, bass, acoustic. And my dad said I have a problem because I only write about love, so I'm working on that now." The album was never released, but the Hawaiian hasn't left music behind and insists she'll never give it up.

When *Pretty Little Liars* was casting, Janel auditioned for Spencer, but ended up being offered Mona instead. Despite her Bratty past, she sees the vulnerability in Rosewood's cattiest mean girl: "I've played the mean girl before, but none like Mona. She *is* a mean girl and can definitely be inconsiderate, but it all stems from her insecurities, which I think makes her different from the typical mean girl. Deep down inside, she's just terrified that she's going to go back to being invisible."

"Laredo" from their 2010 album *Infinite Arms*.

- Emily's dad, Lieutenant Colonel Fields, is stationed in Camp Phoenix, a NATO base operated by the U.S. army, in Kabul, Afghanistan.
- In Mark Twain's *The Adventures of Tom Sawyer* (1876), Tom Sawyer watches his own funeral, discovering what people have to say about him after his "death," like A does at Alison's memorial.
- Hanna tells Aria to stop "pining for the fjords," a line from the Monty Python parrot sketch, and to "carpe hottie," a play on the Latin phrase *carpe diem*, meaning "seize the day."
- Lucas drops another *Star Wars* reference: Count Dooku is drawn to the Dark Side by Darth Sidious, which means as little to Hanna as do the designers she rhymes off to Lucas.
- Alison likely never saw *Das boot*, the 1981 German World War II submarine film, but that doesn't stop her from making a das booty joke.
- Maya and Emily spend more time making out than watching *I Walked with a Zombie*, a 1943 horror flick about a nurse who comes in contact with a woman who may be the victim of an evil voodoo zombie spell.

BACK TO THE BOOKS Em's dad being in the army is a departure from the books, where Mr. Fields was a Typical Rosewood Dad. After running into Noel at a séance in *Heartless*, Aria decides he may not be the Typical Rosewood Boy, and they start dating.

SLIP UPS The crate for the memorial sculpture is absurdly large for the sculpture itself. Ashley says they are a one-paycheck family living a two-paycheck lifestyle: does Hanna's dad not pay any child support or alimony? Why were we shown the flashback to Aria and Ezra's conversation at the homecoming dance? "Ezria" moments are well remembered; replaying that scene felt like filler.

PLL IRL The L.A. Lakers NBA final was on while the memorial scene was being filmed, and the "obsessed" Ashley Benson kept begging for breaks to grab a couple minutes of the game, and extras were signaling her updates as she tried to do her lines. The actress admitted, "I was distracted the entire time." She needn't have worried: the Lakers took home the title. Parker Badgley plays Ali's brother, Jason. Parker's also appeared in *The Guiding Light*, *Law & Order*, 2010's *A Nightmare on Elm Street*, *Consent*, *Detention*, and *Grimm*. Sean's short-lived band is named after unit production manager Skip Beaudine.

Qs & A Why did Toby call Ali's cell the night she was murdered? In what way is Jason "even worse" than Alison? Is he a threat to the girls? Why did Ian show up at Ali's memorial? Who destroyed the memorial? Who made the copy of Alison's bracelet for the girls to find in the forest?

1.09 THE PERFECT STORM

(AIRED AUGUST 3, 2010 | WRITTEN BY OLIVER GOLDSTICK | DIRECTED BY JAMIE BABBIT)

Emily: "I loved her as more than a friend."

Most students have prayed for a freak storm to cancel their tests or essays or SATs, and in Rosewood it actually happens! But as what seems like half the town's population shelter in the high school, tension flares like the lightning outside, and our foursome is tested in ways that make standardized tests seem like a relief. What's particularly interesting about this episode is that instead of A stirring the pot, the drama is driven by natural events, the perfect storm of factors coming together.

Throwing all these characters into close quarters was genius, because metaphorically, a storm was brewing already, with pressure mounting and winds rising. That pressure is most obvious in Emily; still keeping her sexuality under wraps, the sweetest of the foursome is more irritable than we've ever seen before. Hanna already knows, but our girl next door is still hiding it from everyone else. A's texts and the flashbacks they inspire only add to the pressure, forcing Emily to face things she's trying to bury. It's heartbreaking that she's forced to come out to her friends under Wilden's coercion, but her "more than friends" admission might dissipate some of the pressure she's been feeling. Unfortunately, where Wilden is concerned, Emily's just elevated herself to the status of suspect.

With the return of Mr. Fitz, we see another two weather systems collide. Noel Kahn takes up his guitar (that old trick) and finally makes some romantic headway with Aria, and in the proud tradition of musicals, their tender moment comes in the form of a song. With Ezra's ill-timed intrusion, these age-appropriate sparks flicker out like the school's lighting, and the confrontation that has been brewing finally takes place. It's a rapid-fire exchange, all arms-crossed fury and short, accusatory sentences flying. But in the end, Ezra decides to act like an adult and walk away from the relationship. Soon after, the teacher also falls prey to the confessional intimacy of darkness and small spaces, when he ends up in the storage closet with Aria's newly single mom, who's eager to talk about her daughter and introduces some slight sexual tension with her offhand comment about getting into his lap. Ezra keeps stiffly trying to shut down the awkward conversation, which gets more intimate as Ella bares her anxieties.

PLL's focus is mostly on the high school crowd, so glimpses of parental problems are rare, but in this episode the cracks start to show, and we see that being an adult in Rosewood isn't much easier than being a teen. They have the same battles with relationships, reputations, and the urge to be perfect, and the pressure doesn't lessen with the years. In fact, for the older generation, there's less room for mistakes. From Mrs. Hastings hiding her cancer scare to Byron and Ashley getting gun-shy when their candlelit meet-cute ends abruptly, no one wants to appear vulnerable or take a chance.

Forcing confrontations and confessions, "The Perfect Storm" acts like a tornado, stirring up the characters and sending them in new directions. When the air clears, will Rosewood residents be able to find the proverbial calm after the storm, or will they be too busy surveying the damage?

HIGHLIGHT Veronica Hastings laying the legal smackdown on Detective Wilden's shoddy protocol and constant harassment. Second place points to Hanna: Spencer might be the group's natural leader, but she has trouble with authority figures; Hanna, on the other hand, leaps to Emily's defense like a chained-up rottweiler.

EXTRA CREDIT
- Emily's *Great Expectations* text from A is signed "xoxo," the sign-off of another famous faceless spy, Gossip Girl.
- Ali wants to live in Paris and take a nap in the Louvre, one of the world's most famous art museums and home to the *Mona Lisa*.
- Mona and Hanna both make references to *The Wizard of Oz*. Its most prominent theme is the need for confidence and self-awareness, since all the characters ask the Wizard for something they already have. And while Hanna accuses Mona of not having a heart, it's nice to see Hanna discover her own, and some courage as well, as she stands up for Lucas and faces the same anxieties that Mona's still avoiding.
- Veronica tells Spencer she's had too many sidecars, a cocktail made of cognac, orange liqueur, and lemon juice.
- The storm should've had a supporting actor credit: it was in almost every scene, with rain pelting the windows, or the dark, rainy blues of the outdoor world dominating the indoor palate.

SLIP UPS Emily changed her clothes after her muddy memorial visit; why didn't she change her shoes? If the police had plenty of photos of Emily at the memorial, shouldn't they have photos of her breaking it if she's the culprit?

PLL IRL Lucy Hale got to show off her vocal chops singing "Who Knows Where the Time Goes," a 1967 song by Sandy Denny that's been covered by numerous artists including Eva Cassidy, Nancy Griffith, Cat Power, and Nina Simone. Brant Daugherty, who plays Noel Kahn, took guitar lessons in high school but had to brush up on it for this episode. Joked Brant, "I had a bit of a working knowledge of it, I guess in the way a carpenter could have a working knowledge that wood makes a house."

Qs & A Who destroyed the memorial? Why were Lucas's shoes so muddy? Where did the Gloved Wonder get the footage of Ali?

GREAT EXPECTATIONS

"That was a memorable day to me, for it made great changes in me. But, it is the same with any life. Imagine one selected day struck out of it, and think how different its course would have been. Pause you who read this, and think for a moment of the long chain of iron or gold, of thorns or flowers, that would never have bound you, but for the formation of the first link on one memorable day." So relates Pip, the protagonist of Charles Dickens' 1861 classic novel *Great Expectations*. "The memorable day" in question is the first time he meets Estella, the haughty, cold-hearted girl he falls in love with early in the novel. But it's a quotation that could apply just as easily to our PLLs meeting Alison, who, in life and death, would change the course of their lives completely.

Pip's life does change dramatically, though it's not due to Estella so much as to a chance encounter at the book's opening. Pip, alone and visiting the graves of his family, is accosted by an escaped convict who coerces him into bringing food and tools to unlock his shackles. It's a favor the criminal never forgets. Soon after, Pip meets Estella and sets his sights on self-improvement, and conveniently, a mysterious benefactor gives Pip money to go to London and become a gentleman. But he squanders it, rapidly accumulating debt, and in the end is saved from his own overindulgence by two unlikely heroes: the convict, who is his true benefactor, and Joe, the blacksmith who raised him.

Pip is what Estella disdainfully calls "common," whereas Estella, under the care of the rich Miss Havisham, receives a good education and lives in a gothic mansion full of fine things. But Pip's love for Estella makes him want to raise himself above his circumstances, to become a gentleman. Once again, we find an obvious parallel in *PLL*, with Alison befriending the girls, instantly giving them social cred, though, especially in Hanna, we see how hard they still work to maintain her esteem and affection.

Emily gets to play Pip to Alison's Estella, a parallel driven home in "The Perfect Storm" when Alison reads Emily a passage from the novel that no doubt hits close to home: "I loved her against reason, against promise, against peace, against hope, against happiness, against all discouragement that could be." Yet this irrational love doesn't apply to Emily only, but the others too. Their love, like Pip's, seems to be in part aspirational: they love Ali because they start to see themselves in her It-Girl image. But with each Ali flashback, her careless, often cruel actions erode her good qualities a little more, and as Ali brings out their mean-girl qualities, they begin to question whether being like Ali is something to strive for after all. For despite Alison's professed admiration for *Great Expectations*, it seems she got caught in the silly names and missed the main message: that kindness and loyalty trump social status every time, and that character is defined not by our appearance or possessions, but by our actions.

It's a message that Mona, in some ways Ali's heir, would also do well to consider. Mona is only supporting cast in *PLL*, but in *Great Expectations*, she'd be the star of the show: Pip's desire for self-improvement and social climbing would be all too familiar. Like Pip, once she has jumped up a few castes, Mona's also afraid of being too closely associated with her past untouchable status. She may not be as far from it as she'd like: she's still buying second-hand designer goods, and her constant need to cut down others suggests a fragile ego. Hanna, defending Lucas, hits the nail on the head, when she says, "What has he ever done to you except remind you that two short years ago, we were him." But in *Great Expectations* Pip discovers that the very people he tried to distance himself from are the most generous, reliable people in his life, and perhaps Mona needs to take a cue from Hanna, and remember that popularity is not a measure of character. (After all, who wouldn't choose to hang with Lucas over Sean or Ben?)

With convicts and kidnapping, manipulation and attempted murder, *Great Expectations* is also a story concerned with guilt and innocence, though it takes Pip an entire novel to sort the real criminals from the benevolent ones, the cruel from the caring. But as A's web gets even more intricate, we may have to wait a while before we can have similar revelations in Rosewood. In the meantime, *Great Expectations* reminds us to look beyond our own prejudices, beyond the surface of things — a useful reminder for the PLLs and for sleuthing viewers themselves. To that end, Pip's lawyer offers a helpful maxim, whether for judging character or hunting for killers: "Take nothing on its looks; take everything on evidence. There's no better rule."

1.10 KEEP YOUR FRIENDS CLOSE

(AIRED AUGUST 10, 2010 | WRITTEN BY I. MARLENE KING | DIRECTED BY RON LAGOMARSINO)

Ella: "People aren't dolls to be played with."

With a harrowing cliffhanger, "Keep Your Friends Close" shows us how far A is willing to go in an episode that's all about seizing opportunities, regardless of the consequences. Control over their own lives is harder and harder for the girls to maintain, as A toys with them and takes them for a wild and potentially deadly ride.

Hanna tries hard to balance the competing forces pulling at her: she wants to be a good friend to Mona but that means skipping class and spending cash, two things that go against her instinct to be a good daughter, especially while her mom is seriously stressing over money. By rekindling her friendship with

Emily, Aria, and Spencer, building a new friendship with Lucas, and hiding the A secret, Hanna's unintentionally distanced herself from Mona. Mona was her friend back when no one else was, but their united quest for social status is no longer a top priority for Hanna, something she realized after winning homecoming queen. Though it seems superficial, the rumor A starts about Hanna getting lipo cuts to the foundation of Mona and Hanna's friendship: they worked hard and sacrificed to become Rosewood's It Girls, and if Hanna cheated then and doesn't even care about her status now, what's left between the two? Despite not connecting with Mona the way Hanna does, the other girls respect how important that friendship is for Hanna. She won't accept A messing up her life: she decides to stand up to A — and gets mowed down for knowing too much.

Spencer tries to do the right thing by mending her relationship with Melissa: she apologizes for the Wren incident but keeps her tryst with Ian a secret (a decision the rest of the girls support). It's nice to see the Hastings girls declare a ceasefire, but is it really in Melissa's best interest to date a guy who had *two* secret relationships with 15-year-old girls? Probably not. *Especially* since he's in the video from the night Ali disappeared. At the very least he's keeping secrets that could help find Ali's killer — if he's not the killer himself. Shouldn't Spencer warn her sister?

Spencer feared that the girls would react to her secrets the way Ali did — declaring her a "skank" if she was into Ian — but they are accepting of her. And after seeing "Ali hearts Ian" carved into the tree, Spencer now realizes Ali was being hypocritical when she judged Spencer. Emily chooses to keep her big secret from her family: she seems to want to open up to her dad, especially after his "the truth shall set you free" speech, but she can't — she's still too afraid of how she will be judged. And the way her mother looks at those photos of Maya and Emily kissing, Emily may not be wrong in fearing her mom will freak out.

Like Spencer, Aria tries to make amends for her past mistakes; she gives her mother a heartfelt apology for keeping the

NIA PEEPLES AS PAM FIELDS

Can you picture Pam "Straight-edge" Fields wearing a gold lamé suit and dancing in a music video? Watch Prince's "Raspberry Beret" and you won't have to imagine it. California-born triple threat Nia Peeples has been performing since she was a child and in the mid-1980s, she landed a part on *Fame*, the NBC TV show about a New York City performing arts school that was *the* coolest series. From there, Nia's career took off and instead of dancing in other artist's music videos, she recorded and released three albums herself. As well, she kept acting and doing hosting gigs, like the Arsenio Hall–produced dance program *The Party Machine with Nia Peeples*. In the 1990s, her career took a turn into action-star territory. Nia loved doing stunts and fight sequences, adapting her dance training so that she could be physical in a different way on set. More recently, she's garnered recognition for her long-running stints on *Walker, Texas Ranger* and *The Young and the Restless*.

Her career has taken her from dance-partying teenager to strict no-nonsense mom, but that's not the tricky thing for Nia on *Pretty Little Liars*. "It's a funny thing being a recurring character on the show," said Peeples, "because I'm gone more than I'm there. A lot of times, as an actor, I'll show up on set and read the script and think, 'Hmm, what has gone on between today and the last time I was on the show and how much does Pam know?' So it's always really interesting and a precarious position as an actor to pick and choose those things, because I don't really know where my character is going." When she's not in Rosewood, filming on another project, or doing charity work, Nia works to promote a fitness and health regime that she's designed for women over 40, eager to share her secrets and break the myth that only the young should be considered beautiful. A mother of two with a three-decade career as she hits her 50s, Nia Peeples may not play the perfect character on *Pretty Little Liars*, but for the younger actresses she works with she's the perfect role model for a long, interesting, and satisfying life in Hollywood.

truth from her, realizing that it was a big mistake to do so. Ella shows her daughter forgiveness, but that's something that Aria is initially not ready to give to Fitz. For Aria, hiding feelings is just like lying, and she is angry with Fitz for allowing her to believe that he didn't love her. As far as the girls' problems go, this is a pretty sweet one to have — especially as Fitz explains to her that he was looking for a way for them to be together — and her anger melts when he leans in for the kiss. Until Fitz finds some other job, their relationship is verboten, and A's not the only one who knows about them: Hanna saw them together, and if the hooded figure who wrote on the window of the car is *not* A, then someone else knows too.

Secrets from the past — from within their group, from Ali, from A, from Toby — continue to surface and shake their understanding of what's going on. The girls try, for the most part, to do the right thing, but it's hard to navigate a world full of cryptic clues, red herrings, shifty suspects, and plain old lies. And it's even harder when the truth doesn't set them free but gets them run over.

HIGHLIGHT The steamy reuniting of Fitz and Aria. Those two love to make out in his car! Second place is Aria's line to Spencer, spoken like a true best friend, "You're a freak and I love you."

EXTRA CREDIT
- The FBI agent assigned to Ali's case is Agent Cooper, a reference to David Lynch's *Twin Peaks*. In that creepily awesome TV series, Kyle MacLachlan's Agent Cooper came to a small town to investigate the murder of a popular blonde teenager who was hiding more and darker secrets than Alison DiLaurentis.
- Emily tells Cooper that Alison thought secrets kept them close, something we heard Ali say in the pilot episode.
- The scenes of Ashley stealing Mrs. Potter's money and driving through town with it are an homage to the opening of

Hitchcock's *Psycho* (1960), where Janet Leigh's character nicks $40,000 from her workplace to solve her financial problem.

- The title of Ezra's poem, "B-26," refers to the song on the bar's jukebox when he first met Aria.

ERIC STEINBERG AS WAYNE FIELDS

Bringing Emily's stern but loving dad to life is Washington, D.C.-born actor Eric Steinberg. The son of two university profs — his dad in Asian Studies and his opera singer mom in the music department — Eric's been working steadily in the film and TV industry since the mid-1990s, in Hollywood, New York, and in Thailand on occasion. Though he's been on shows like *24*, *Charmed*, *Without a Trace*, *Days of Our Lives*, and *Torchwood*, he's most often recognized for one of two roles: the sci-fi fans recognize him as Setan from *Stargate SG-1* and the soap-opera fans as Ji Min Kim from *The Young and the Restless*. Besides enjoying the comfort that a regular gig offers, Eric liked getting to know the cast and crew on the set of *Y&R*: "The sound guy, for instance, did a couple of films with Ingmar Bergman, one of the great filmmakers of our time, and here he is sitting in the booth at *The Young and the Restless*. They have these stories, the cast and crew, that only come with the regularity of working this kind of schedule. Theater is similar but this is much more gratifying in that way. I love being exposed to this audience." *Stargate* and *Y&R*, though very different shows, have one thing in common with *Pretty Little Liars*: a devoted and hard core fanbase. Eric can expect the *PLL*ers to start recognizing him as Emily's Major Dad.

BACK TO THE BOOKS The moment Toby shows up in Emily's car was a big surprise for book fans: in *Flawless* Toby is found dead. Mona feels ditched by Hanna in *Perfect*; details like the restaurant name, Rive Gauche, and the two backup bitches, Riley and Naomi, are pulled from the books. The villainous A starts a lipo rumor in *Perfect*, but it's about Mona, not Hanna. The cliffhanger moment is pulled straight from *Flawless*: after Hanna gets run over, the other girls get a text from A that "she knew too much." In *Perfect*, "I See You" is written in condensation on glass, but it's a message for Emily, not Aria and Fitz.

SLIP UPS Maya's comment to Emily that Alison brought Toby's dark side to the surface and is in someway responsible for her own murder is a little too "blame the victim" for comfort. Emily and Aria's crazy blowouts disappear after the gag, and their hair returns to its normal height and volume. Toby has "friends in all the wrong places," and "misery loves company"? Let's stick to one cliché per line, *PLL*! Would Ashley really leave her purse open, full of stolen money and visible on the seat next to her? It's pretty easy to zip up that evidence.

PLL IRL Showrunner Marlene King actually went "glamping," and she thought it would be fun to write into an episode.

Qs & A Is Toby's story the truth: that the night Ali disappeared he met her to thank her for getting him away from Jenna? Were Spencer and Ali secretly seeing Ian at the same time? Who turned Toby in to the police? Who did Hanna see writing "I See You" on the window of Fitz's car? Who is A?!

1.11 MOMENTS LATER

(AIRED JANUARY 3, 2011 | WRITTEN BY JOSEPH DOUGHERTY | DIRECTED BY NORMAN BUCKLEY)

Alison: "Go ahead and try it. Be honest. See what it gets you. . . .
Take it from me. You're always better off with a really good lie."

In a show about the dangers of keeping secrets and telling lies, you might think honesty is always the best policy. But in this fascinating episode, a dead girl known for lying is perhaps the voice of truth: honesty isn't as simple or as easy as it seems, and it certainly doesn't guarantee that people won't get hurt.

Though "Moments Later" is filled with dramatic revelations like Melissa and Ian running away to tie the knot, Hanna's drug-induced encounter with a candy-striping Alison acts as a centerpiece to the episode and to the season as a whole with its focus on the central tension of *PLL*: the relationship between truth and security. The girls often think there's safety in secrecy, but they are constantly threatened by the consequences of their lies being exposed. Similarly, while there should be safety in honesty, honesty means vulnerability, and in this drug-induced dream, Alison cautions against coming clean. She offers the tantalizing clue that "telling the truth to the wrong person at the wrong time" is how she wound up six feet under, and warns Hanna against baring the truth.

Hanna might agree with Alison, especially after her distressing conversation with Lucas. She tries to do right by him in the long run and keep him as a friend by telling him she's just not that into him. So far, Lucas has been one of the series' straight shooters: his directness and honesty are part of what makes him so endearing. But when even Lucas wants to be lied to, honesty starts to look a little less benign. Poor Han, trying to turn over a new leaf, but nothing takes the little bumps out of your tapioca like breaking a heart and losing a friend.

But when it comes to not handling the truth, Emily's parents make Lucas look like a champ. Though her father tries, both parents struggle to reconcile wallet-picture Emily with the grown-up version. To his credit, G.I. Dad realizes that at heart, his little girl is still the same — "I just need a new picture" — and even after Emily's confession, he takes the same tack with his wife. But Mrs. Fields wants that static, simplistic version of her daughter back; she wants the future they planned for her. It doesn't help that this part of her daughter flies in the face of her values, rigid black-and-white mores she can't believe her husband is even thinking of reexamining. While it's hard to watch her anger and her total lack of understanding, her perspective is important for the writers to include. With the still prevalent anti-gay sentiment in the U.S. and beyond, Pam Fields' reaction is a very real part of many coming-out stories. Emily overhears every word of her parents' heated debate, and no doubt she wonders if the honesty was worth the price. She may never again be the picture-perfect daughter they thought she was. But by the end of the episode, she's at least resigned to the consequences of her revelation, telling her friends, "I don't know what it's going to be, but it's going to be different."

Aria also finally comes out with the truth about her relationship with Mr. Fitz, though not by choice. And based on the crossed arms and furrowed brows in the hospital room, she's not faced with the most sympathetic crowd either. (At least she didn't have to tell Mr. and Mrs. Fields.) But by the end of the episode even Spencer, the group's judgiest, is coming around. Honesty was certainly the harder path here, but will it ultimately be the better one? Maybe the reactions and advice of her BFFs are important: it's easy to get caught up in the romance of being star-cross'd lovers and lose perspective. Still, even if the girls are excellent at staying mum, Aria's dangerous secret just got much harder to keep under wraps.

HIGHLIGHT Emily's pained admission to her father is beautifully portrayed by Shay Mitchell. And on the lighter side, Mona's

THAT'S SO GAY

In 1989, the baby boomer drama *thirtysomething* aired an episode called "Strangers" in which two men are shown lying beside each other in bed, not touching, with one smoking a cigarette. The implication that they had just had sex caused five regular sponsors to pull their advertisements, costing the show $1.5 million in revenue, and the episode was also left out of the summer rerun schedule. There were gay characters, and occasionally gay couples, on primetime TV, but different rules applied to them — no visible "more than friends" behavior. Even well into the '90s, shows with fairly prominent gay characters were never seen hugging or kissing. Susan and Carol got married on *Friends*, but they never got their wedding kiss.

That's not to say two people of the same sex *never* kissed onscreen — women did occasionally; in what is now known as "sweeps lesbianism," a show might resort to a one-time titillating scene meant to boost ratings (one of the first involved Holly Marie Combs, a.k.a. Ella Montgomery, in 1993 on *Picket Fences*). Marti Noxon, the writer who penned the landmark relationship between Tara and Willow on *Buffy the Vampire Slayer*, explained to NPR, "You can show girls kissing once, but you can't show them kissing twice . . . because the second time, it means that they liked it." The first boy-on-boy kiss didn't grace network TV until 2000 on *Dawson's Creek* when the openly gay Jack McPhee locked lips with Ethan. (Jack's kiss actually happened before there was smooching on *Will & Grace*, a show with a gay character in its title!)

Twenty years after that sensational scene in *thirtysomething*, ABC Family debuted a new teen series with a female lead who would soon admit that she was gay. There was a bit of a stir from some camps, notably the Florida Family Association, who announced the show "sends the wrong message to these young girls, a message that reinforces and legitimizes this homosexual lifestyle," and pressured some companies to withdraw their advertising. But for the most part, people were unfazed.

As people nationwide start to openly embrace their sexuality at a younger age (the average coming out age is now 16, dropping from 19 to 23 in the '80s), it's only natural that TV shows reflect the more open reality of teen life by including gay characters. And they are: *Glee*, *Gossip Girl*, *Degrassi: The Next Generation*, the new *90210*, *Greek*, and *Skins* all have main characters who are gay, and a 2010 study by GLAAD (Gay and Lesbian Alliance Against Defamation) revealed that four percent of all series regulars are gay. That might not seem like much, but there are two important parts to that: first, that the characters are regu-

lars, and second, that they are treated with the same respect as straight characters.

And that's where *Pretty Little Liars* really shines. Because even though Emily is a lesbian, she's not treated any differently than her hetero friends. Just as Aria, Spencer, and Hanna have interests and issues outside of boyfriend drama, Emily isn't a one-note token character. Showrunner Marlene King explained that it was important she didn't have "any stereotypical look or vibe for a gay woman. She's a pretty little liar just like any other pretty little liar on the show." Shay Mitchell praises the way *PLL* has kept her character completely grounded and real: "Most of the time on TV and in movies, you see the girl who is the weird one and that's the one who is gay or a lesbian. And you see two hot chicks making out and it's glorified. And this isn't. It's just simply what it is. And it's humans finding each other and feeling something."

Emily actually dates more than the other liars, which Marlene thinks is key because Emily is trying to figure out what kind of girl she likes. "She's not blowing through these girls like a box of chocolates. But she's definitely searching and looking," said the showrunner. Executive producer Oliver Goldstick puts it simply, stating that she's "forging an identity." And surely that's something that's relatable for all teens.

It helps that Emily is played by someone who is able to see the character for who she is: just another girl. Shay explained, "I've been in relationships before where I've loved somebody, I know what it's like to have a crush on somebody, I know what it's like to kiss somebody. So with all those things, how would it be any different for my character? Even if she's kissing another girl, she's not kissing another girl being like, 'Oh my gosh I'm kissing another girl.' She is falling for that person."

Emily's journey is one that has resonated with fans across the globe, and after Emily came out, Shay was bombarded with messages from people who related to the story line. Playing such a prominent gay role comes with great responsibility, but Shay has handled it with sensitivity and compassion, even appearing in an "It Gets Better" promo for the Trevor Project. "If I can represent the gay community in any small way, I'm proud to do that," she said. "But I have had a lot of girls even on the street that recognize [me] . . . and they ask me for advice. I don't feel in any position to [give it], but I'm just saying be true to yourself and that's what the character is doing . . . just live as much of an authentic life as you can." Which is great advice for any teenager, regardless of sexual preference.

Marlene has noted the story line's popularity across a broad audience. "I'm actually happy to say gay woman *and* gay men love this show," she said. "And I hope it is a special experience for gay women, to be able to watch these characters who are beautiful inside and out, relating to each other in such an accepting way. We all want that unconditional love by our friends and our family. And that's what we're creating here. Hopefully it becomes a role model for other people."

underwired white flag and tale of Hanna's barfy bow managed to be perfectly in character and still touching.

EXTRA CREDIT
- *The Twilight Zone* was an iconic sci-fi TV series that originally ran between 1959 and 1964 and, due to its popularity, was revived twice after that. Each week *The Twilight Zone* explored strange events in the "fifth dimension" and often ended with a plot twist to drive home an overall message.
- The internet offers great resources for people considering coming out. Try starting out at the National Coming Out Day site (hrc.org) or EmptyClosets.com.

BACK TO THE BOOKS In *Perfect*, A leaks Emily's secret by posting the picture of Emily and Maya kissing all over the school natatorium. Emily doesn't come out to her parents; A outs her instead. In the same book, post-hit-and-run Hanna forgets the identity of A . . . until the next volume. In *Unbelievable*, Lucas kisses hospital-bed-bound Hanna, and she returns his romantic feelings.

PLL IRL "Moments Later" was *Pretty Little Liars*' winter premiere and the highest rated episode of season 1. Lucas's Sleeping Beauty kiss was shot as both a forehead kiss and an on-the-mouth kiss. But, according to Ashley Benson, they decided to go with the forehead because it "was a little sweeter and not as creepy." For Hanna's broken leg, Ashley had a five-hour fitting for four casts. She had to keep it on all day and had to use crutches and a wheelchair to get around.

Qs & A Why was Noel Kahn lurking in the hallway when Fitz was working late? Ali says that the girls already know what happened the night of her disappearance, or would if they put all their knowledge together. But haven't they done that already? Unless, of course, they're hiding things to protect their own pretty little secrets. Whose lipstick is on the cup by Hanna's bed? Was someone actually in the room with Hanna pretending to be Alison?

LAURA LEIGHTON AS ASHLEY MARIN

A could learn a thing or two from Laura Leighton's best-known character, the one and only crazy, manipulative, and conniving Sydney Andrews from the original *Melrose Place* (a role she revived for the short-lived reboot in 2009). Before Laura made her mark on pop culture history in that part, she grew up in slightly less scandalous Iowa before making her move to California to be an actress. She was busily working as a waitress before landing what was originally only a two-episode gig, but Sydney Andrews became her breakthrough role, and one for which she earned a Golden Globe nomination in 1995. Shortly after Sydney "died," Laura appeared on sister show *Beverly Hills 90210* then moved on to roles in films, TV movies, and other series. Laura describes her onscreen alter ego in *Pretty Little Liars* as a woman who has "a bit of an edge. She's very matter-of-fact and she places a very high value on appearances." A real-life mom (she has two kids with husband Doug Savant), Laura brings her maternal instincts both to her part as single-mother/business-woman Ashley Marin and to her TV daughter. Said Ashley Benson, "Laura's become like my second mom; we talk all the time. She helps me out with my personal life; she gives me really good advice. We have so much fun on set together, she's great. She is very motherly to me; I like that a lot." And just like the relationship between the Marin women onscreen, Laura's having just as much fun with her younger costar: "We're having a good time. It's funny because we're completely different generations but it's great to make a new friend and we have plenty of stuff to laugh about and talk about."

1.12 SALT MEETS WOUND

(AIRED JANUARY 10, 2011 | WRITTEN BY OLIVER GOLDSTICK | DIRECTED BY NORMAN BUCKLEY)

Hanna: "Everyone has a life that no one else knows about."

Home is supposed to be a place free from threat, judgment, or attack, but in Rosewood that cozy, safe feeling is far from commonplace. For Toby, his home is now his prison, with Jenna and the Rosewood PD confining him there. Though Jenna got what she wanted, he can still keep from her what she really wants, and his rejection of her advances is one of the first salt-in-wound moments in a sometimes deliberately uncomfortable episode.

In a story line that shows respect for life's complexity and for realism, Emily has her first major "out" moment: Maya comes for dinner. Emily is terrified (and, secretly, so is Maya), worried that her parents will be disapproving. Even a boy with Maya's unconventional family background would have a hard time winning Pam Fields' approval; add homosexuality to children born out of wedlock, tattoo wedding rings, and political protests, and it's a miracle Mrs. Fields made it through the first course before hiding in the pantry holding back sobs. But on the surface, the dinner seems like a relative success, because of Pam's need to keep up a polite façade no matter how difficult the situation. That moment of private panic provides a glimpse of what life *could* have been like for Emily if she'd chosen to bottle up her feelings and hide her sexuality instead of opening up to her parents and braving the fallout. With Emily's dad called away to Texas at the end of the month, soon it will be Emily and her mother alone again in that house, Mrs. Fields sickened by her daughter's relationship with Maya. In a depiction surprisingly nuanced for network TV, Pam's perspective is shown without condoning her opinions or actions, and the effect of her blunt words on Emily is palpable. For Em, home is not a place free from judgment.

Aria is also dealing with "coming out" fallout now that the

girls and Noel know about Fitz. She kept it from the girls to honor her promise to Fitz, but that choice, to Hanna at least, felt like a betrayal. Hanna feels like a chump for trying to help Aria get over her non-existent Icelandic beau, and, not surprising for a girl who used to be best friends with Alison, Hanna wonders if she and her friends seem really immature to Aria now that she has an older boyfriend (with "hot faculty parties"). Aria successfully reassures Hanna and the girls, but Noel remains a wild card. How bad is he? Is he A, or is he just after an A in English? With that devilish smile it's hard to know if anything he says can be trusted.

Shell shocked after being run over and now confined to a wheelchair she doesn't quite know how to use, Hanna feels incredibly vulnerable with her broken leg and the feeling that A is among the partygoers. And she's right — the stolen loot and the note in the pill bottle mean that A *was* there — and Hanna's putting her money (if she had any) on Noel Kahn as the prime suspect. But even sweet Lucas proves to have dark secrets and a temper to match. Jealous about Sean and hurt by Hanna's honesty with him, Lucas is cruel, making fun of Sean the way Lucas himself is made fun of; he drinks too much; and, in a *major* confession, he admits to smashing the memorial. He hated seeing Ali commemorated as anything other than the leader of a teen torture squad. Hanna gets it, and she promises to keep his secret, adding it to the growing list of things she keeps hidden.

In Rosewood, relationships are easily destroyed: in flashback, Ali kills Noel's relationship with that girl using just one text, and A kills Spencer's with Alex by sending in the tennis application. By taking away their boyfriends, Spencer thinks A wants to force the girls to self-destruct, making them like four lobsters trapped without food — and A keeps turning up the heat.

HIGHLIGHT "You know you have to boil that, right?" When Spencer is affectionate, it's just about the cutest thing ever.

EXTRA CREDIT

- Emily says her parents change the channel when *Ellen* comes on. The stand-up comedian-turned-actress-and-talk-show-host made TV history in April 1997 when her character came out on *The Ellen Show*, making her the first openly gay lead. (Ellen herself had publicly come out two months earlier on *Oprah*.)

- Mr. Fitz's class is reading *The Great Gatsby* and writing papers on its "themes of change and loss." There's a lot in F. Scott Fitzgerald's 1925 classic that resonates with the entitled and immoral goings-on of our fave fictional Pennsylvania town, but the paragraph from the end of the novel that Fitz has on the board is well chosen: "I couldn't forgive him or like him but I saw that what he had done was, to him, entirely justified. It was all very careless and confused. They were careless people, Tom and Daisy — they smashed up things and creatures and then retreated back into their money or their vast carelessness or whatever it was that kept them together, and let other people clean up the mess they had made . . . ."

- Mona calls Hanna "Baby Jane," a reference to *What Ever Happened to Baby Jane?* (1962), a psychological thriller where the title character (played by Bette Davis) is paralyzed from the waist down and becomes paranoid and violent.

- In his drunken state, Lucas is in Margaritaville, so called after the classic 1977 Jimmy Buffett song, but that doesn't stop him from his "meta-geek" cracks about Sean and Hanna like "Me Tarzan, you Jane Austen."

- Hilton Head is a resort town in South Carolina with a number of oceanfront golf courses.

- Hanna trapped in her wheelchair powerless against an intruder was another nod to Hitchcock, this time to *Rear Window* (1954) where James Stewart's character finds himself in a wheelchair with a broken leg fending off a murderer.

BRANT DAUGHERTY AS NOEL KAHN

Born August 20, 1985, in Mason, Ohio, Brant Daugherty took an uncommon approach to becoming an actor: he studied writing and directing at Columbia College in Chicago. While he was studying what went on behind the camera, he actually ended up doing a lot of acting, playing roles in over 50 of his classmates' films.

After college, he got a job as a production assistant. ("I graduated school, I had a concentration in writing and editing; what can I do? Make coffee!" joked Brant.) He worked a few random jobs, but it was on the set of *Bring It On: Fight to the Finish* that one of the film's stars, Holland Rollen, encouraged Brant to go to a meeting with her agent. "She had a lot of faith in me," said Brant. "I was really impressed that somebody would look at their assistant on set as I'm getting them sandwiches and think, 'You know what, I think you could be good for this.'" The agent took him on, and Brant started auditioning.

When *PLL* came up, he auditioned for Ezra but was told he was too young (though he is actually older than Ian Harding). Then he tried for Toby, but Keegan had that one locked down. Luckily they had another part for him: master-of-the-unsettling-stare and steamy window vandal Noel Kahn. At the time, Brant thought he might only get one episode, but Marlene King had bigger plans for him.

The *PLL* experience ended up being everything he had hoped

for. Says Brant, "There's something so powerful about coming to work and knowing that what you're doing is really resonating with people. . . . Every time I walk into that place I feel like something magical is happening."

When he's not creeping around Rosewood as Noel, Brant's playing a starring role in *Private*, Teen.com's web series adaptation of the bestselling novels by Kate Brian (also an Alloy property). And Brant's still using his film school skills to write — he's written two feature-length films and one short. With his wide range of experience, he's keeping his mind open about the future: "I'm not anticipating sticking to any one thing, television, internet, film. I'm just in it to act. However I can express that is wonderful."

BACK TO THE BOOKS In *Unbelievable*, Em's parents invite Maya to dinner, but it's Emily who feels uncomfortable, not Mrs. Fields. Mona plans Hanna a post-hospital party but it's *way* more elaborate and not a surprise.

PLL IRL On the subject of smashing the memorial, Marlene King said, "That was a very interesting departure for us, but a great surprise. I think the majority of the person you're seeing *is* A, but every once in a while — when it's organic to the story — we'll reveal those to have been someone else. Often those are a surprise even to us." (Hmm, does that mean Lucas is definitely *not* A?)

Qs & A Very suspicious the way Noel writes "A" on his English paper — is he A? Were Ian and Alison together at Hilton Head right before she disappeared?

1.13 KNOW YOUR FRENEMIES

(AIRED JANUARY 17, 2011 | WRITTEN BY I. MARLENE KING | DIRECTED BY RON LAGOMARSINO)

Mike: "You lie and cheat but draw
the line at hypocrisy. Such a role model."

This episode's title is a play on a common expression, but its origin is less commonly known, coming from an ancient Chinese military text, *The Art of War*. The actual translation goes, "If you know neither yourself nor your enemy, you will always endanger yourself." And on *Pretty Little Liars*, neither part of that equation can be discounted. Of course, the main problem is that the main enemy, A, is proving difficult to get to know. But sometimes understanding ourselves can be just as tricky. In "Know Your Frenemies" several characters are forced to confront the enemy within.

Mr. Fitz faces blackmail from the relentless and creepy (and relentlessly creepy) Noel Kahn. With the threat of an almost-certain disgraced dismissal, Fitz has to decide if he'll compromise his values and stoop to Noel's level. In the end, he refuses to become the enemy simply to win this battle. But there's even more to it. He refuses to allow Noel's threats and judgment to taint what he declares to be "the most real and honest thing in my life." As he eloquently explains to Aria, "Even if this doesn't look right, it has always felt right. And I will not let him change this into something that feels wrong." As it turns out, Mr. Fitz's career (and Aria and Ezra's relationship) gets a stay of execution from Public Frenemy #1, A, but it's good to know the English teacher's moral blind spots only involve underage loves.

In a battle much closer to home, Emily finds a formidable enemy in her mother. Although she backs off temporarily, Mrs. Fields hasn't expanded her narrow view (made nicely literal by her misleading peep through Emily's door) and only entrenches herself more deeply. Just a few episodes ago Emily wouldn't even admit to herself she might be gay; now she dares anyone to challenge her right to a relationship unrestricted by gender. Like Mr. Fitz does with Aria, Emily refuses to let her mother's disapproval (or given her public cafeteria kiss, anyone else's) taint her feelings for Maya. Though Mrs. Fields' meddling gets Maya packed off to the wilderness, the girls' goodbye is tender and warm. Sure, it's a catalogue of clichés, but it answers the other PLLs' cafeteria queries: girl-on-girl romance looks much the same as any hetero Harlequin fantasy.

Hanna's enemy is more complicated, since it's her own self, as she's been fighting a battle against food for a long time. A bribes her into facing those cupcakes and her fear of becoming a piggy herself but underestimates Hanna's resolve. Further, Hanna ends up admitting her problem to Aria, a sign that she's seeing it more clearly and is no longer totally under its power. The flashback is interesting because it helps us understand some of Hanna's allegiance to Ali, who manages to seem supportive and benevolent even as she's directing Hanna down a road to self-destruction. Hanna didn't need tips on throwing up so much as she needed the kindness Ali offered, and luckily Aria can step up as a more worthy replacement. Hanna refuses to let her enemy control her body, gaining a victory more important than finding the Benjamin Franklins in the paper towel dispenser.

HIGHLIGHT The pair of heartfelt goodbyes in our two forbidden romances as these two couples found a way to use their love to fuel the fight.

EXTRA CREDIT

- In a nod to one of the show's oft-noted predecessors, Hanna calls Spencer Veronica Mars, the teen sleuth who solves mysteries when she's not solving algebra problems.
- "Gatsby: The corruption of the American Dream" is on Fitz's blackboard. The American Dream is the notion that every person can succeed, regardless of who they are or where they came from.

SLIP UPS If Ian and Melissa needed to have a top secret chat, why didn't they do it in the barn? How much time has passed since the last episode? Ian and Melissa have gone on a honeymoon, Emily's dad is gone, and Hanna's leg has healed, but Han and her mom talk about the missing money like it just happened. Hanna kicks the stall door shut in the bathroom at Lucky Leon's, a pretty aggressive move for a girl whose broken leg *just* healed.

PLL IRL The two boys eating ice cream, frightened by Toby, are Marlene King's songs, Emerson and Atticus. Marlene points to Spencer seeing Toby in the alley as the turning point in their relationship: "Spencer was the one who was like, 'The devil has a name, and it's Toby Cavanaugh.' She was by far the most judgmental of Toby. . . . [But] now there's a little opening there for her to get to know Toby. And maybe realize she was wrong about who he was." Ashley Benson loves going into flashback mode to play Hefty Hanna: "She's my favorite character, I get really great emotional moments with her." To play the role, Ashley wears a fat suit, although at the beginning the wardrobe department just used bulky layering, which didn't look as real.

BACK TO THE BOOKS In *Perfect*, Maya doesn't get sent away; instead Emily has to go to "gay rehab." Instead of A saving Ezria from Noel Kahn, in *Perfect* Aria's boyfriend calls the cops on the couple, after a photo from A tips him off. In the first book, Aria dismisses a group of jocks who are bothering her by saying, "Have fun playing with your balls"; Aria makes a similar comment to the snorting jocks bugging Hanna outside Lucky Leon's.

Qs & A A uses the same "get rid of it" phrasing to Hanna that Ali did. Coincidence? Who was watching the girls through the window?

1.14 CAREFUL WHAT U WISH 4

(AIRED JANUARY 24, 2011 | WRITTEN BY TAMAR LADDY | DIRECTED BY NORMAN BUCKLEY)

*Caleb: "The rich girls steal, the pretty
girls lie, the smart girls play dumb . . ."*

There's a warning in this episode's title — there's a price to pay
if you get what you want — but the girls are trapped in their
own A-athon, unable to heed the warning even if they want to.
Hanna, desperate to earn back the money for her mother, is A's
prime target. Unable to get a proper job, A offers Han a well-
paying solution . . . at a price. The stakes are high enough for her
that alienating Sean (again) and toying with Lucas's heart seems

RYAN MERRIMAN AS IAN THOMAS

Born April 10, 1983, in Choctaw, Oklahoma, where his parents still live, Ryan Merriman has a list of credits that spans over two decades, over 20 films, and many TV shows as well. He began his career at eight years old with local commercials and print ads, and by age 12 had met a manager, gone to L.A. for pilot season, and had a recurring role on the television series *The Mommies*. He's won a handful of Young Artist Awards and has acted opposite screen legends. Though he's lived in California for close to a decade, his heart is still in Oklahoma and he thinks of Choctaw as his home. He's a self-described down-home, country, "boot-scootin' kind of guy" and returns to his home state to support charitable causes, particularly around children's hospital fundraising.

Though a different actor played Ian in the pilot episode of *Pretty Little Liars*, Ryan has made the character his own. "He's kind of a bad boy," said Ryan. "A snake with blue eyes is what we call that. It's great. You know, a lot of the stuff I play is guy next door or jock or whatever. So it's just cool to play a role I can have a little fun with. Sometimes the things he says don't really mean what they mean, you know what I mean? The writing on the show is so fun; you know, it's very tricky to follow it." But Ryan was comfortable with his costar Torrey DeVitto; the two also worked together on a film called *Cheesecake Casserole* (not yet released).

He's been in movies like *Halloween Resurrection*, *The Ring Two*, and *Final Destination 3* as well as meatier fare like *The Deep End of the Ocean*. But one recent project stands out as close to the actor's heart. In *The Fifth Quarter*, which is based on a true story, Ryan plays a high school football player who loses his way after his brother dies in a car accident, but over the course of a football season gets his game back and leads his team to a surprise championship victory. Drawing on his junior high days on the field as well as his decades of acting experience, Ryan delivered a critically acclaimed performance. But the actor, an old pro though still shy of 30, takes it in stride: "I'm just lucky I get to do what I love."

like her only choice. Just like Alex walked away from Spencer after one of A's games, Sean has reached his limit, telling Hanna "something sick" is going on. He thinks she is the one treating them like her playthings when really Hanna is just a puppet, with the vicious A pulling the strings. Hanna comes across — to Emily, Lucas, and Sean — as a girl enjoying her power as someone who is attractive to both the guys, but Hanna's secret is that her power has been stripped from her. Dancing with Lucas all night is cruel, knowing she doesn't reciprocate his romantic feelings, but also a dream come true for him. Will he fall harder for her or feel manipulated by her hot-and-cold act?

Aria's insecurities and fears kick into high gear when her mother matchmakes Simone and Ezra. When Aria feels threatened, she acts her most immature and, ironically, highlights the age difference between her and Fitz. The usual discomfort of a teenager being reminded how recently she was a child is even more mortifying when it's done in front of the hot English teacher who also happens to be her secret boyfriend. But Aria's feeling that she has to compete with Simone feels a little forced in the wake of the bigger problems on her plate and it ignores what she should know, what the audience knows, and what Fitz reminds her of in the parking lot — he's in love with her. The actual complication in their relationship — that it's imbalanced because he, as her teacher, wields power that she does not — goes ignored.

Just as Spencer cuts in to prevent Aria from a public Fitzplosion, the girls' attempts to be forthcoming are thwarted at every turn, most notably when the Ian video disappears from Spencer's laptop. Even the moral center of the group, Emily, sees her *in vino veritas* moment made meaningless; she confronts Ian, but Spencer covers it up afterward with a lie that Emily's accusations are only about their kiss. At the end of the night — as Emily drifts off into a drunken slumber, missing Hanna's confession about A's latest prank — it turns out not to matter that the right thing to do would be to clear Toby's name. No matter how hard they wish or try, no matter if they behave worse than Alison, the girls will only get what A wants them to have.

HIGHLIGHT "Was that tree always here?" Drunk Emily is a definite highlight; seeing normally straight-laced Emily get wasted is something we may never see again, so cherish the messy moments!

EXTRA CREDIT
- Hilariously, the first movie Spencer thinks of in her lie to Ian is *Tootsie*, the 1982 Dustin Hoffman comedy where he plays a cross-dressing actor.
- Simone says she made Aria turn off *The O.C.*, Fox's excellent teen drama, and pick up Emily Brontë's 1847 novel *Wuthering Heights*, but Aria remembers it was *The Exorcist*, the 1971 novel that the more well-known film was based on.
- Aria's song request is not a Backstreet Boys hit but "We're OK" by the Rescues from their 2010 album *Let Loose the Horses*.

SLIP UPS At the dance, the paper says "DJ Sign Up Sheet," but it's a list of song requests. Hanna says to Lucas that the dance-athon is for a "good cause," but fundraising for their own class trip is not exactly charity work.

PLL IRL During the dance-athon, the music playing while they filmed was so bad that Ashley Benson requested new tunes. No wonder: Chuck Hittinger (Sean) described it as "a mariachi band meets line dancing music." All of the post-dance scenes were shot in the pouring rain; between takes, crew members had to wipe down the car Emily gets into. Looks like Norman Buckley is the go-to director for Rosewood dance eps: he also helmed "There's No Place Like Homecoming." Aria's former babysitter Simone is played by Alona Tal, who's had recurring roles on *Cane*, *Supernatural*, and *Veronica Mars*.

Qs & A Did Ian steal the laptop and delete the video? Who is following Alison in that photo? Ella gives A his/her coat, so Ella can't be A. Also she didn't *seem* to recognize him or her, but the Gloved Wonder is someone who fits right in at the school dance — student or chaperone?

1.15 IF AT FIRST YOU DON'T SUCCEED, LIE, LIE AGAIN

(AIRED JANUARY 31, 2011 | WRITTEN BY MAYA GOLDSMITH | DIRECTED BY RON LAGOMARSINO)

Spencer: *"What is a leader without any followers?"*

"Watch your backs, I didn't," says A's warning at the end of the last episode, a good encouragement to play it safe and look out for yourself. But the liars are starting to realize that the best defense is a good offense.

The episode starts with Hanna still running scared, and no wonder. When she finds her mom in the kitchen looking more beaten than the eggs she's crying over, Han realizes that whatever her mom may say, the daughter is the caretaker now. The stakes are high: she's terrified that her remaining parent will leave her, and though certainly conflicted, Hanna decides to consign Aria to collateral damage.

But Mrs. Montgomery's history class provides some insight from events long past, as the class studies British Prime Minister Neville Chamberlain's policy of appeasement after World War I. Familiar with the power plays of high school, Spencer can easily translate for the rest of the class: "Giving in to a bully never works. . . . Your only choice is to stand up to them, even if it costs you something." Hanna gets the message, and thanks to help from Caleb, she avoids starting a war in the Montgomery household.

Spencer, of course, speaks from experience. As the flashback reveals, she chose to face her opponent head-on in a thrilling throwdown, so she knows that standing up to a bully isn't pretty, especially if that bully has a god complex like Alison did. Often the chairwoman of the Liars 2.0, Spencer knows a few things about leadership, and even in the past she realized Ali's dependence on her posse: "It seems to me the question isn't whether we will exist without you, but whether you will exist without us." Later in the night that proposition takes a sinister, literal twist. Ali does in fact cease to exist, and it is the remaining four girls who are now the keepers of Alison's memory.

Emily, who used to fear conflict like Spencer fears getting a B, takes a more diplomatic tack, though she's no less fierce or unmovable than Sergeant Spencer. While her friends nobly offer to help out after Paige taunts her, Emily wants to take on Paige herself. She plays fair: she doesn't bring in teachers, but stands her ground and refuses to let Paige bring her down. And Emily doesn't just stand up to Paige, she also stands up to Spencer, who hadn't acknowledged that Em's no longer the girl under Alison's thumb.

But despite this week's triumphs, there's one bully who's not willing to show up for a set-piece battle. A's sticking to guerilla warfare, relying on surprise, sabotage, and secrets to win a war without any clear objective or rules: just four pretty little targets.

HIGHLIGHT Spencer standing up to Ali in the flashback. It was about time someone took Ali down a peg.

EXTRA CREDIT
- The episode title comes from a popular proverb, "If at first you don't succeed, try, try again," that likely originated from a 19th-century teacher's manual by Thomas H. Palmer and was popularized by Edward Hickson later that century with his "Moral Song."
- Hanna wanted some tequila with her sunrise, referring to the

cocktail known for its color gradations that look like a sky in the morning.

- Mr. Hastings doesn't know the difference between a Monet and a mojito. Claude Monet (1840–1926) was one of the most prolific and celebrated of the impressionist painters. A mojito is a rum cocktail, heavy on the lime and mint. The two things are hard to confuse, but after too many mojitos, the world does start to look a bit like a Monet painting.
- Widely believed to be one of the contributing factors to World War II, Chamberlain tried to appease Hitler by allowing him to annex part of Czechoslovakia, a bold move that only added to his strength.
- Hanna puns on "The Princess and the Pea," a Hans Christian Andersen fairytale about an unnamed princess who unknowingly proves her princessly super-sensitivity by feeling a pea beneath 20 mattresses.
- Ali says to Spencer, "Trying to get me voted off the island?" referring to the mother of all reality shows, *Survivor*, which premiered in May 2000. It's an unfortunate reference, since Ali's torch is extinguished before the night is out.
- In the bead lady's home are a bunch of dream catchers! Spencer's quip from earlier in the episode was bang on.

SLIP UPS Emily's one of the top swimmers on the team, but she didn't think to move backward underwater to escape her near-drowning at the poolside?

PLL IRL Lindsey Shaw was nervous about the drowning scene, so she and Shay came up with a signal in case Shay was really running out of air. Shay wanted it to look legit, but in the end Lindsey still held her down a bit long, and Shay told the *New York Post*, "The terror on my face in that scene is honest." Hanna tells Caleb he doesn't "understand the Biebs. Or his hair," but Ashley Benson probably does: her boyfriend, Ryan Good, is the "swag coach" for the teen pop heartthrob.

Qs & A The bead lady tells the Gloved Wonder s/he has "such expressive eyes." Who could it be?

1.16 JE SUIS UNE AMIE

(AIRED FEBRUARY 7, 2011 | WRITTEN BY BRYAN M. HOLDMAN | DIRECTED BY CHRIS GRISMER)

Spencer: "Toby Cavanaugh hasn't cornered the market on lying."

An episode full of new connections between characters and the importance of friends and allies is projected against a backdrop of Rosewood's favorite pastimes: persecution, competition, and betrayal.

Emily thinks Spence wants a fight about Toby, but Spencer has a new understanding of what it's like to be framed and realizes she jumped to conclusions about his guilt. She's eager to right wrongs and sees him as a potentially useful ally. With Toby, the liars could put their various pieces of the puzzle together to find A. Emily's reluctant and Toby has reason to be so as well. Just as Melissa and Ian are convinced Toby is guilty, other folks in town show their cruelty by smashing the Cavanaughs' mailbox and vandalizing their house. In the court of public opinion, he's been convicted. Someone apologizing for saying and thinking terrible things about him, someone acknowledging how scary it is to be framed, is likely precisely what Toby needs to hear. Spencer and Toby have been watching each other (and not in a creepy way) for a while now, and during their tête-à-tête, they realize what they have in common: knowing something you're not supposed to makes you a target.

In a great scene, Spencer ponders the mysteries of Toby while answering Emily's science homework questions: she is intrigued by him. He's different from what she expected, and if nothing else, Spencer has learned this past year that things are usually *not* what they seem. Toby shuts off his public connection with Spence, returning the book to her, and it's all but certainly because of Jenna. Spencer can't be Toby's tutor, but she can be his secret ally.

Aria knew something was not right about the whole art gallery thing, paranoid that her mother saw her with Fitz. It's fun watching Ella, Byron, and Aria dance around the truth and be super cagey with each other, because we know that Hanna's the only one who's in hot water. When Aria discovers Hanna's betrayal — thanks to A — she's hurt that Hanna let A pit them against each other. At least for now A has won and Aria is not speaking to her friend. Luckily, Hanna and Caleb's new connection goes beyond snarky one-liners and calling in favors. She accidentally finds out his secret and opens up her home to the "stray." Caleb proves to be a good friend, and not just a sketchy hacker, as he sits on the stairs with Hanna, silently comforting her.

And Rosewood's newest creepily happy couple keeps doling out the surprises, and they hit Spencer with a big one: Melissa is pregnant. She knows about Ian's flings with Ali and Spencer, and she's forgiven him. Nothing Spencer says can convince Melissa that her little sister's "sabotage" is about real danger, not about jealousy. The sisters have always been competitors, and Melissa thinks Spencer is capable of trying to destroy her happiness out of spite. That spirit of extreme competition has been hugely destructive for them, ruining even their earnest moments of caring for each other, and the same drive to outdo everyone else seems to be driving Paige McCullers off her little rocker too.

Emily wants to win anchor position — even if she needs Spencer to tell her it's "okay to admit that" — but Emily has a healthy attitude toward swimming, one she's charitable enough to share with Paige. Back in "Can You Hear Me Now?" Toby asked Em why she swims, and then, as now, it isn't because she has something to prove, but because Emily still remembers how to have fun.

HIGHLIGHT All the great one-liners: "You reading that fast or fanning yourself?"; "You can fit all of *that* under a cap?"; "Han, my dad's about to have dinner with someone *in the dark*. Move it."; "A owes me: hospital bills, pain and suffering, tire marks on my cleavage."

EXTRA CREDIT
- Appropriately attired in a French-themed wardrobe this episode, Spencer lends Toby *L'Attrape-coeurs*, the French edition of *Catcher in the Rye*. Spence saw him reading *Catcher* at the Apple Rose Grille in "Reality Bites Me."
- When Spence tells him that she keeps ending up on her ass

The creepiest casa in Rosewood:
Jenna and Toby's.

after thinking she knows something, Toby says, "*C'est dom-mage*" which translates to "That's too bad," and she replies, "*C'est la guerre*" — "That's war."

BACK TO THE BOOKS There's a big swim meet in *Perfect*, and, in a slight change, Rosewood High's swim team is called the Sharks, instead of the Hammerheads of Rosewood Day.

SLIP UPS Toby says he can't go anywhere because of his ankle monitor, but in "Know Your Frenemies," he was walking down the street and Spencer saw him being jeered at. Does Toby tuck his jeans *into* his ankle monitor? Seems like he'd be more likely to wear his pants over it, but the ankle monitor needed to be visible for the shot. While the chase through the school at night was fun and scary, wouldn't Caleb have just said, "Hey Hanna, stop running"?

PLL IRL Shay got a swimming coach a couple of weeks before her onscreen swim meet to help perfect her stroke. The in-pool scenes, which were shot on location rather than on the WB back lot, took 12 hours to film, and Shay laughed, "By the time I got out, I was a complete raisin!"

Qs & A What do the Braille marks on that paper that Toby found in Jenna's room mean? On the Gloved Wonder's desk there is a wrench, a candlestick, a rope, and a lead pipe, four of the murder weapons from the board game Clue. Is the object we see the weapon that killed Ali or is it a piece in A's murder mystery game? Why is the Gloved Wonder also learning French? Just to taunt us with no name after the repeated "*Je suis*"?

1.17 THE NEW NORMAL

(AIRED FEBRUARY 14, 2011 | WRITTEN BY JOSEPH DOUGHERTY | DIRECTED BY MICHAEL GROSSMAN)

*Caleb: "Knowing the right questions
is better than having all the right answers."*

In "The New Normal," everyone tries hard to act like it's just business as usual, but there's more posing and fakery in Rosewood than onstage at a beauty pageant.

Case in point: Caleb. He's a phone hacker and detention regular, a bad boy by reputation, but he's been nothing but nice to Hanna, who's brought this stray dog home. But the others aren't quite so ready to categorize him as cuddly. Emily tries to warn Han about him, but Hanna reminds the others that they've judged too quickly before, noting that "it seems to me we once had this conversation about Toby." Touché, Han.

Afraid of the implications of a resurgence of old feelings, Ella and Byron are busy trying to act like there's nothing going on between them, but of course Byron's touchiness as they talk about Mr. Fitz and his hostility at the parent-teacher conference means he's fooling no one but himself. But beyond jealousy, there might be another force at work. He tells Aria, "Every English department has one, full of charm and promise." Perhaps Mr. Fitz looks a little too much like Mr. Montgomery before his fall from grace, and Byron doesn't relish being reminded of the untainted respect and love he used to get from his wife and daughter. Little does Byron know Mr. Fitz has already fallen . . . and he's taken Aria with him.

The scenes between Ashley and Mrs. Potter's nephew are like a fakers face-off. Who can keep up the charade longer? Leland initially seems to have the upper hand: Ashley's so focused on her defense that she doesn't question this long-lost nephew enough. She gets ready to deal with the problem in her usual way (see: Detective Wilden in towel), but the balance of power switches when Ashley decides to trust Caleb (and Hanna's) judgment and ask Leland some questions he can't answer. Looks like Team Caleb just got another member.

All of this fakery and subterfuge only exaggerates the episode's most important and authentic moments all the more. In a jaw-dropping moment, Paige kisses Emily in the car, stripping off her homophobic mask. Turns out her harassment was just fear, jealousy, and a dash of self-hatred. The episode's other moving moment also comes out of a lesbian story line. While Emily tells her mom, "I know what you'd say: it doesn't matter who I am, I'd better get used to people looking at me only one way," her mom surprises her, showing her that issues of Emily's sexuality haven't overshadowed the Emily she knows and loves. Seeing her defend her daughter's integrity so fiercely makes Pam Fields more likeable. She might not be ready to march in the pride parade, but Emily's sold her mother a little short too.

Caleb reminded Hanna of the importance of asking questions, and hopefully that's advice our liars decide to trust.

HIGHLIGHT Spencer's glee at teasing Aria about Mr. Fitz was irresistible.

EXTRA CREDIT

- Aria says they were "punk'd," referring to the 2003–2007 reality TV show of the same name starring Ashton Kutcher, which pulled elaborate pranks on unsuspecting celebrities.
- Byron shouldn't be too upset about Ella and Ezra's not-date: Leonard Adams isn't even a real author.
- Spencer compares Caleb to "The Artful Dodger" (or "Arthur Dodger" as Hanna hears it), the nickname of pickpocket Jack Dawkins in Charles Dickens' *Oliver Twist*, but it's become a reference to describe a person adept at getting away with things.
- Spencer says Aria and Hanna were like *The Real Teens of Rosewood*, playing on the Real Housewives of . . . series that

started with *The Real Housewives of Orange County*, a reality show that followed five rich housewives who make the citizens of Rosewood look grounded.

- As Ella lists off Ezra's virtues to an increasingly annoyed (and jealous) Byron, he asks sarcastically, "Does he play guitar?" And unless Fitzy just keeps one around his apartment for decoration, he does.

SLIP UPS How come the Rosewood sign isn't painted over anymore? Has the graffiti squad pounced on it? FBI Agent Cooper left because Toby Cavanaugh was arrested; why didn't she return when that case fell apart?

PLL IRL Lindsey Shaw gave *Hollywood Life* the scoop on her shocking kiss: "We decided not to do the kiss during rehearsal and save it for the first take. I was so nervous that when I went in to kiss her, I totally got the side of her mouth. It was really awkward, and the camera was shooting us from the side, so you could totally see."

Qs & A The Gloved Wonder brings flowers to Mrs. Potter's grave; did A have anything to do with Mrs. Potter's death?

1.18 THE BADASS SEED

(AIRED FEBRUARY 21, 2011 | WRITTEN BY OLIVER GOLDSTICK & FRANCESCA ROLLINS | DIRECTED BY PAUL LAZARUS)

Emily: "Maybe there are no accidents."

Who can you trust? The school play raises questions about who in Rosewood is acting all the time, pretending to be someone they're not, and hiding dark secrets. People are often not who they seem — bad seeds or good — and Byron has distrusted Fitz in the past, considering him a flake and not an earnestly literary guy (and, yes, that's totally pretentious on Byron's part). Their bonding time is chockfull of unintentional double entendres about "hot stuff" Fitz "exposing" himself to students and "bond[ing] with them in a special way." It's uncomfortable for Ezra, but he doesn't break character, keeping the truth from Aria's dad. Ashley is wary of Caleb, sensing that something's off but she's not in on the secret. In a classic Hanna conundrum, she's being bad for a good cause; her compassion for Caleb convinced her it's okay to go behind her mother's back and to lie to her.

Though it seemed impossible, Spencer is getting even more tightly wound, trying to prove that the roles in which Ian and Toby have been cast should be reversed. Toby is perceived as the bad seed but is innocent, and Spence reaches out to him (literally) in what is probably the first non-violating human contact he's had in ages. On the flip side, Spencer physically recoils whenever Ian is near, convinced he is Ali's murderer and determined to prove it.

Breaking up the Ian tension with tension of a different sort, Aria tries to rewrite her and Fitz's relationship to include scenes outside his little apartment. Their anxiety over the permanence of their relationship is coupled with the difficulty of hiding a private relationship in public. Before an attentive audience, they constantly have to juggle two different dynamics — teacher and student, and boyfriend and girlfriend — and Aria flubs her lines by calling him "Ezra." Though their futures may not be linked, Aria is reminded (by the fleeting peace they enjoy after having found the "murder weapon") that she should "carpe hottie," as Hanna would say. Fitz's potential new job at Hollis is a problem for another day.

Spencer's frantic sleuthing and the girls' quick action in handing over the bloodied trophy to the police only serves to realize their fear faster: the nightmare is *not* over and A's stepping up his/her frame game. A has cast the foursome as pretty little liars and is now directing them deeper into trouble. Like

THE BAD SEED

The play that Mr. Fitz selects for the school production is *The Bad Seed*, adapted by Maxwell Anderson from a 1954 novel by William March. That same year it had a successful run on Broadway; a film adaptation came out two years later and garnered Academy Award nominations for its lead actresses, and there was a TV movie remake in 1985. The story concerns the nature of evil and what to do when we suspect it's lurking right in our own family.

Christine Penmark (the character Spencer appears to be play-ing) is the mother to an eight-year-old girl named Rhoda, who seems to be the perfect child — excellent manners, well behaved and groomed, and charming around adults. No one suspects that she is actually a sociopath who must have her way no matter what. A child in her class wins a penmanship medal over Rhoda, and at the picnic by the pond, Rhoda is seen fighting with him. The boy is later found dead. Hmm. Both the headmistress (Mona's character) and the boy's now always-drunk mother (Hanna's character) come to Mrs. Penmark to ask her about Rhoda, but by the time Christine figures out the truth and finds the penmanship medal hidden not so cleverly in her daughter's desk, Rhoda has already killed the janitor (he knew too much). Rhoda lacks the ability to feel remorse or any sense of morality, and Christine slowly goes crazy, torn between the obligation to stop a sociopath from killing again and the mater-nal instinct to protect Rhoda from harm. The play builds to a climax that is truly haunting.

Was Ali like the girl in *The Bad Seed* — a sociopath born bad? "The Badass Seed" presents as exhibit A the shocking flashback where Ali barely reacts to the news that a girl has fallen down the stairs to her death; instead she gives Ian a *look* and then cavalierly gets the girls a ride home with the cops. Alison was an accom-plished liar with a good-girl façade, and, like Rhoda in *The Bad Seed*, only other people her age seemed to pick up on her dark behavior. Did Alison intentionally target the girl Ian was flirting with? Did she intentionally blind Jenna?

Ian calls Ali a "psycho stalker who wouldn't take no for an answer" — is that an accurate description? In the Kissing Rock video, the rats in their cages, A is in control of the girls, and it looks like Spencer's the first one A wants to take out permanently.

HIGHLIGHT Rub-a-dub-dub, Hanna and Caleb in the tub! Not only is this scene a little steamy, Hanna's sudden shyness makes it just plain adorable.

EXTRA CREDIT

- The book that Spencer fell asleep reading, *Bloody Tantrums*, is a prop, not a real book; its "author" is Francesca Rollins, one of the episode's writers.
- Hanna's mom compares Caleb to Dr. Seuss's Cat in the Hat, who appears when the mother is away and disappears just before she returns.
- Inspired by Tyler Blackburn's floppy hairdo, Mona calls Hanna and Caleb Velma and Shaggy, two Scoobys who are finally dating in the latest cartoon incarnation, *Scooby-Doo! Mystery Incorporated*.
- Byron tells Fitz that "hope springs eternal," a phrase that originated in Alexander Pope's *An Essay on Man* (1734).

Ian seemed happy to flirt with and kiss Ali, definitely not a guy who was rejecting her advances. Ian is the other candidate for bad-seed status: he's an upstanding citizen of Rosewood, now married to a Hastings, but the girls know he's a liar with an eye for younger girls. Is he a murderer too? Spencer's bad dream about Melissa and Ian's baby is another allusion to *The Bad Seed*: the story suggests that the offspring of a killer is likely to inherit that murderous gene.

Spencer's hair styled in two braids is an homage to Rhoda's braids in the film — and a clue that blame will be directed at Spence by the end of the episode. Appearances can be deceiving, but to the folks in Rosewood, it's Spencer Hastings who looks like a bad seed, not a misunderstood-and-framed seed.

TYLER BLACKBURN AS CALEB RIVERS

"When they told me that Hanna was getting a new boyfriend, I said, 'Screen test!'" Ashley Benson remembers with a laugh. "I met with a couple guys, but then Tyler walked in and I knew he was the one. He's amazing."

Born October 12, 1986, in Burbank, California, Tyler Blackburn knew from an early age the direction he wanted his life to take. "I started taking an acting class when I was a junior in high school," Tyler explains, "and I realized that is what I wanted to do with my life. I have always had an interest in it, but when all my friends were applying for college, I decided I knew what I would like to do. I drove to Hollywood once a week for this acting class and I met some managers, through that I got an agent and starting auditioning and the rest is kind of history."

Tyler made his big TV debut on Nickelodeon's *Unfabulous* in 2005, doing two episodes of the show. After an episode of *Cold Case* and a part on the Josh Schwartz web-series *Rockville CA*, Tyler landed on *Days of Our Lives* in 2010, playing "computer geek" Ian in 17 episodes. "We only got one take per scene and that was probably the hardest part. You had to make sure you knew your lines and hit your marks and did a good job," Tyler remembers with a laugh. "Because of that it was really good training. It made me focus really hard and do the best I could do in a small amount of time. They film an entire episode in one day, so they move so quickly."

The move from NBC daytime soap to ABC Family evening soap seemed seamless for the young actor, who generated buzz with the *PLL* audience from his first episode as the new-to-Rosewood sketchy bad boy Caleb Rivers. During his downtime on set, Tyler likes to read and exchange music recommendations with Troian (who has similar taste in music). Though he doesn't watch a lot of TV, Tyler makes sure to tune in to *PLL*: "You film something and you do all these different takes and you wonder what they are going to end up choosing. I also think it is important [to watch], because the fanbase of the show is so awesome and people are so supportive of it — I joined Twitter for the show semi-reluctantly but it's been so cool to hear what the fans say. I want to know what they have seen and what they are talking about too. It's definitely really awkward to watch myself. I don't enjoy it, that's for sure. I watch the episodes alone because I kind of don't want to be in the presence of people while I am watching it."

Caleb fans paying close attention to Tyler's career were a little bit nervous for his future in Rosewood, when in 2011 the actor landed a role in the pilot for an NBC comedy, *Brave New World*. Though that series was not picked up by the network, another of Tyler's projects, the indie film *Peach Plum Pear*, hit the film festival circuit in 2011 and picked up accolades en route.

Fittingly for an actor on a show about a cyberbully, the actor became part of the Delete Digital Drama campaign. In addition to raising awareness for a good cause, Tyler realized just how aware of *him* fans had become: "We had a rally in Glendale and people were literally crying when they met me. I was like, 'I am not Justin Bieber. I am not one of the Beatles.' So that was interesting. Honestly, it's just a testament to how popular the show is. How good it is, because people get so drawn into it and emotionally attached to the story line and the characters and all of that. I think it's great, but it's like 'Take a breath. You don't need to cry.'"

But Tyler wasn't helping downplay his new heartthrob status with his role on the web series *Wendy*, produced by Alloy Entertainment for Macy's. In a modern-day retelling of the Peter Pan story, Tyler plays Pete opposite Meaghan Martin (*Mean Girls 2*, *Camp Rock*, ABC Family's *10 Things I Hate About You*) in the title role. As part of his role, Tyler recorded an original song,

"Save Me," and filmed a music video in advance of the series' online debut. Though it was his first time recording in a studio, music has always been a key part of Tyler's life. "It's kind of like a common thread in my life, and it was just a great opportunity to really try that out. It's something that I've thought about doing professionally for awhile now. I think that song was great for the web series, but I would probably record something a little bit different for a solo project. I'm just in the explorations right now, just figuring out my voice."

But *PLL* fans eager to see Tyler bring his musicality to Rosewood may be disappointed. "I'm not sure that Caleb is necessarily the singing type," jokes Tyler. "He has his own strong points, and I don't think being a musician is one of them."

BACK TO THE BOOKS Spencer is also a regular cast member in school plays at Rosewood Day and plays Lady Macbeth in *Ruthless*.

SLIP UPS Hanna already has tons of mascara on when she asks Caleb to pass it to her in the bathroom. Since when do you need ID to get into a frat party? Why would the cops assume the girls created that trophy or question them so aggressively for simply turning over the suspicious thing they found at school?

PLL IRL Tyler Blackburn wore a loincloth for the shower scene, so Ashley Benson didn't actually get a peek. On the shower scene, Tyler said, "Ashley made it so fun; we were cracking up. The water kept going from freezing cold to burning hot. And it was a one a.m. shoot, so we were pretty slap-happy. [Ashley] and I both are a little like our characters, in that we have a little of that witty playfulness. We get along and have good chemistry because we can keep up with each other."

Qs & A What is in the Neufeld's bag that Ian gives to Jenna? Did Alison kill the girl at the party? Did Ian? With the trophy shenanigans, was A trying to ruin the girls' credibility with the cops for a specific reason, or just for sport?

1.19 A PERSON OF INTEREST

(AIRED FEBRUARY 28, 2011 | WRITTEN BY I. MARLENE KING &
JONELL LENNON | DIRECTED BY RON LAGOMARSINO)

Aria: "Whoever said the truth will set you free never met A."

Taking place in tents, hotel rooms, karaoke dive bars, and distant parks, the setting of "A Person of Interest" mirrors the characters as they bravely explore new territory, even though these bold explorations mean making themselves vulnerable.

The heart of this episode belongs to the parallel sleepovers with seemingly strange bedfellows. Hanna decides to tear up her V-Club membership. Intimacy can be intimidating enough, but Han really lays herself bare when she opens up to Caleb about fat camp. Caleb seems to recognize this, and, in turn, tells her about being abandoned by his mom — parental abandonment is something Hanna understands all too well. Though we've seen the greatest change in Emily in the show so far, moments like this one highlight that Hanna's also transformed. She's not the guarded, snippy teen queen she was: she's softer and more sensitive, a kinder gentler Hanna who's left a lot of her former superficiality behind. You can also see it in her choice of partner: she's traded her homecoming king for a hobo-hatted outcast, and the change looks good on her.

While Hanna goes all the way, Spencer takes it at her own

pace, but her party for two is just as exciting. In a sense, Spencer's taking the bigger chance, spooning with the former enemy. It's endearing to see our model of composure lose her shirt and tie, and let someone in (even if she still has to be the big spoon — no surprises there). The scene helps us warm up to Toby too, who is still making up ground he lost in his days as prime suspect and for his pseudo-incestuous past. What's a little sibling action compared to besting Spencer at Scrabble? He's taking a chance too — after all, Spencer was a mean girl involved in blinding his sister. Their light-of-day, public parking lot kiss is as brave and trusting a move as Han and Caleb's campfire embrace.

Aria's leap of faith isn't about physical intimacy (and it's still unclear whether Aria and Ezra have crossed into illegal territory there), but about emotional intimacy. She comes clean about her involvement in The Jenna Thing, and Fitz handles it

as well as he handles screaming parents in the cafeteria, calmly and sensitively. His absolution is more important than any between-the-sheets action, and this relationship, the most scandalous of the series, emerges as the most solid.

With Emily and Paige, we see two people unwilling to take chances. Paige is into Emily and willing to take a chance on the relationship, but fears the fallout of being openly gay. Emily, on the other hand, is willing to venture into dive bars and onto a karaoke stage, but she won't be revisiting her old stomping grounds in the closet. She's come too far on her journey and isn't about to backtrack now. She won't let having to be secretive about something make her feel like it's wrong.

As we approach the season finale, the girls' new confidence in this episode has changed the landscape dramatically. Will these new alliances make them stronger in their battle against A, or, as Caleb's sketchy phone call suggests, have they let their guard down at exactly the wrong time?

HIGHLIGHT Pink's soulful "Glitter in the Air" beautifully unites scenes of three lovers taking chances on one another.

EXTRA CREDIT
- Hanna refers to the group as Charlie's Angels, referencing the 2000 movie adaptation of the popular late-'70s TV show. Calling Spencer Lucy Liu is actually a pretty good fit: the Asian-American actress played Alex, the most serious and aggressive of the Angels.
- Jenna tells Aria Mr. Fitz should add George Orwell's classic 1949 dystopian novel *Nineteen Eighty-Four* to the reading list, and adds, "Big Brother's always watching you." Constantly surveyed by two-way telescreens, the people of Oceania have no privacy, their every move is monitored: our pretty little liars would certainly sympathize.
- Caleb says Hanna's like Dora the Explorer, referring to the main character in the wildly popular children's cartoon of the same name. Though Caleb's referring to her camping skills, it's not a bad analogy considering the episode's theme.
- The episode's closer seems like a visual reference to the villain of 1980s cartoon *Inspector Gadget*. Dr. Claw was just an arm in an empty chair, a fitting image when A is just as faceless and, like Dr. Claw, can see all.

SLIP UPS When Toby and Spencer rush out of the hotel room, the coffee mug on the bed is standing up, but when the camera

LINDSEY SHAW AS PAIGE MCCULLERS

Once *PLL* had established itself as one of the hits of the season, most actors would have done anything to nab a role on the show: for Lindsey Shaw that meant a dramatic makeover. The natural brunette became a vibrant redhead, with shortened locks and a blunt bang. It seems redheads have more fun, and Lindsey isn't looking back: "Now that it looks awesome, it's my personal life and my professional life."

Born May 10, 1989, in Lincoln, Nebraska, Lindsey "loved to be in the center of attention and performing," so her mom started taking her to agencies and talent competitions, and she earned herself an agent at age 11. She made her mark on Hollywood a couple of years later playing best friend next door, Moze, on Nickelodeon's hit comedy *Ned's Declassified School Survival Guide*. More plum starring roles followed, on CW sitcom *Aliens in America* and ABC Family's *10 Things I Hate About You*, but neither show made it beyond its first season.

Her role on *PLL* only guaranteed one episode, but eventually evolved into a six-episode arc, as Emily's swim team rival revealed some pretty little secrets of her own. Though we're introduced to Paige as a bully, Lindsey sees beyond it, explaining that her character "is totally and completely scared, just like every single person in high school. There's this underlying fear of not being accepted."

We find out why when Paige comes out to Emily with a crashing kiss in "The New Normal." Lindsey jumped at the chance to have a lesbian story line, hoping she could be an example to other teens struggling to face their sexuality, just like her character. "I just wanted to be as emotionally truthful as I could, even if I've never experienced these things firsthand," said Lindsey. "This wasn't just another role for me. It was a big opportunity to speak to people and change their attitudes, and to speak to kids who are maybe struggling with their sexuality and to say, 'You're wonderful. And you're not alone.'"

switches angles it has fallen over. It looks like Jenna left her glasses in the hotel room: she may be blind, but you don't need to look in a mirror to know something's not on your face. Also, back in "To Kill a Mocking Girl," Hanna was hilariously "not woodsy," but here she camps like a pro.

BACK TO THE BOOKS Spencer does see a therapist in *Perfect*, an experience that gives her new insight on what may have happened with Ali.

PLL IRL The writers referred to this episode as the "romance episode" because everyone was hooking up. It was also the first time they got a note from the network that something was "too suggestive." So Hanna and Caleb's tent scene lost a couple of seconds to the cutting-room floor. Shay Mitchell loves karaoke, so much so that her parents bought her a karaoke machine when she was 11. The karaoke vocals were recorded before filming the scene, but Shay and Lindsey Shaw still had to sing live in front of crew and extras. Shay called it "really fun and embarrassing." But she said that shooting the scene with the police cars in front of Spencer's house gave her shivers and reminded her of the first episode.

Qs & A What was Jenna doing in room 214? Or if she wasn't actually there, why is A playing hot and cold with them? Who is Caleb working for? Is the Gloved Wonder watching a live feed? Where are the cameras located?

TAMMIN SURSOK AS JENNA MARSHALL

With a career spanning two continents, a platinum album to her name, TV roles on comedies, dramas, and soap operas, and numerous film roles, Tammin Sursok might have even more determination than her *PLL* alter ego Jenna Marshall. Perhaps that's because she learned it at a young age, when her family emigrated from South Africa to Australia and had to start new lives in a foreign country. "We couldn't take any money out so we had to start over in Sydney with just the four of us and four suitcases," recalled the actress.

Born August 19, 1983, in Johannesburg, Tammin always knew that she wanted to be a performer. She told Wetpaint, "I have been acting since I've been talking. I didn't really think that there was another option for me, as a career. I was six years old and I remember telling everyone to sit down because I was going to put on a little song-and-dance performance for them. It was just something that I loved, and I wanted to be involved in it, from a very young age." The ambitious young actress started doing musical theater at age seven and continued honing her musical and theatrical skills on the stage and in acting classes for the next eight years.

At age 14 she landed an agent and after her first audition, for

Aussie soap *Home and Away*, she got the part. She immediately threw herself into it, switching to homeschooling so she could work with the network's schedule and play Dani Sutherland for the next five years. When she finished her story line on *Home and Away*, the teenager was signed to Sony Australia and produced a pop album, *Whatever Will Be*, which spent 11 weeks in the top 100 albums chart. Though she had a seven-album deal, she found the label was not giving her next album enough support, and Tammin switched her focus back to acting and headed to America. But she hasn't given up dreams of another album. She explained, "I've gone through the process before and I think it can be really hard to do the music that you want to do . . . In time, I'd love to do music again, but I'd want to do the music that I've written and that I play on the guitar — that would be amazing!" The singer likens her sound less to her pop productions of the past and more to the dark, edgier songs of performers like Tori Amos.

On arriving in Hollywood, Tammin didn't find any work for an entire year, but then she died her hair dark, and in the same week she booked two films and *The Young and the Restless*. Though she was worried about her career getting stuck in soap operas, filming on the classic daytime show ended up being valuable experience.

She needn't have worried about being stuck in daytime television; the next phase of her career would be defined by a new, younger audience. Tammin was able to show off her pipes when she was cast as one of the leads in Nickelodeon's show choir TV movie *Spectacular!* The actress calls that job her favorite to date. "When you're doing a dance film, everyone's singing and dancing, so everyone is on this natural high, all the time. We had all this energy and we bounced off each other. It was a really good thing to be a part of," said Tammin.

Then along came the terrific tandem of *Hannah Montana* and *Pretty Little Liars*. On *Hannah Montana*, Jenna played Siena, girlfriend to Jackson Stewart; she came into the hit show toward the end of its run and had a great experience, even though she often had to juggle shooting schedules with *PLL*. Though the Aussie import was at first worried about being the odd man out, she insisted, "They were such a family on set. I thought it would be so difficult to only join for the final season, but they were really welcoming."

As for *Pretty Little Liars*, Tammin came into the process quite late, just before the pilot was set to be filmed. Unlike many of the cast members, she passed on reading the books, preferring to get an idea of the character from the scripts alone, something perhaps especially important for a villain if they are to be even a little bit sympathetic. "It's very easy to just label characters as 'good' or 'evil,' and not really know their backstory. I made my own back-story and tried to find a vulnerability in Jenna, because you need to have somewhere to go with the character — you need a reason why she acts that way and how she reacts to all the girls. A lot of that comes from pain, and being bullied," noted Tammin.

The biggest challenge to playing the character isn't playing the bad girl, but the blind girl. "I've learned a lot about body language, about what happy looks like through your body or what being on edge looks like through your hands, or through your mouth — I've had to act from the nose down! . . . It's been difficult, but I'm up for the challenge." Based on the knowing smirks that come from those bow lips, it seems she's doing just fine.

The role has also given her a window of insight into the daily challenges of the visually impaired. "I have so much empathy for visually impaired people," stated the actress. "I shut my eyes for most of the scenes I shoot so I don't accidentally see objects out of the corner of my eyes. I find it so difficult, and I admire anyone who lives this way."

But it seems that even losing her sight wouldn't hold back the assertive Aussie. She's been acting for 20 years, and she doesn't plan on backing off any time soon. Noted Tammin, "My manager and agent tell me to let go a little bit, but you're only young once, and you only have one career. There's always someone who's more talented and more beautiful, who's going to have more drive than I do, so I just have to run my own race and be the best I possibly can. For me, I want to keep going."

1.20 SOMEONE TO WATCH OVER ME

(AIRED MARCH 7, 2011 | WRITTEN BY JOSEPH DOUGHERTY | DIRECTED BY ARLENE SANFORD)

Aria: "Everyone's entitled to privacy."

The sense that someone is watching over you is either sweet and comforting . . . or super unsettling. And for the girls, it's mostly creepy. They've long been spied on by A, but now they are under the microscope from all angles. The police search Spencer's house and room, prompting her to do a quick edit of her inbox. Between the threat of the cops and Aria's text slip up, Rosewood's resident Lolita hides her Fitz memorabilia, realizing that her privacy may not stay private. Trust issues abound, and the line between being protective and invasive gets murkier as we near the season finale.

Ella trusts her kids and respects their privacy, but Byron feels that extra diligence is called for when there is a killer loose and cops circling. In the Montgomery family, keeping secrets is nothing new and, historically, it has been destructive. Mike is so scared of his family falling apart again that he urges Aria to lie to make the problems go away. A fake boyfriend is an appealing solution for Aria, but Emily knows firsthand how harmful it can be to have someone pretend to be into you. And she sees shades of her relationships with both Alison and Ben playing out in Paige and Sean. Paige is in the place Emily was when we first met her: hiding the truth from her parents, scared to admit she's gay, and going on a date with a boy just to keep up appearances.

There's no greater example of the damage that comes after trust is broken than in Hanna's destroyed happiness. The owl pendant isn't a gift symbolic of her and Caleb's first night together; it is a symbol of his betrayal . . . and a memory key. As long as she can, Hanna holds on to her trust in Caleb — the alternative is too heartbreaking — but the truth, which he admits, is that he betrayed her. Ironically, toying with someone's heart in exchange for cash is just what Hanna did to Lucas at the dance-athon, but because of how far she's gone with Caleb — inviting him to live in her home, risking that her mom's secret could get out, and having sex for the first time with him — the fallout is crushing. Caleb and Jenna may not be the *X* factor that solves for A, but the equation of Hanna and Caleb may have just become unsolvable.

Hanna loses more in Caleb than a hot boyfriend (as when A drove Sean from her). She's lost having someone who's there for her, watching over her — not spying on her. It's what Spencer has found in Toby, who asks her to come to him before ever running away (*aw*), and it's what Spence is reassured she has in her mother, who's not always so affectionate with her youngest daughter. Spencer's mom trusts in her innocence, believes she's being framed, and will continue to handle the cops and lawyers. As Emily tells Paige, who turns to her for advice and comfort, none of them is fearless, but with loved ones whom they can trust, they're able to be brave.

HIGHLIGHT Spencer and Toby by the fire, quietly talking about running away with Cat Power's cover of "Sea of Love" in the background.

EXTRA CREDIT
- "Someone to Watch Over Me" is a jazz standard written by George and Ira Gershwin in 1926; the title was also used for a 1987 police thriller directed by Ridley Scott.
- Aria hands over an exhaustive pile of Ezra-related paraphernalia to Emily for safekeeping (most of which couldn't be linked to Mr. Fitz anyway), but she holds on to the Sherwood Anderson book, which we first saw in "The Homecoming Hangover."

BACK TO THE BOOKS With the A of it all, Spencer can't concentrate on her schoolwork, which is what drove her to steal Melissa's essay in *Flawless*.

SLIP UPS Do people keep disposable take-out coffee cups in their house? They do in Rosewood! After Toby gets Spencer to bring coffee to the cops, the Montgomery parents walk down the street with the exact same coffee cups in hand.

PLL IRL As Ian walks by Spencer's room, he creepily takes a sip from a glass of milk, and Troian did not let Ryan Merriman get away with it. "I made fun of him for a day with that milk," said Troian. "I was like, 'Get out of here with the milk!'" Ashley Benson stands by Hanna's decision to slap Jenna across the face in the girls' bathroom: "Don't feel bad for Jenna, she deserved that."

Qs & A Forget all that Spoby motel room action: 2-1-4 is Caleb's locker combination — one mystery solved. How did threads from Toby's blood-stained sweater get on Spencer's bracelet?

1.21 MONSTERS IN THE END

(AIRED MARCH 14, 2011 | WRITTEN BY OLIVER GOLDSTICK | DIRECTED BY CHRIS GRISMER)

Hanna: "Fool me once, shame on you.
Fool my friend, you're dead freakin' meat."

With the penultimate episode of the season, the darkest secret yet is revealed: Rosewood was founded by a bunch of freaky clowns. Why else would their Founders' Day celebrations be a carnival of creep? But while in any carnival it's the clowns who should be the spectacle, the opening scene of this episode shows the clowns crowded outside the Grille window, because in Rosewood it's our liars who are the main attraction.

With A lurking in the shadows watching the quartet's every move, *Pretty Little Liars* has always been about voyeurism and the power that comes with it. Being a watcher, especially an undetected one, is an active position, and while the watcher may not be able to control the situation, s/he can control the *information*. Further, the watchers in this episode aren't just Officer Garrett or a certain know-it-all blackmailer, but the everyday citizens of Rosewood who can make or break a reputation. And so, as our liars become aware of their audience, they refuse to be passive objects of anyone's gaze any longer.

After the café opening, the focus is on Spencer first, who's getting a refresher in Rosewood 101 from her mom and sister. Veronica suggests she should stop hanging out with everyone's favorite suspect, Toby Cavanaugh, and make nice instead by volunteering at the carnival. Spencer fights back, saying she doesn't care what people think, but her mom reminds her that "most verdicts are decided in living rooms." But by the end of this ep, Spencer's through with the living room crowd, and with a bold public liplock declares to all of Rosewood that *she's* the only judge of character to worry about.

Aided by Hanna the web-stalking genius, Aria takes a turn as watcher, tracking Fitz's former fiancée on not-Facebook. But in the end she can't handle the subterfuge and decides on the direct approach instead. The ex-files are opened, and Ezra reassures Aria that what's past is past. But Ezra, sensitive poetry-writing soul that he is, wisely deduces that Aria's distress isn't all about a ring from the Ponte Vecchio, but about the fact that they can't post their relationship on the internet for all the world to see. Interestingly, Aria wants to be seen, but only in a way she controls. So she improvises a compromise, and while the couple's turn as the paperbag prince and princess is a little sad, it's still a small rebellion.

Meanwhile, Emily may have been an unwitting secret keeper for Alison, but she refuses to become one herself. She dismisses Paige's drama and her shame, announcing, "I don't want to be your secret." While A points out the "love me, lie for me" similarities between Emily's relationships with Alison and Paige, this time Emily's not going to let anyone convince her to hide who she is.

The episode ends with the girls in a strange position, spying on their past selves as they watch the videos on the flash drive Jenna tried so hard to find for herself. And though this new perspective exposes how long they've been spied on and makes them feel vulnerable, it also gives them information and, hence, power to take on Ali's killer and maybe even shine a light on the ultimate voyeur, A.

HIGHLIGHT Spencer trapped in that cylinder of doom was one of the most heart-pounding moments of the series so far, though her audacious smooch with Toby is a close second.

EXTRA CREDIT

- The episode's title nods to the 1971 *Sesame Street* classic *The Monster at the End of This Book*: the book's loveable blue Grover spends the whole book warning of a monster at its conclusion, but when the reader arrives there, it's Grover himself! Grover's embarrassed. This episode encourages the characters to make no such mistake: have a good look and decide yourself whether something's as scary as it's made out to be.
- Aria's comment on Caleb's espionage — "He didn't invade Poland" — refers to the Nazi's first major act of aggression, the 1939 invasion and division of Poland, an event that marked the beginning of World War II.
- After being crushed by Caleb, Hanna listens to Elliott Smith, an American singer/songwriter known for his melancholy acoustic guitar ballads.
- Aria's rented *Runaway Bride*, a 1999 Julia Roberts–Richard Gere rom-com about a bride with chronically cold feet; *Top Secret Affair*, a 1957 comedy about a journalist trying to catch an army general in a dangerous liaison; and all five seasons of *Big Love*, the critically acclaimed 2006–2011 HBO series about a modern polygamist and his wives.
- Ezra bought Jackie's engagement ring on the Ponte Vecchio, Florence's famous medieval bridge that is home to numerous

jewelry shops, though the Italian city is better known for blown glass than diamonds.

SLIP UPS Every time one of the characters says website, their lips are saying Facebook. According to Marlene King, the dub order came down from the ABC Family legal department. Maybe Mark Zuckerberg is uncomfortable having his program on a show about constant surveillance? Was Hanna in a sound-proof tent? Couldn't she hear the conversation between Caleb and Mona? Who has been paying for Ali's storage locker?

Qs & A Melissa is caught in a lie about Hilton Head: is she lying about anything else? Did Ian do something to Spencer's phone after he picked it up in the cylinder of doom? Who filmed the videos on the flash drive? What is the Gloved Wonder going to do now that s/he has the key to Fitz's apartment?

1.22 FOR WHOM THE BELLS TOLL

(AIRED MARCH 21, 2011 | WRITTEN BY I. MARLENE KING | DIRECTED BY LESLI LINKA GLATTER)

Jenna: "You have no idea who you're dealing with."

A season finale that managed to deliver answers while raising even more questions, "For Whom the Bells Toll" proves once again that in Rosewood nothing is as it seems. As if murder wasn't bad enough, as if A wasn't bad enough, the girls are faced with the epic creepiness that they have been watched and filmed for years, and they weren't the only victims.

Information is power, and now that they've seen the videos, the girls aren't afraid to confront Jenna. Jenna could have been a sympathetic character: she was mocked by Ali and the rest of the girls, isolated, feared, hated, blackmailed . . . and blinded! But the video footage of her threatening Toby with false accusations of rape and forcing him into a sexual act shows that she's as accomplished a liar and manipulator as Alison was. Like Ali says to Jenna about Ian, "You think you know people. And then they surprise you." Jenna's connection to Garrett is a big surprise, and shows that even though the PLLs have the videos, Jenna has more weapons in her arsenal. Is her relationship with Garrett heartfelt, or is she using him?

As we learned in the flashback (which for the first time is from Jenna's perspective rather than one of the girls'), Ali evaded responsibility by blackmailing her victim, and the girls mimic Ali's tactic but with a very different goal — to make Ian pay for his crimes. The girls are unable to corner him, despite what seems like a decent plan, and in a twist he manages to corner Spencer in the darkened church, determined to kill her to keep her from revealing his secrets. Ian says he's doing it because he loves Melissa, but killing his sister-in-law to protect his marriage is pure crazycakes, even for Rosewood.

Fortunately not all romance on *Pretty Little Liars* is as twisted as Ian's is with the Hastings' women — but most are just as plagued with honesty issues. Aria cuts to the core of her parents' "it's complicated" relationship status by demanding that her mother face one question: does she love Byron enough to want to fix the marriage? Aria's frustration comes from her own Fitz-related drama, discovering that he had a fiancée and she's at Hollis too, just as his new job there was about to promise them less sneaking around. While Spence battles with her family — her feelings about Melissa's baby are misunderstood as motivated by petty cruelty — what she has with Toby shines as an example of all the good that can be in a romance. He is her escape and solace, a person to be open with. The scene in her bedroom is a lovely change of pace in the otherwise tense finale, giving us a moment to rest along with Spencer (though, sadly for us, not in Keegan Allen's arms).

The season ends with lots of things hanging in the balance — and one thing notably not hanging where it should be. Ian's

*Rosewood's chapel, host to weddings,
funerals, and disappearing bodies.*

missing corpse puts the girls back in the spotlight as the little liars everyone thinks they are. Is Ian really dead? Will Emily have to move to Texas? When will Caleb get back? (Thank you, Lucas!) Though we still can't be certain who killed Alison DiLaurentis, or who A is, the first season of *Pretty Little Liars* wraps up with a satisfying episode guaranteed to bring us back for more.

HIGHLIGHT Spencer and Ian's battle up the bell tower; it's been a slow and dramatic build between these two and to see them come to blows was scary and awesome.

EXTRA CREDIT
- There are notes about Hemingway on the blackboard in Fitz's classroom to go with the Hemingway-inspired title for this episode. *For Whom the Bell Tolls* (1940) tells the story of an American soldier in the Spanish Civil War (1936–1939) and fittingly explores the nature of political conflicts, mortality, and the brotherhood that exists between soldiers under wartime conditions.
- Hanna says to Jenna, "The truth. Can you handle that?" in a variation on the famous line from *A Few Good Men*, the 1992 film (based on the 1989 play of the same name) written by Aaron Sorkin and starring Jack Nicholson, Tom Cruise, and Demi Moore. The story follows a military court trial of two marines accused of murdering a fellow marine.
- In Spencer's room, Toby is reading Jack Kerouac's 1958 novel *The Dharma Bums*, and he is able to give Spencer a moment of peaceful transcendence in a day otherwise spent stressfully tracking down her creepy and murderous brother-in-law.
- In "Moments Later," Lucas told Hanna that she deserved a better boyfriend; by going after Caleb to bring him back to Rosewood, Lucas is staying true to that sentiment: even though Hanna doesn't like Lucas romantically, he has a big enough heart to make sure she's with someone else who loves her.

- In another reference to *PLL*'s favorite auteur, the bell tower scene was shot as an homage to Hitchcock's *Vertigo*.

SLIP UPS The video of Jenna coercing Toby calls into question the contents of his psychiatrist file found in "There's No Place Like Homecoming." Why would Toby lie to his shrink? It's out of character for the honest guy.

BACK TO THE BOOKS Ian is also accused of Ali's murder at the end of *Unbelievable*, but he maintains his innocence, and in *Wicked*, the girls find his body in the woods, but when they return with the police it has disappeared.

PLL IRL The finale was the most intensive shoot of the season, especially the bell tower sequence, but Marlene said it went "beyond all of our expectations" seeing it cut together in the finished product. Troian told *Entertainment Weekly* that what she loved about Spencer's finale arc was that "even though she's falling down the rabbit hole in a sense, she's also falling in love, and finding a true connection with somebody. . . . It's really beautiful. It's fun for me to play the dichotomy of having some of the best moments of your life come immediately after or before some of the worst."

Qs & A When Ian is telling his story of how Spencer killed Ali, he says Ali was killed from a blow to the head, but Spencer corrects him, saying she died of suffocation. If Ian killed Ali, shouldn't he know how she died? Ian seems to recognize the hooded figure who pushes him to his (maybe) death: had they been working together? Where did Ian's body go? Did A take it or is Ian still alive? If Ali didn't talk about Spencer when she went to see Jenna in the hospital, how did Jenna know that Spencer had stood up to Alison? Who crashed their car into Melissa and Spencer's? Will Melissa's baby be okay? Why is Noel Kahn back? Who is A?!

"When you *love* someone, it's *worth* fighting for, no matter what the odds."

— Aria

"It won't be that easy, bitches."

— *A*

"You're *always* better off
with a really good *lie*."
— *Alison*

Season 2

2.01 IT'S ALIVE

(AIRED JUNE 14, 2011 | WRITTEN BY I. MARLENE KING | DIRECTED BY RON LAGOMARSINO)

*Hanna: "I feel like I have a hangover
and I never even went to the party."*

In a show with the word liars in the title, it's not surprising that it's hard to know who to trust in Rosewood. And in this dramatic season opener, when bodies have disappeared, people seem to be back from the dead, and our liars are cast as, well, bigger liars, the facts can't be trusted any more than A. So, in the high-stakes game A has created, how do you decide who to believe and trust?

Near the beginning of the episode, our girls face an *Intervention*-style gathering of all their parents in Spencer's living room. Already a stark contrast to the cozy slumber party upstairs, the scene becomes increasingly tense as we start to understand that the parents are worried for their daughters, but they don't actually believe their story. When Spencer, always the direct one, asks point blank, "Do you believe us?" there's a lot of shuffling and looking at feet from the assembled adults. Though they love their children, they can't empathize with them enough to see beyond the facts (MIA corpse) and how this looks to the rest of the town. Though Ella says, "We heard you," it's clear they've heard without listening.

Ezra, on the other hand, is one adult who's never had a problem listening — to Aria at least. In fact, he believes Aria from the start (it's almost the first thing he says to her when she visits). Aria, unfortunately, can't quite do the same for him. He's lied by omission, but to make up for it he opens up completely, makes himself naked — nicely visualized as his first time shirtless on the show. "Ask me anything," he says, and he answers quickly and honestly. In this case, a combination of openness, respect, and love are enough — for Ezra at least, and hopefully Aria can follow his lead.

Like Ezra, Melissa is an adult not far from her own teen years. Unfortunately, she's prompted by the loose ends of the case, and not by her love for her sister, to finally come to Spencer ready to really hear her side. She also reiterates one of the episode's central threads, saying, "I wasn't listening. But now I am." Always vying for parental praise, the two Hastings girls haven't had mutual trust in a long time, but at least here they take a few wobbly steps toward it.

With her "good shoes" character and readiness to listen, Dr. Anne emerges as an adult that could be trustworthy, though A has done his or her best to convince the girls that the "talking cure" is just a road to more problems. The counselor respects them and genuinely wants to listen: so much so that she separates them to encourage each girl to speak.

Hanna says, "I'm not going to a shrink. That's what friends are for." It's a perfect line for this episode about listening and trust. Even though the girls have lied, even though they've kept their own dark secrets, they've listened to one another, trusted one another, even when things didn't make sense. Their restored friendship is the most significant departure from the books, and one of the best ones, for Alison may have brought them together, but the relationships they've built have kept them together and prevented them from going it alone.

HIGHLIGHT Caleb's heartfelt speech may not have won over Hanna just yet, but who could resist him for long?

EXTRA CREDIT
- The title is a reference to Mary Shelley's 1818 classic novel *Frankenstein*, in which Dr. Frankenstein, like the liars, learns the destruction that can come with the pursuit of forbidden knowledge.
- The word "believe" is used eight times in this episode.
- On the blackboard in Mr. Fitz's classroom: the class is still talking about Hemingway, referencing critics Leslie A. Fiedler and Rena Sanderson. But it looks like Mr. Fitz (or the set decorators) didn't do too much homework: what's on the board is copied directly from the Wikipedia page.
- Looking at Ezra's desk, Hanna mistakes a *Playbill* for a *Playboy*, but there's no confusing a theater magazine with Hugh Hefner's infamous skin rag.
- On Aria's nightstand are *What Really Matters* by Tony Schwartz, *Evening* by Susan Minot, and *Border Music* by Robert James Waller. The last selection seems a bit mainstream for offbeat Aria, but maybe Waller's star-crossed lovers struck a chord.
- The horror movie moment with Spencer in the kitchen is a nice reversal from last season: the person outside is still Toby, but this time he's a friend, not a foe.
- Dr. Anne works in the same building as Dr. Mark Goldstick, a name that's surely a nod to writer and executive producer Oliver Goldstick.

SLIP UPS When Caleb visits Hanna at her house, the clock reads 11:40, making it awfully late when Hanna goes to the Grille to confront Mona, whose date is starting past most teens' curfew.

BACK TO THE BOOKS In *Killer*, the girls are accused of

lying about Ian's death after his body disappears from the woods. Melissa starts receiving IMs from someone claiming to be Ian, and Spencer makes him confirm his identity by revealing a name only he would know (his embarrassing middle name). The girls go see a grief counselor in *Wicked*.

PLL IRL Said Marlene King on writing "It's Alive": "Writing the first episode back was really almost like writing a pilot all over again, because this season felt like it was a new beginning in a lot of ways. We're starting a whole new set of stories." Brant Daugherty (Noel Kahn) described the cast reactions at the table read of this script to Wetpaint: "Many of us were reading it for the first time, and we got to that scene, and it reads, 'Noel walks in and kisses Mona' — and I remember Lucy Hale audibly gasped, 'Oh my God!' If we can get [her] to gasp, we can get the fans for sure." Annabeth Gish, who plays the girls' psychiatrist, Dr. Anne Sullivan, has some experience with unexplained phenomena and serious drama: her past credits include *The X-Files*, *The West Wing*, and *Brotherhood* as well as roles in the films *Double Jeopardy* and the '80s classic *Mystic Pizza*.

Qs & A Now we know what A did with Mr. Fitz's stolen apartment key: s/he stole his diploma and planted in it Dr. Sullivan's office to prove to the girls there is no such thing as privacy in Rosewood. What are Jenna and Garrett afraid Jason is looking for? What is "The Jason Thing"? Is Ian still alive? If not, who moved the body and who is texting Melissa? Is it significant that Ian (or the person posing as Ian) texted, "Ask me anything," which is precisely what Ezra said to Aria?

DREW VAN ACKER AS JASON DiLAURENTIS

If this season Jason DiLaurentis looks bafflingly unfamiliar and familiar at the same time, it's because there's a new actor in the role — Drew Van Acker — but he's not an easily forgotten face. Born in 1986 in Philadelphia (not too far from Rosewood, perhaps?), Drew got into acting in high school, but his main focus was on soccer and he was good enough to land a scholarship to Towson University in Maryland. But Drew was drawn back to performing off the field, and soon enough he made his way to Hollywood. As well as having an active (and often shirtless) modeling career, he's been in episodes of *Greek* and *Castle* and he had recurring parts on both the short-form series *The Lake* and Cartoon Network's *Tower Prep*. As the second coming of Ali's older and troubled brother, Drew landed his highest-profile gig yet. "I like doing the creepy stuff," said the actor of his character whose suspicious behavior comes under scrutiny by the PLLs. But he admitted, "Jason might see it another way." But like her character, Lucy Hale understands the appeal of Drew as Jason: "I think all girls are drawn to the bad guy. I mean, it doesn't hurt that he's flawless and beautiful."

2.02 THE GOODBYE LOOK

(AIRED JUNE 21, 2011 | WRITTEN BY JOSEPH DOUGHERTY | DIRECTED BY NORMAN BUCKLEY)

*Jason: "One way or another, people
are gonna mind their own business."*

No one likes to say goodbye, and as the girls are driven apart "for their own good" their abandonment issues flare up. The PLLs each have valid reasons to feel insecure, and it makes giving someone a second chance difficult, especially for Hanna.

Though none of the girls likes being separated, Hanna takes it the worst, realizing that pretending to avoid each other has the same net effect as actually avoiding each other: they are isolated. So soon after the Caleb breakup, Hanna has lost Mona too; these were both people she trusted who betrayed her in different ways. But no one has had a deeper impact on Hanna than her father, who returns — it seems to her — only when she's in trouble. Hanna's an expert at giving him the teenage cold shoulder, and it's not undeserved. She is incredibly blunt with him, telling him that because he lied to her, she doesn't trust him. But she is willing to listen to him, even if she won't immediately forgive him. His claim that he acted with the best intention and made mistakes sinks in, and Hanna's able to reach out and forgive Mona, believing that while her bestie shouldn't have destroyed Caleb's letter she did it to protect Hanna, not to hurt her. With Tom Marin sticking around Rosewood to make up for lost time, Hanna at least has one more person on her otherwise shrinking team.

With a move to Texas on the near horizon for Emily, she's anticipating being even further removed from everything she cares about — her friends, her swim team, and her possible romance with Samara. Will the Danby scout be the answer to her worries? It's reassuring enough for Emily that she goes out on a date with Samara, risking getting close to her despite the "ghosts of girlfriends past" and her uncertain future.

Aria is on shaky ground at the beginning of "The Goodbye Look," and Ezra's pleas for a second chance — an opportunity to convince her that leaving his job isn't the same thing as leaving her — don't seem enough to convince her to take the risk. But his goodbye speech in the classroom, a thinly veiled aria to Aria, brings her to realize how much Fitz means to her. With the weather giving the English teacher and his star student a nice moment of pathetic fallacy, the storm passes, the sun breaks through clouds, and then, after their whole relationship spent in secret, Ezra and Aria share their first public and passionate kiss in the school parking lot. And in slow motion no less.

Only two episodes into the season, the plots are ramping up — break-ins, texts from dead guys, a flicker of chemistry between Hanna's parents, and a nosy dog sniffing in the DiLaurentis's yard. Rosewood may look peaceful and picturesque from Spencer and Toby's lookout spot, but Toby is right — monsters lurk within.

HIGHLIGHT Aria and Fitz's smooch in the parking lot is beautifully filmed, epically romantic, and set to the perfectly chosen soundtrack, "Please Don't Leave Quite Yet" by Adam Agin.

EXTRA CREDIT
- The episode's title is the name of a song written by Steely Dan's Donald Fagen about being left behind, and also the title of a crime thriller by Ross Macdonald about a burglary of a wealthy family, a suspicious son, and how the past catches up to the present in a world of riches and trouble. The "goodbye look" is the change in expression when someone is about to shoot to kill.
- Danby University (along with its excellent swim program) is fictional.
- In the flashback, Ali's brother calls her friends the Powerpuff Girls; silly Jason doesn't remember that there were only *three* kindergarten superheroes in the Cartoon Network's hit show

(1998–2005) — Bubbles, Buttercup, and Blossom.
- In his goodbye speech, Mr. Fitz quotes Joseph Campbell (1904–1987), a writer whose theories on myths and the hero's journey have made him influential in popular American thought and literary theory.

BACK TO THE BOOKS Hanna's dad doesn't wait quite so long to try to reconnect with her in the book series; after the hit-and-run he shows up at the hospital — rather than sending her a plant that dies. Since the girls don't reconnect in the books like they do on TV, when things with Mona fall apart Book Hanna is often lonely, striving to regain the friendships she's lost.

PLL IRL Said Ian Harding of "the kiss": "When we were shooting that — we actually shot that on a back lot at Warner Brothers — literally there were tour buses driving by. I don't know what it was, it was like National Teenage Girl Day, because all of them were filled with every female between the ages of 13 and 21. And it was the most epic kiss in the world. Norman Buckley, the director, said, 'Hey, why don't you spin one way and then spin another way.' And I was like, 'Oh, this is going to look so ridiculous,' but it actually came out pretty well." If the Danby scout looked familiar, it may be because actor Greg Cromer had a recent and memorable role on *Community* as Dr. Rich.

Qs & A Is Ian the one breaking into Rosewood houses? Since the Gloved Wonder is way nicer to that puppy than Jason was, can we safely assume that Jason is not the Gloved Wonder? Why is Jason so cagey and secretive? What is (or was) buried in the DiLaurentis's front yard? Ali said she has tons of hiding places: are there still secrets hidden in and around that house?

2.03 MY NAME IS TROUBLE

(AIRED JUNE 28, 2011 | WRITTEN BY OLIVER GOLDSTICK | DIRECTED ELODIE KEENE)

Ashley: "Things change. People grow."

Ashley's message to her daughter might seem as obvious as Spencer's attempts to get her mitts on Melissa's phone, but in a show where the characters are imprisoned by the secrets of their past (with A as jailer), change and growth are vital to stepping out of Alison's shadow. And in this episode, that growth shows up as empathy, with characters reaching out in ways they never would have imagined not so long ago.

Once a disciple of Alison's philosophy of popularity, Hanna has switched her image from haughty mean girl to friend of the people. She's really trying to make things up to Lucas, and she quotes her mother's wise words and reminds him that she doesn't want to be tethered to her past, held down by her "biggest mistake." She spares Mona the same fate, forgiving her for her misguided meddling. Mind you Hanna's not so self-aware: she doesn't see she's guilty of the same faux pas as Mona when she deletes Isabel's lovey-dovey text. But oh well, two steps forward, one step back. No one said growth was always a forward march.

Like Hanna, Spencer's ambition has often meant personal relationships become collateral damage on her quest to reach the top. Spencer was always so focused on her sister's benchmark achievements that she lost sight of Melissa herself. With her hair swept up in a messy bun and her junior executive armor cast aside for softer pjs, Troian shines as a verge-of-tears Spencer, making a touching plea to her sister to remember the relationship they once had, to make it a priority. Though she's partially motivated by fear for her own safety, the nature of her conversations with her sister have dramatically changed from last season.

Aria's always bemoaning her age, desperate to escape her high school years, but despite her adult tastes, she's still taking her own wobbly steps toward maturity. After running from her romance with Fitz (and then charging at it in the school parking lot), she's learning to stay put and work on her relationship. But more importantly in this episode, Jenna starts to help Aria see things in a new light: literally and figuratively. In the dark pottery studio, Jenna's not all smug smiles, knowing snark, and brother seduction, but someone who's mourning what she's lost, someone who will always see the past more clearly because her present is shrouded in darkness. Aria sees that even someone who seems sinister can be vulnerable too.

With her rescued growth chart featuring in many scenes, Emily's story offers the most obvious example of embracing change. While she considers faking the Danby letter, Emily fought to be honest with her parents last season, and she's not willing to give up those hard-won gains. She really doesn't want to move to Texas, but if anyone's learned that the unexpected can sometimes be a welcome surprise, it's Emily.

But if personal growth were measured on that wall chart, Pam Fields would have grown several feet in the last little while. Faced with a box of baby clothes and early artwork, Pam is finally realizing what her husband caught on to right away: regardless of who Emily loves, of how much she may have changed, Emily is still Emily, someone to be treasured. Pam's able not only to accept what has happened, but to empathize with her daughter's journey, and acknowledge her own role in that struggle. It's a turning point in one of the show's most realistic relationships. Change might not be easy, but it is possible.

HIGHLIGHT Ali's moment of vulnerability in Spencer's kitchen: it's a reminder that she's not as confident and untouchable as she may act. Her reactive jab at the Hastings family's apple selection also gives us a taste of what Ali's like when she feels threatened.

EXTRA CREDIT
- Spencer says Emily's talking like founding father, scientist, statesman, and philosopher Ben Franklin, meaning she's speaking in aphorisms, though Emily's actually paraphrasing psychologist Abraham Maslow, who said, "I suppose it is tempting, if the only tool you have is a hammer, to treat everything as if it were a nail."
- Emily tells Spencer she has to stop playing Harriet the Spy, referring to the classic 1964 children's novel by Louise Fitzhugh (or its 1996 film adaptation) about a precocious young girl who keeps tabs on the people in her life in a notebook.
- Jenna gets Aria to light her candle, a subtle nod to Aria's involvement in the fire.
- Though Rosewood is fictional, the Pennsylvania references are factual: Yardley, where Toby's job offer is, is a small community in Bucks County, and Tom jokes that Isabel wants to rent Veterans Stadium, once home to Philadelphia's major sporting and concert events.

SLIP UPS Parenting demerit points for the elder Hastings yet again: who leaves their daughters alone after a near-death experience and a violent break-in?

PLL IRL There is a real Hollis college in Hollis, New Jersey, but the establishing shots of *PLL*'s Hollis College are actually Ohio State University. Playing Lucas's yearbook love interest, the "appendix" named Danielle, is Amanda Leighton, who has also appeared on *Criminal Minds*, *Grey's Anatomy*, *House*, and *90210*.

BACK TO THE BOOKS Spencer has a similar tender moment with her sister in *Unbelievable*, and Aria takes a "Mindless Art" class with Jenna, but Aria soon identifies herself to Jenna. In *Unbelievable*, Emily's parents have a change of heart about her sexuality after Emily runs away from her aunt and uncle's house.

Qs & A What is Jason hiding in his house? Whose blood is on the gauze in Jason's garbage? The flashback is the first time we see Alison vulnerable, and it seems to be genuine. What happened with Jason and his friends to upset her, and what could she say about him to get him written out of her grandma's will? What did Wren give Melissa and who was watching them in Jason's house? What does the Gloved Wonder want with Melissa's engagement ring? Is it telling that the pawnbroker thought it was his/her ring and not Spencer's?

2.04 BLIND DATES

(AIRED JULY 5, 2010 | WRITTEN BY CHARLIE CRAIG | DIRECTED BY DEAN WHITE)

Mike: "Things aren't how they used to be, and they never will be."

Maturing along with the girls themselves, *Pretty Little Liars* continues to step up its game in season 2 with stronger writing; a tone that's more confident, funny, and heartfelt; and way more shirtlessness — a whole basketball court full! The girls are also more proactive about solving the mysteries that plague them, and that means more hiding in the bushes doing the spying themselves rather than being the ones spied on. But a show about secrets and lies would be nothing without a constant stream of new, juicy material and "Blind Dates" takes the idea of lying for others to the extreme.

On the more innocuous side, Emily is faced with the lie she didn't even tell as her mom turns into Danby's number-one enthusiast. Instead of hiding the truth from Samara like the girls have chosen to do in the past with A-related trouble, Emily opens up, telling her a *version* of the truth that protects her from A backlash, and Samara proves willing and able to help Emily out by redirecting Momma Fields' enthusiasm and encouraging Emily to play the college field.

Aria inadvertently stumbles upon a secret her brother has been keeping: he's up to *something* and it's not playing basketball after school. In a scene that proves girls aren't the only ones who will resort to blackmail to protect themselves, Mike threatens to rat out Aria to their parents if she rats him out. And Aria does keep her brother's secret. She also shares a moment with Jason DiLaurentis that looks like it could turn into trouble for the Ezria fans: she is flattered that he remembers her pink hair and that he admired her.

The one PLL who is ready to let go of who she was when Alison was the head mean girl is Hanna. She's been resistant to the idea of therapy with Dr. Sullivan, but after she goes through with her fake date with Caleb so Lucas can potentially find happiness with Danielle, she realizes that she's on the verge of a breakthrough. Caleb and Hanna agree that what's holding back

CLAIRE HOLT AS SAMARA

The actress who plays Emily's new love interest, Samara, understands the joy of swimming just like Em does: Claire Rhiannon Holt, who was born July 7, 1988, in Brisbane, Australia, was a competitive water polo player in her teen years and loves sports. Her first acting role was as Emma Gilbert, the accidental mermaid in the Australian kids show *H2O: Just Add Water*, which had a huge audience — 100 million viewers in over 100 countries. Her experience with water polo and love for swimming helped her to play a mermaid, from keeping up during the physically demanding shoot to the tricks of the trade: putting a few drops of milk in her eyes to stop the chlorine burn. After leaving her fish tail behind after two seasons of *H2O*, Claire landed roles in a couple of movie sequels, *Messengers 2* and *Mean Girls 2*, and an independent film *Blue like Jazz* (not yet released) before moving back to TV with her recurring roles as Samara on *Pretty Little Liars* and Rebekah on *The Vampire Diaries*. Luckily for the Australian transplant, her friend from *H2O*, Phoebe Tonkin, also made the leap to Hollywood and landed a role on *Vampire Diaries* sister show *The Secret Circle*. As Claire has grown from straight-out-of-school actress to accomplished 24-year-old, her parts have become more complex and layered — and that suits her just fine. From a 1,000-year-old vampire to a social justice seeking college student to Emily's guide into the world of acceptance, Claire is proving she can swim with all kinds of fish.

Lucas is caring so deeply about what other people think, to the point of being paralyzed by his lack of self-confidence. In confronting her lingering attachment to Alison, Hanna is able to let go of worrying about what Alison would do or say or think. In Hanna's imagined conversation with Alison, Alison prays on all of Hanna's insecurities and fears, but Hanna is now strong enough to choose solitude over mistreatment. She gets the difference between a true friend and a total frenemy. But whoever ransacked the doctor's office wasn't so pleased with Hanna's new independence.

But the major reveal at the end of the episode ups the ante: Melissa, thinking she's about to run away with Ian, instead finds him dead, a gun in his hand and a suicide note beside him. The girls who cry wolf are going to have to call in the cops on this one.

Rosewood's go-to restaurant, the Apple Rose Grille, unless you're Mike and prefer Sausage Heaven. This storefront was formerly used as Luke's Diner on Gilmore Girls.

HIGHLIGHT "That was easy." "Well, I'm not." Caleb is going to have to work if he wants Hanna back.

EXTRA CREDIT
- The billboard with the eerie slogan — "Someone's watching you so look your best . . ." — and the ever-watching eyes is reminiscent of the billboard in *The Great Gatsby* featuring the eyes of Dr. T.J. Eckleburg that watch over the characters like the watching eyes of God.
- Instead of going to therapy, Hanna wants to watch *Intervention*, the A&E reality program that's been on since 2005 where various kinds of addicts are forced to confront their problems.
- The hospital where Wren works, St. Anthony's in Philly, is fictional.

BACK TO THE BOOKS Melissa finds Ian's body in *Wanted*, but it's an even more gruesome scene than the suicide tableau on TV.

SLIP UPS Why did Aria dress up like an inner-city youth to go to the poor side of town? Definitely "unexpected" but definitely not cool.

PLL IRL One of Marlene King's favorite scenes is Hanna talking to "Ali" in Dr. Anne's office, and the showrunner says just thinking about Ali spinning around in that chair gives her goose bumps.

Qs & A If Mike hasn't been playing pickup after school, what has he been up to? (Wild guess: no good.) The girls don't see but we do: above the door in the barn where Ian lies dead there's a missing horseshoe, just like the one Spencer got at the pawnshop. Did A have something to do with Ian's apparent suicide? The Gloved Wonder puts a red phone in the purse (presumably Spencer's) on the drivers' seat: why and is that Ian's red phone, seen in "For Whom the Bells Toll"? Who trashed Dr. Sullivan's office, and is it significant that the clock was stopped at 6:05 p.m.?

2.05 THE DEVIL YOU KNOW

(AIRED JULY 12, 2011 | WRITTEN BY MAYA GOLDSMITH | DIRECTED BY MICHAEL GROSSMAN)

Ella: "I guess we see what we want to see."

Ian is dead (no question about it this time), the girls are no longer Rosewood's most wanted, and the parentals have relaxed the besties ban. Seems great, but since this is *Pretty Little Liars*, things aren't as they seem, and the girls can't, as Spencer suggests, take a break from looking over their shoulders. The episode takes its title from an old proverb: "Better to deal with the devil you know than the devil you don't." It suggests that facing the known (even if unpleasant) is better than facing the unknown.

Alison DiLaurentis has been front-page news since her disappearance, a blemish on the town's picture-perfect image and on its psyche. Rosewood's residents are looking for answers, for someone to blame, to feel like the order of things is restored. Ian's death becomes like an old-fashioned witch trial, an attempt to purge the town of the fear they've borne for over a year. We see the effect it has had on the parents when Ashley breaks down in this episode, telling Hanna she's been terrified of losing her to the same fate as Ali. Now that the devil has a name, and he's dead, Ashley can rest a bit easier.

In the Hastings household, Ian's death has crushed Melissa, paralyzed by her husband's death and her so-I-married-an-axe-murderer realization, but it's done a lot to repair Spencer's relationship with her family. Her mother's visit to Spencer's bedroom to apologize has all of the softness that's normally missing from the Hastings manse, and the closing shot, with Spencer scurrying into her mother's open arms, and her mother telling her she loves her, is a brief moment of solace. The conversation between Hastings daughters later in the episode offers hope for the same thing between them — until derailed by A, perhaps permanently.

Jason also knows the terrifying grip of the unknown, haunted as he has been by the possibility that he might have killed his own sister. He's on the verge of man tears talking to Aria, a move that makes Aria's sympathy more understandable, but not enough to wipe away his recent sketchy behavior. Jason may be happy to embrace Ian as the killer, but viewers won't be able to forget Jason's blackout night as easily as he has.

Despite Ian's story arc being put to rest, the girls can't wash their hands of the whole thing as easily as they brushed off the dirt from Ian's grave. Emily (and A) won't let them. The most loyal to Ali, and probably the one who loved her most, it makes sense that Emily's the one who keeps pursuing her killer. With her *Wheel of Fortune* prowess, Emily reopens the case they'd been so desperately trying to close. In the final scene, the girls end up back at the graveyard, and in a sense, back to the beginning — surrounded by death, with Ali and A just beyond their grasp.

HIGHLIGHT As if the misty cemetery weren't creepy enough, seeing the director's cut of the Ali video was a chilling finale.

EXTRA CREDIT
- The girls are reading *The Heart Is a Lonely Hunter* in English class. The 1940 novel by Carson McCullers has become a Southern Gothic classic. The novel focuses on the isolated lives of four acquaintances of a deaf-mute man, spinning out from the central but unknowable character, who is something different to each of the characters. Seem familiar?
- Hanna and Ashley try to keep their *Eat, Pray, Love* moments for when they're alone. *Eat, Pray, Love* is a 2006 bestselling

memoir by Elizabeth Gilbert about her life-changing travels in India, Italy, and Bali. It was adapted into a film in 2010 starring Julia Roberts.

- Hanna gets most of the series' good one-liners, but in this ep Aria's comment to Mr. Fitz when he wanted to speak to her post-funeral showed she can zing with the best of 'em: "Should I round up the rest of the student body so you can address us as a group?"
- Hanna says Ashley is a partner at Dolce, Gabbana & Leibovitz. Dolce & Gabbana is a high-end Italian fashion line started by Domenico Dolce and Stefano Gabbana. Annie Leibovitz is an American photographer whose iconic images have graced the covers of *Rolling Stone*, *Vanity Fair*, and *Vogue*. Han also threatens to unleash Erin Brockobitch on Janet, referring to Erin Brockovich, the legal clerk turned environmental crusader made famous by the 2000 movie dramatizing her story.
- Caleb has a date to watch cult classic adventure flick *The Goonies* (1985) with Lucas.
- Teenagers sneaking into a graveyard "is like chapter one of every Stephen King book." The famous American horror writer is publishing royalty and has over 50 books to his name, so chances are he included a few teens in graveyards.
- The ABC Family website also lists this episode as "Don't Kill the Messenger."

PLL IRL Top marks to costume designer Mandi Line for four more fabulous funeral outfits. Even in basic black, the girls' personalities still shine through, from Hanna's fascinator and daring décolletage to Spencer's Victorian choker and neckline.

BACK TO THE BOOKS In *Unbelievable*, it's Spencer, not Jason, who realizes that she has suppressed her memory of the night Alison disappeared and worries that maybe she was the one who killed her. In *Killer*, Aria connects with Jason by talking to him about Ali and her death, something that others seem scared to do.

Qs & A The handwriting on Jason's anonymous note is the same as on Ian's fake suicide note (pay special attention to the Ts and Is to see the similarities). Why has Mike traded lacrosse and basketball for breaking and entering? Who sent Jason the note? Was it A or someone else? What was Jason up to on the night that Ali died? What new info was Melissa about to share with Spencer before Ian's phone interrupted them? And most importantly, if Ian didn't kill Ali, who did?

2.06 NEVER LETTING GO

(AIRED JULY 19, 2011 | WRITTEN BY BRYAN M. HOLDMAN | DIRECTED BY J. MILLER TOBIN)

Aria: "How many times do we have to put her away?"

In the opening scene the girls move from talking about whether Ali's killer is dead or still on the loose to recapping Hanna's recent kiss with Caleb; it's a great microcosm of the girls' reality — how their lives have played out since Ali's body was discovered, buried in the DiLaurentis's backyard, and A began to terrorize them. On the one hand they are obsessed with finding out the truth and wriggling out from under A's thumb, but on the other they keep living their lives, both to keep up appearances and to actually, you know, *live their lives*. Romance and family drama and an endless pile of homework. But the ever-present Alison/A situation has meant that "letting go" is impossible. Aria says to Jason that every time they try to make peace, someone says something ugly about Ali's death. The grieving process for the PLLs and for Ali's family has been far from peaceful: a year spent hoping Ali is alive, a violent death revealed, the park memorial destroyed hours after it was dedicated, a family friend accused of murder, and for the girls, the realization that the crime has not actually been solved. Now the fashion show the girls were reluctantly a part of turns quickly from a meaningful moment to a public condemnation of Ali, as devil imagery dances onscreen and the words "bitch" and "monster" slash across the carefully chosen photos of her angelic face.

Which is, of course, the last thing Ali's mom needs. The intensity of her grief is uncomfortable for the girls, particularly for Hanna. A mother unable to let go of her daughter, her emotion is right on the surface, and she clings to the girls like she does to Ali's dresses, hoping to keep her daughter "alive" in some way. It's interesting — and intriguing — to see the distance between Jason and Jessica DiLaurentis and how differently they handle themselves. Jason came back to Rosewood for answers, and he's taking Ian's confession as an indication of his own innocence. He wants to move on, let go, and try to be happy — in Rosewood and with Aria, if that glint in his eye is any indication of romance a-brewing. But the girls are suspicious of Jason — Spencer and Emily in particular. Does he really not remember the last day he saw his own sister? When Jenna and Garrett talk about The Jason Thing, do they mean his blackout or that note? Assuming that Jason isn't a killer, he could be good for Aria in ways that Fitz hasn't been: Jason gets the Ali stuff, they can be seen together — sort of — and he proves to be a useful confidant and protector from the eternally suspicious Noel Kahn.

Spence says she was always a romantic, but the girls can see the Toby Effect. He chills her out without diminishing her feelings and provides a perspective the other girls don't have. And she's not the only PLL to find happiness: Hanna opens up to Caleb in the end, realizing that giving second chances and granting forgiveness aren't a sign of weakness but of a person's willingness to let go of the past. And it seems like her mother has come to the same conclusion about Tom.

Even though the fashion show was derailed by A, and Ali's memory tarnished again, there is a sweetness to "Never Letting

Go": despite A's best efforts to control the girls, they have each other, they have burgeoning romances, and they have parents who believe in them and know that they were not responsible for the fashion show hijacking. Maybe it's time for A to let go and move on to another game.

HIGHLIGHT Mona's bossy fashion show takeover ("Are your legs always that short?") and Spencer's desire to yank the side ponytail of a girl who's "five feet of insidious snark."

EXTRA CREDIT
- Aria makes a point of returning for her hair products, which are all TRESemmé; this product-placement advertisement was part of a larger *PLL* tie-in campaign that featured commercials where Hanna and Mona talked boys and fave conditioners.
- The Gloved Wonder buys (from the fictional website Taback Decker New York) brown Tory Burch riding boots, which just so happen to be the same pair Dr. Anne Sullivan was wearing in "It's Alive" (Hanna makes a comment about them).

PLL IRL The only other time Alison's mom appeared was at Ali's funeral in the pilot episode; she was played by Anne Marie DeLuise in that episode, but here is portrayed by Andrea Parker. Costume designer Mandi Line describes the fashion show as having three distinct segments. The first pass is "resort" looks, which Line calls "high-end" and "a little obnoxious." The second pass was supposed to be "New York going out," but Mandi points out that the girls go to school looking like that. For the final look, which Mandi designed herself, she went more over the top, with what Troian calls "post-apocalyptic-Mad-Max-Burning-Man-pirate-wench." Ali's old dresses were haute couture, and these were Lucy Hale's favorite outfits. Both Aria and Hanna are in Alexander McQueen, Em is in Catherine Malandrino, and

Spencer is wearing a design from Anthony Franco's collection. (Sadly Ali was wrong: unlike the PLLs, these dresses are not one of a kind.)

SLIP UPS In Spencer's inbox, there's an unread message from Melissa with the subject line "lunch"; not only is Melissa out of town, but after the huge "never forgive you" blowout the sisters had, it's unlikely big sis would email Spence about lunch plans. Gloved fingers don't work on track pads, but somehow the Gloved Wonder manages just fine.

Qs & A Was the slideshow tampered with before or after Noel got it? Jessica says Jason came into family money; in "My Name Is Trouble," Ali said she could get her grandma to write him out of the will — did Grandma die? What is going on between Peter Hastings, Jessica DiLaurentis, and Jason? Why is the Gloved Wonder buying the same boots as Dr. Anne? The boots will be shipped to an address that starts with 5214 (bringing back the 2-1-4 mystery number from season 1).

Rosewood City Hall, which also doubles as its police station.

HOW TO DRESS A LIAR

When *Pretty Little Liars* made its debut, our liars looked, well, pretty, but their wardrobes didn't have fashion blogs all atwitter or people flocking to the malls. It was no *Gossip Girl*. But in episode 3, that changed with the appearance of one accessory: *the* feather earring.

Along with the earring came the show's new costume designer Mandi Line, who had plucked the earring from her own ear and handed it to a skeptical Lucy Hale. The actress's first thought was "I look like I have a peacock in my hair!" but everyone reassured her. In the end, ABC Family agreed with its star: it had to go. But with the episode in the can, it was too late — and once "To Kill a Mocking Girl" aired and the earring became *the* earring, *Pretty Little Liars* rocketed into the fashion stratosphere, and Mandi Line and her bold creative instincts were there to stay.

A graduate of the Fashion Institute of Design and Merchandising, Line had been fixated on fashion from a young age. But growing up she didn't have much money, so she had to be resourceful, and in fact, managed to never wear the same outfit twice. She explains, "I grew up with nothing so I used to go to Goodwill and thrift shops. I once pinned terry cloth flowers all over my jeans. I was always about mixing vibes and genres. I was a little Siouxsie and the Banshees and a little bit hippie. Oh, and I won best dressed in high school." She came to *PLL* with some experience under her belt: she'd already worked on other ABC Family projects like *10 Things I Hate About You* and *Greek*, Lifetime's *Drop Dead Diva*, and a number of films, but in this teen drama she saw an opportunity to make style a main attraction.

"At first they were like, 'Who is this person we just hired?'" recalled Mandi. "Not that anyone was hesitant, but I wanted to sell them on the idea that you've gotta have a show where viewers will tune in for clothes." But since *PLL* is a drama and not a runway, all the girls' looks have to suit their characters, and hopefully extend those characters, as well.

Mandi worked to develop a distinct style that suited the personality of each girl, though this can vary within an episode, and like a good costume designer, Mandi notes, "The tone of the script dictates how far I take it." The style isn't static either — as the girls change, their styles do too.

The designer identifies Aria's look as closest to her own: a little punk, a little boho, a little vintage — edgy, experimental, and one-of-a-kind. Line calls it "vintage eclectic, very tactile," and notes, "Everything is very textured, but really done in an elegant way, with little granny boots and fishnets." As the show has gone on, especially in season 2, Aria's style has settled down a bit, becoming a little more romantic as Aria enters a mature relationship and gains more distance from her pink-highlights past. For Aria, Line shops flea markets and integrates high-end vintage finds, adding her own flourishes and adjustments for the tiny Lucy Hale: "We cut, we sew, we alter and chop. Any time she is in a fitting, we have three pairs of scissors." Mandi and Lucy have actually become pals in real life. "We literally text each other, like, 'Okay, you bought this? Cool. You ate this for lunch? Cool,'" revealed the designer.

Dressing Queen Bee Hanna was a challenge because with a $10,000-per-episode budget the designer couldn't buy Hanna all the things the character would buy (or steal) in real life, so often Line ends up "upcycling," adding her own twists to elevate less expensive items. Hanna started the show with lots of color and flowy fabrics, but after the first 10 episodes she gets a little edgier. It's partially a reflection of Hanna becoming a bit more grounded as a person, but Line also clarified, "If you think about it, the It Girl is kind of edgy these days too." (The style transition is also appropriate for Hanna's developing taste in male accessories, swapping squeaky-clean jock Sean for bad boy Caleb.) Line shops boutiques and gives brands Alice + Olivia and Foley and Corinna a special shout-out as being perfect for season 2's Han.

Line calls Spencer's style "funky prep," and in the beginning got a lot of her clothes from American Apparel, J.Crew, Urban Outfitters, and Izod, but by the second season she switched her focus to vintage pieces and smaller brands like ASOS, aiming for a look that was less mass-produced. It's a transition that fits, since by season 2, Spencer's no longer obsessed with competing with her sister and impressing her parents. We see more belting and mixing of patterns, and keep your eyes peeled for the animals Mandi has snuck into Spencer's outfits every episode! Of Troian, the designer notes, "No matter what she does, [she] has a vintage feel to her because she's got this timeless body, beautiful hair, and classic face," and she praises the actress for having an excellent sense of her own style.

Emily's style can be the most challenging for Mandi, "because overdoing things is my thing, and she's more simple." Since former model Shay is also far more glamorous than her character, the designer also has to tread carefully. "Oh my god, she's a vixen. She's a hip-hop video girl," exclaims Mandi. So she tries to steer the actor away from straight-up sexy toward a Cameron Diaz or Jennifer Garner look. Luckily, Emily's style, originally defined by a sporty, all-American aesthetic, is evolving right along with the girl. In the beginning, the stylista explains, "Her clothes are approved by her mom and she doesn't do anything to rock the boat," but coming out gives Emily more fashion freedom, a chance to explore who she is and not who her parents want her to be. Her shirts are slipping off the shoulder, her accessories are getting bolder, and the designer has started to integrate some leather and beadwork. Mandi based Emily's emerging style on one of her friends who's a high-profile club promoter, and explains, "Slowly we're taking her a little Johnny Depp–ish, with scarves and the V-neck, very American Apparel." The designer hits stores like Alternative Apparel, AllSaints, Puma, Adidas, and American Eagle for the foundations of Emily's look.

Overall, Mandi wanted to focus on style that was accessible for ABC Family viewers. She notes *Gossip Girl* fans could never afford Serena's or Blair's costly couture, but Mandi shops at Macy's, Bloomingdale's, and Nordstrom regularly, avoiding swankier department stores like Barneys or Saks. Sometimes this even means tweaking the pieces to add her own flair, which transform items into one-of-a-kind Mandi Line.

Thanks to Mandi's resourcefulness, creativity, and willingness to take chances, in 2011, *Pretty Little Liars* earned a spot on *InStyle*'s list of the most fashionable TV shows of all time, and as the designer had hoped, people *do* tune in for the fashion. "She's just got a mind unlike any other I've come in contact with," said Lucy. "She really was born to do this."

2.07 SURFACE TENSION

(AIRED JULY 26, 2011 | WRITTEN BY JOSEPH DOUGHERTY | DIRECTED BY NORMAN BUCKLEY)

Caleb: "There's a difference between
being honest and being suicidal."

Science buffs know surface tension as the phenomenon that causes some molecules to bind together (think rain droplets on a car) and others to repel (think oil and water). Certainly this is an episode that explores the ties that bind, and the things that threaten to push people apart. And on *Pretty Little Liars*, nothing brings people together like a secret shared, and nothing divides them like one withheld.

The centerpiece of this ode to tension is the bizarre love triangle happening at the Montgomerys' dinner party. Whether it's their bouquet offerings or their two-wheeled travels, Jason and Ezra try to outdo each other, though neither knows about the other man's secret tie to Aria. She's drawn to both — one man represents who she wants to be and one man is tied to who she was — but she can't continue to be pulled in both directions.

Family ties are another major source of tension, with Mike's less-than-legal extra-curricular coming to the attention of the Rosewood PD and his parents. We see instant conflict between Byron and Ella over how to handle the situation, and things between Aria and her brother boil over after she realizes he hasn't kicked the B&E habit. Things aren't much friendlier at the Hastings household, where Spencer and her father's fireside confrontation illuminates Mr. Hastings' desire for closure at the expense of truth. Spencer is powerless to save the field hockey stick from becoming kindling, nor can she find out what her father is hiding. Though letting her in on the secret might bring the family together as a united front, Mr. Hastings' secrecy means Spencer instead finds herself turning against her own father.

There aren't many relationships that are immune to the tremors of tension running through Rosewood, but the ones grounded in trust seem to weather the storm best. Hanna and Emily may squabble during their new stint as roomies, but Emily's wise enough to put some space between them. Similarly, Hanna and Caleb disagree about his entrepreneurial efforts, but when he opens up about his past, the sketchy part of it is put in perspective, and a few more walls come down in Haleb town. She even keeps his secret from Emily, who's feeling the strain of her own secret load and tells Hanna, "I've got all the secrets I need right now."

After all the incendiary public antics from A last episode, "Surface Tension" is a welcome retreat back to our girls' private world, grounding the characters with relatable stories once again.

HIGHLIGHT The always-honest Toby lies for the first time, 'cause that's how much he loves Spencer.

EXTRA CREDIT
- A's gift basket has a stuffed pig in it — looks like A won't let that one go.
- *Guess Who's Coming to Dinner* is a 1967 drama starring Sidney Poitier, Spencer Tracy, and Katharine Hepburn. It's notable for its positive representation of interracial marriage (which was then still illegal in 17 states).
- Ezra went to Ireland because it's the homeland of James Joyce, a key modernist writer famous for his stream-of-consciousness style in now-classic novels like *Ulysses* (1922), and Samuel Beckett, a novelist and playwright best known for his existentialist comedy *Waiting for Godot* (premiered in 1953).
- Jason biked the coast in Kona district on the Big Island in Hawaii, home of the Ironman World Championship.

SLIP UPS The penmanship on the board in Ella's classroom with the Carson McCullers lesson goes from boyish printing to a flowing cursive. Not the work of the same teacher.

PLL IRL This episode marks the debut of Hanna's bedroom. Scenes at the Marin house always took place in the kitchen, front hallway, and bathroom thus far. Ashley Benson was thrilled to get a bedroom of her own and notes that her two favorite colors are black and pink, like the feathers on the wallpaper, and she says that one of the stuffed dogs on the bed looks a bit like her own dog, Olive.

Qs & A The meeting of the moms reveals some gossip on Peter Hastings: he has a habit of paying people off to get what he wants — is that why he's at odds with the DiLaurentis family? Was the field hockey stick the murder weapon? What is the Gloved Wonder injecting in the tube of cream?

2.08 SAVE THE DATE

(AIRED AUGUST 2, 2011 | WRITTEN BY MATT WITTEN | DIRECTED BY CHRIS GRISMER)

Emily: "A is taking us down, one at a time."

A great episode with a *lot* going on, "Save the Date" centers on Emily who has been even more stressed than Spencer. Not only has A *given her an ulcer* but s/he's endangered her health further — as well as her swimming career, college plans, reputation, and relationship with her parents — by sneaking steroids into the pain cream that Emily's been slathering on. Emily feels like there's no safe place — not home, school, or the hospital — nowhere that she's out of A's reach, so her desire to run away to Texas is understandable. What keeps her from ditching Rosewood, more than her friends rallying around her, comes in the beautiful scene between her and her father. He shows her that his love is unconditional, that scholarships and swim team standings mean nothing to her parents if her health or happiness is affected. Emily and her parents have come a long way in the past season and a half, and this moment of acceptance means the world to her. But her dad's well-timed speech means that the secrets Emily was ready to spill stay hidden, and A still holds hostage the truth about Danby and her medical results.

In a contrast to the moment "Emmy" has with her dad, Ella's attempt to force a conversation with Mike turns ugly. Closed off and fuming, his fear that she'll leave again comes out not as hurt but as aggression, and Ella doesn't know how to handle his raw anger at her. To Mike, Ella's love and presence is conditional — on his behavior, on Byron's, and on Aria's. Hanna's been dealing with her parents' breakup and the absence of her dad for a long time now, but she bought into the fantasy of her family reuniting just as her mom did — until that "save the date" card showed up. Ashley's decision to push Tom back to Isabel, because she needs a man who knows what he wants, echoes Hanna's breakthrough in "Blind Dates" about Alison. Ashley, like Hanna, will be okay alone: it's better than being mistreated. For Hanna, it feels like she's losing her dad again, and her family will never be united and perfect like that one outside Lucky Leon's. That fear of losing someone she loves is also what kept her from telling Caleb about the guy tailing him. But just as Spencer forces Hanna to talk in the elevator, Hanna forces Caleb — and both are better off for opening up. In Rosewood, good things are often fleeting, but that doesn't mean unconditional love doesn't exist.

But does it between Aria and Fitz? She's cooled off on him and it's only made him scramble harder to win her back, acting a little too desperate for her attention. He's not ready to lose her, but Jason seems to be creeping between them.

HIGHLIGHT Spencer and Aria sneaking into the morgue in candy striper outfits. Spencer Hastings never wastes an opportunity for a little detective work!

EXTRA CREDIT

- Emily realizes that when the girls saw Jenna buying black lace lingerie in "The New Normal," it must have been for Garrett.
- Ezra's joke that he wanted to find Aria at the potter's wheel and sing "Unchained Melody" is a reference to the famous scene from *Ghost* where Patrick Swayze's spectral character has a moment with his still-alive wife, played by Demi Moore.
- A has been lacing Emily's pain cream with human growth hormone, which has been used as a performance-enhancing anabolic steroid by athletes since the '70s; non-medicinal use has all kinds of nasty side effects from enlarging organs and bones to triggering diabetes and affecting fertility.
- Spencer steals candy striper outfits for her and Aria. In "Moments Later," in Hanna's dream when she was in the hospital, Alison is wearing the same uniform.
- Ashley calls her time with Tom her "week of magical thinking," alluding to Joan Didion's award-winning memoir *The Year of Magical Thinking* (2005) and the idea that if you hope hard enough for something you can change an otherwise inevitable event.

PLL IRL The scene where Spencer and Aria break into the morgue is one of Lucy Hale's favorites. Episodes 2.07 and 2.08 were filmed simultaneously, and two of *PLL*'s frequent directors, Norman Buckley and then-new-to-Twitter Chris Grismer, took the opportunity to engage in a friendly tweet-war, posting photos and busting each other's chops. Both directors think Twitter is a huge part of *PLL*'s success. "I think it's amazing that fans get to interact so directly with the cast and crew of the shows they love," said Grismer. "Some shows that I've been on tell the cast and crew not to tweet about the show or send pics from set and I think they're making a huge mistake. You can build a pretty big following by communicating with the fans."

SLIP UPS Spencer and Aria act as if they thought the blow to the head killed Alison, but they've long known the cause of death was suffocation. In "The Jenna Thing" it's in a news report and in "For Whom the Bells Toll" Spencer corrects Ian when he says that Ali died from a blow to the head. What they didn't know was the horrifying detail that Ali was buried alive. It's not that gross to eat cookies in a morgue ("They stay fresh," says Spencer), but to use the gloved hand you've been touching hospital garbage with to eat said cookie? Super gross. A save-the-date card for a wedding is sent out way more than six weeks beforehand; up to a year of nuptial notice is generally provided.

Qs & A Spencer's top murder suspect is Jason: is he guilty? What did Jenna mean when she asked Garrett if the girls "know" about Jason? Who stole page five of the autopsy report and why? Who did the guy tailing Caleb call? Does Rosewood have reanimated corpses or was the Gloved Wonder hanging out under a sheet in the morgue? How long had s/he been there? Did s/he overhear Spencer and Aria snooping?

2.09 PICTURE THIS

(AIRED AUGUST 9, 2011 | WRITTEN BY JONELL LENNON | DIRECTED BY PATRICK NORRIS)

Emily: "It's already so bad, how could it get worse?"

Photography is the art of capturing light and of balancing it with darkness, and in "Picture This," with its focus on photography and surveillance, the interplay of light and dark is especially important. And that's an even more interesting lens when focused on the men of *PLL*, who get more screen time than ever in this episode.

Though the show's strength is its fabulous foursome, the

guys are really starting to become more than crushes and/or men of mystery. The most interesting is Jason, he of the conveniently repressed memories, home fortress building, and washboard abs. Certainly there are lots of reasons to suspect Jason, and all of the girls except Aria have no problem picturing him wielding the skull-crushing hockey stick against his own sister. (In Aria's imagination, Jason is otherwise engaged . . .) When Emily and Spencer enter his shed-cum-darkroom and discover close-ups of Aria's oblivious face (which eerily echo the close-ups of Alison in *PLL*'s opening credits), things look bad. We also have Veronica Hastings' decisive judgment — "All you need to know is that the DiLaurentis family is not to be trusted. Jason included." —

egging on Spencer's own suspicions. But in Jason's moments with Aria he's docile and sensitive, and we can't forget that Toby once looked pretty suspicious too.

Mike Montgomery didn't get much attention until he smash-and-grabbed himself into some screen time, but now it seems like he's spent a bit too long beneath that dark hood, and his own battle is with what seems like the darkness of depression. He literally can't handle the light of his lamp and asks Byron to turn it off. Byron's take-no-prisoners attitude shifts into a more empathetic, gentle approach when Mike's behavior reminds him of his brother, Scott, mentioned for the first time. There's an implication that Scott descended so far into the darkness that he was swallowed by it.

Ezra's in the dark in a different way. With Aria's hot-and-cold (and occasionally crazy) behavior, he knows something's going on (and he suspects its name is Jason), and it's clear a little lace and vending snacks aren't going to fix it. This has been a relationship always lived in the dark, but within it they were open and honest. Now, as they try to move toward being more open, Aria finds herself less willing to risk full exposure.

Luckily in Caleb, we find some light. His story also involves a photo, one of his long-lost mother, and he looks at it, bitter and unsure whether he should intrude on such picture-perfect bliss. But Hanna wisely reminds him that "looks can be deceiving." When he's deciding what to do, our failed delivery boy is sitting on a swingset at the playground just like a kid, and what he needs from Hanna is a pep talk and someone to hold his hand. When he comes to say goodbye, he's lost his slick, laid-back confidence, and in his glazed eyes and quivering lips, we see a new Caleb.

Of course the one camera we can't account for is the one belonging to A, who turns some close surveillance at Emily's window into a deft poker night power play, reminding us s/he's always been in charge of what develops in Rosewood.

HIGHLIGHT The show's sexy dream sequence opener might have been all sizzle and no steak, but it was an easy way for the producers to avoid a hot-button issue while dialing up the heat. The mid-episode reprise, while just as fiery, is a lowlight, crossing the line into annoyingly gimmicky.

EXTRA CREDIT
- Hanna and Emily are wearing the same yellow nail polish — a nice touch for the new roomies.
- Caleb's mom lives in Montecito, a community just outside

Santa Barbara, California, which is one of the wealthiest areas in the U.S. And yes, talk show host, entrepreneur, philanthropist, and all-around powerhouse Oprah does have her primary residence there.

PLL IRL Fittingly, the iTunes bonus featurette that came out with this episode was on cinematography: the art of lighting and framing a TV show or movie. Caleb and Hanna's goodbye scene was one of Ashley Benson's favorites to shoot, even though she had to cry for the five hours it took to film it. Cody Christian, who brings Mike Montgomery to the small screen, has a resumé that includes modeling, commercials, and guest spots on *True Blood* and *Grey's Anatomy*.

SLIP UPS If Jason's so secretive, wouldn't he have a less obvious hiding spot for the shed key? When Spencer and Emily leave the Hastings house it's daylight, but as they approach Jason's shed it's darkest night. Looks like they walked next door really slowly. Can't Caleb read? He's right next to Hanna, looking at her laptop, and yet he's somehow incapable of reading the photo's caption himself.

BACK TO THE BOOKS In *Wicked*, Aria revives her girlhood crush on Jason, but their romantic prospects are quickly squashed. There's a strange tension between the Hastings and DiLaurentis families in *Heartless*, which Spencer's determined to get to the bottom of.

Qs & A Why do the Hastings parents think the DiLaurentis family isn't to be trusted? What does Jason know that Jenna and Garrett don't want him to share? How did the Gloved Wonder hide a camera in Jason's darkroom without Jason knowing? Or does Jason know . . . ?

2.10 TOUCHED BY AN "A"-NGEL

(AIRED AUGUST 16, 2011 | WRITTEN BY CHARLIE CRAIG
& MAYA GOLDSMITH | DIRECTED BY CHAD LOWE)

Spencer: "Sometimes you have to hurt someone to help them."

Another excellent episode, "Touched by an 'A'-ngel" hits the exact mix of incredibly unsettling and earnestly heartfelt that makes *Pretty Little Liars* appointment TV. The girls spin off in different directions rather than sticking together — Hanna off with her stepsister-to-be and Mona, Aria navigating her beaus, Spencer "The Terrier" Hastings digging up secrets and secret clubs, and Emily left alone . . . with A.

The college fair gives Ezra an excuse to return to his old stomping ground of Rosewood High, but Jackie Molina (ugh) is in tow. Though Fitz is blind to it, Aria can see that Jackie's

Rosewood's main street before set dressing.
The second storefront becomes Lucky Leon's.

MUSIC ON *PLL*

"It's haunting, it's romantic, it's gorgeous, it's dark, it's kind of scandalous." Sounds like a description of our favorite show, and that's how Chris Mollere, music supervisor on *Pretty Little Liars*, describes its musical tone.

Chris Mollere credits his parents for his love of music, counting his father's diverse collection of records as a major influence on him as he grew up in his military family, traveling the world. Chris went to University of Texas at Austin and got deeply involved in Austin's music scene. He went to live performances and worked with bands in the areas of production, promotion, and management. After college, he moved to L.A. and began working with Emmett Furla Films as a producer's assistant in 2005 and 2006, slogging work but an invaluable experience. Chris realized the job of a music supervisor would combine his interests in music and film, and soon he was working on independent films, supervising commercials, and assisting a TV composer because "you have to pay your dues." The first series he worked on as music supervisor was ABC Family's *Kyle XY*. He's also worked on projects like *Greek*, *10 Things I Hate About You*, *The Vampire Diaries*, *The Box*, *The Haunting of Molly Hartley*, and *Dead Like Me: Life After Death*.

Step one for any music supervisor on a TV series is figuring out the musical identity of the show, and with *Pretty Little Liars*, Chris and the producers wanted the songs to create another narrative layer, adding to the storytelling in the way music does on shows like *The O.C.* and *Grey's Anatomy*. Unlike with some series, it wasn't about choosing big-name artists but about finding the right musical fit. As Chris explained, "You don't have to be signed on a major record label to actually be good for the project." With the fast pace of episodic television production, Chris doesn't have a lot of time for mulling over song choices, which means it's crucial that his sensibility for the sound of the show aligns with the director's and the showrunners' visions. Permissions to use a song are cleared about a week before an episode goes into sound mixing, earlier for more complicated situations or for songs that are attached to major labels. With not a lot of time to get the paperwork done, Chris's strong relationships with artists, publishers, and label representatives are incredibly important. In order to get into music supervision, not only do you need a love of music but, Chris stresses, "the most important thing is to learn the [permission] clearance side. Most people think music supervisors just put music into scenes for TV and film. They don't think about the business and legal aspects. You can get into a lot of trouble if you don't know them." When he's not sorting out contracts, Chris is listening to music and going to shows and music festivals.

Chris never wants his song choice to "stick out" — "We try to make it feel organic so it's not as noticeable, so it's accentuating and not overtaking the score." — and the best feeling is when an artist sees a huge increase in downloads and sales after a track appears in an episode. "It's awesome. That's my goal, you know — I started as a music fan and musician first — so seeing that happen and to be able to help in the process is exactly what I love to see happen. It's the ideal situation." For *Pretty Little Liars*, a lot of the song selections come from singer/songwriters, and Nashville has been "very good for the show." One of Chris's favorite placements in the show so far is Brooke Waggoner's "Fresh Pair of Eyes" (from "The Jenna Thing," when Fitz and Aria make out in his car); for Chris, the song's "cinematic feel" pulled viewers in and added another layer to the epic moment. The show's most identifiable song — "Secret" by The Pierces — came to be the main title "by fans, actually, of the books, who for years have said that that is one of their favorite songs, this should be the main title. It just fit spot-on." That song was, of course, included on the *Pretty Little Liars* soundtrack album that was released in February 2011; the album included 12 tracks heard in the series, including an exclusive recording of "Your Love" covered by Fay Wolf.

Not all of the music heard on *Pretty Little Liars* is licensed; the musical cues are the work of Michael Suby, who has composed for films like *The Butterfly Effect*, and for TV series as diverse as *Keeping Up with the Kardashians*, *Robot Chicken*, *Kyle XY*, and *The Vampire Diaries*. Amazingly, it only takes Suby about a day to write the musical cues for one episode of *Pretty Little Liars*. Part of that creative speed comes thanks to a schedule where there is no room for second drafts (in contrast to film where a longer schedule allows for many changes). "I write the best when I'm under tremendous

pressure," said Suby. But he always has music cues in his head, so scoring for film and television just comes naturally. "When I watch a scene, I hear it," explained Suby, adding that he is "essentially copying" what's inside his head.

still into him, and the unofficial status of their relationship leaves them open to "outside threats" — like that kiss from Jason DiLaurentis. It takes Spencer directly confronting Ezra about the danger she thinks Jason poses to make him step up his game, and Fitz gives Aria what she wants: a pledge to make their relationship public. (Of course, that is what Aria wants *before* her mother tells her the idea of a relationship between Fitz and one of his students would leave her feeling disappointed and betrayed.) Spencer's digging also forces a few other crucial confrontations: Jenna shows up in her living room, telling her to let it go, and Garrett shows up on Jason's front door, a six pack of beer in hand. Jason's right about Rosewood: someone saying precisely what they mean is a rarity, so the fact that there are so many frank conversations in this episode is strangely foreboding.

But trust Hanna to keep things messy. On her mission to make nice with Kate, Hanna opts not to be direct (with an apology for her past bitchiness) but instead slips into old habits of trying to impress, aided and abetted by Mona in her triumphant return. When Hanna finally does let her real feelings out, she has an unintended audience in Kate, who proves to be a prototypical mean girl on the phone that night. Just what Hanna needs: another blonde bully in her life.

With the girls off on their various missions, an already isolated and anxious Emily feels abandoned. Without her swim team, a huge part of her identity and social life has been cut off, and she's left feeling like the weak link A says she is. Already exposed and vulnerable, what with the dirt A has on her, Emily's situation only gets worse: temporarily blind (facedown on the massage table), naked, and clueless, Em literally has A's hands all over her, a violation that's sure to keep her out of spas for the rest of her life. It's a bold move, even for A. Though the result is Emily is too scared to tell Dr. Sullivan the truth about A, it also brings the girls corralling back around Emily in support, reunited after their time apart.

The girls are at a place in their friendships where a misstep is no longer an unforgiveable betrayal. And Aria and Spencer's lovefest ("You're really tiny, and I love you!") is a prime example of how strong the girls are together. The foursome has a bond that A can no longer touch.

HIGHLIGHT Despite everything that A has done, somehow sneaking in and giving Emily a massage is the worst. Shudder.

EXTRA CREDIT
- *Touched by an Angel*, which ran from 1994 to 2003 on CBS, was a TV show about caseworkers/angels who helped mere mortals with their personal drama. With next to no "bad touches."
- Ashley calls out Hanna on getting up super early to watch William and Kate's wedding on April 29, 2011.
- Spence says she almost joined the Madrigals, a small choir that performs Renaissance music and sometimes involves costumes. C'mon Spence, it'll look good on a college application.
- Hanna doesn't know who Pollyanna is, a derisive term for a foolishly or naively optimistic person, but she and Mona both know a Rebecca Minkoff when they see one; Kate's sold-out handbag is by America's number-one accessories designer.
- Spencer's translation of *Nos animadverto totus* (as *we see all*) is not wrong, but could also be translated to *we perceive, or turn*

the mind to, the whole — which is way too philosophical and not disturbing enough for Rosewood.

BACK TO THE BOOKS The cop with a history tied to Jason and Ian is Officer Wilden, not Garrett who was added by the show writers. The faux friendship between Kate and Hanna plays a big part in Sara Shepard's series.

SLIP UPS Kate's friend Margaux speaks French almost as terribly as Mona does; let's assume her family's French heritage is a few generations back.

PLL IRL The horseback-riding-gone-wrong scene between Hanna and Mona is Janel Parrish's favorite. This is the first episode directed by Chad Lowe, a.k.a. Byron Montgomery. On the actor's stint on the other side of the camera, Shay Mitchell said, "He's obviously an actor first and foremost, so he's an actor's director. He's really, really great to work with; he gives you a lot of time, so it's been fun working with him." Asked for his theories on who A is, Ian Harding said, "I feel like if it is just one student, let's look at the kid who is failing out because he is obviously not doing homework! But he is obviously spending his time [as A]; Emily had a box full of cereal [with only As] and then had something inside it and it was hermetically sealed as well. You plan that months in advance! How did that happen? It's either a group of people or somebody is a mastermind or has a crazy split personality." Born January 25, 1988, Canadian Natalie Hall brought the drama of her two years as Colby on *All My Children* to the role of evil stepsister Kate. (A different actress played her in "To Kill a Mocking Girl.") Natalie has also appeared on the Broadway stage in *The Sound of Music* and done guest spots on *Law & Order: Special Victims Unit* and *The Good Wife.*

Qs & A Did the NAT club do more than act as peeping Tom filmmakers? Are they responsible for killing Alison? Are they

A? Jenna says to Garrett that Spencer and Toby were looking at yearbooks — how does she know that? Does she have her sight back or was she listening in somehow? Garrett asks Jason if they are "still cool" — about what? With the hoodie and gloves on the coatrack, and the first-person angle, it's clear that Dr. Sullivan is seeing A — is s/he a new patient or a regular?

2.11 I MUST CONFESS

(AIRED AUGUST 23, 2011 | WRITTEN BY OLIVER GOLDSTICK | DIRECTED BY NORMAN BUCKLEY)

Aria: "A's everywhere. Constantly on us. Like a shadow."

In the Roman Catholic tradition, confession is an essential ritual: a way to face your sins, repent, and be absolved. In this aptly titled episode, the thing that's more important than the actual confessions is what prompts them: facing something you'd rather not and accepting responsibility for your actions. The girls find the courage and wisdom to confess without being blackmailed by A (in fact, in spite of A), and we can see that our liars are really maturing.

Emily's the rock of this episode. After living in fear of A most of the season, Emily refuses to be a victim anymore and leads the girls to confide in Dr. Anne. Emily also recognizes when someone else needs to get something off their chest and offers a sympathetic ear to Ashley. With Maya's return, we have a good reference point to compare the Emilys of season 1 and season 2. She admits, "There were things — people — I was afraid of. . . . But I'm not afraid anymore," and her resolve is unwavering. Emily's taken the worst of A's bullying all season, but she listened to Dr. Anne's lecture. She's not going to live in fear anymore, and she's attempting to create a safe space of her own.

Though she accidentally gets drunk and barfs on a very expensive wedding dress, Hanna still gets some maturity points this episode. She attempts to make nice with Kate despite her evil stepsister-to-be's threats of revenge. She's actually more mature than her sassy grandmother, who urges Hanna to ditch all wedding festivities. Thus it's all the more tragic when Tom can't see past the ruined gown to his devastated daughter (a failing highlighted nicely by Grandma Regina, who instantly sees Hanna's side).

Meanwhile in the Montgomery household, Mike continues his downward spiral, and while his parents squabble over the best approach and Ella hides her injury, it's the children who face what their parents can't. Mike opens up to Aria, finally acknowledging that something's wrong, and Ella's cover-up reminds Aria that she can't protect Mike by hiding how bad things have gotten. Notably, Aria is the one to call the family meeting, and Mike follows her lead by coming down to literally face his family (rather than keeping them in his parental rearview mirror) and metaphorically face his problems.

After their willingness to open up and face things head-on, the liars don't really need their therapist anymore — and it's a good thing, because thanks to A, she may be gone for good.

HIGHLIGHT The cinematic confrontation between Toby, Spencer, and Mr. Hastings took tension to new heights for *PLL* in this surprisingly real and emotional moment.

EXTRA CREDIT
- Regina says Ashley looks like Condoleezza Rice, the secretary of state under George W. Bush. It's a compliment: Rice made history as the first female African American to hold that office.
- Maya makes a surveillance joke with the centerpiece — something Emily would find less funny if she knew that she'd recently been bugged during therapy.
- The surveillance bug was hidden on Dr. Anne's bobblehead of Sigmund Freud, the father of psychoanalysis.

SLIP UPS Ashley takes cups that were on a tea towel upside down (presumably drying) and then puts them in the dishwasher. Clean freak or blooper?

PLL IRL That confrontation between Toby and Spencer and Mr. Hastings may have been chilling, but it was one of Troian's favorite scenes to film, with director Norman Buckley telling all the actors to really dial up the aggression.

BACK TO THE BOOKS In *Flawless*, Kate double-crosses Hanna in a different way: she spots the painkiller Percocet in Hanna's purse and asks for one, but then later rats her out to Tom and Isabel.

Qs & A Will there be any consequences to Emily ignoring A's demand that she expose Aria and Fitz? What was Jenna talking about on the phone? Has someone crossed her? What does the DiLaurentis family have on the Hastings? In the patient file Dr. Anne believes is A's, 1994 is part of his/her birth date, making the suspect a contemporary of the PLLs. What happened to Dr. Anne?

2.12 OVER MY DEAD BODY

(AIRED AUGUST 30, 2011 | WRITTEN BY I. MARLENE KING | DIRECTED BY RON LAGOMARSINO)

Jenna: "She deserved to die like that."

For the midseason finale, *Pretty Little Liars* pulls out all the stops, as A gives the girls tasks and a time limit, or else the good doctor dies. Or so they think. Despite a police investigation that doesn't make much sense if you think about it even a tiny bit, the episode's nonlinear timeline keeps the tension high straight through to the end.

The idea that the four girls are dolls or possessions to be toyed with — in the past by Ali and now by A — has come up in past episodes, but A sending them the creeptastic dolls complete with commands couldn't be more clear. A believes s/he can force them to do whatever s/he wants, and in "Over My Dead Body" the girls are forced to do things they would never do, but which, in a clever turn, outsiders would believe the girls capable of. As Spencer realizes, A is being the ultimate frenemy by making the girls take what s/he thinks they want, but knowing that there will be huge consequences to their actions. Each girl's risk is extreme and they stand to lose a lot: Hanna's dad, Toby, Ezra, and Emily's life. From the outside, Aria, Hanna, and Spencer seem to behave like crazy, self-centered liars — Aria blackmails, Hanna sabotages her father's relationship (and his wedding), and Spencer outs herself as a liar — while Emily is given the suicidal card to play. But in the end, it seems like these tasks were just an opening act for the real show: giving them the murder weapon and having them arrested. It's clear that Jenna and Garrett played a key role in this plan, and Garrett seems to be on the police force for the sole reason of extracting and planting evidence in Ali's murder investigation. The way that Jenna and Garrett gloat over their plot against the girls makes them top suspects as A. But it remains a distinct possibility that they are only partially responsible, perhaps having piggybacked on A's scheme.

Jenna is chillingly unrepentant — about what she and Garrett have done to the girls and about Ali's violent death — but she's alone with that attitude. The *PLL* parents are particularly open to admitting faults in "Over My Dead Body": Ella apologizes to Aria for asking her to lie about Mike, telling her daughter that sometimes no matter how hard she tries to do right, she just gets it wrong. In a scene that only makes it harder for Hanna to later interrupt the wedding, Tom Marin admits his past mistakes and makes an earnest plea for future familial accord. He says to Hanna that he's trying to break his bad habit of sabotaging good things before someone else can. Both parents' words of wisdom may come back to haunt the girls, who madly commit acts of self-sabotage at A's behest. Except for Emily . . . A's bored with her.

What Emily gets is an exhaust-fueled, near-death dream of Alison. Just as Hanna seemed to have actual communication with Ali in her hospital dream sequence in "Moments Later," after we see Ali pull Emily from the barn, she tells Emily that she knows who A is but won't reveal her identity. While Emily does want to be completely free of A, she's not willing to die for it. But is the alternative jail? The girls are told that their situation doesn't just look bad, it *is* bad. As Jason says about Alison, A is an expert at keeping secrets and punishing people with the truth — and the girls are once again persons of interest in Alison DiLaurentis's murder.

HIGHLIGHT The girls in their dirt-covered dresses sitting in the interrogation room, Spencer staring at the two-way mirror like she could burn a hole in it. Perfection.

EXTRA CREDIT
- Maya knows all the words to "What a Friend We Have in Jesus," a Christian hymn about the solace found in sharing secrets and worries through prayer.
- Hanna mocks the people at the True North camp by comparing them to the squeaky clean image of the Osmonds, the family music group who had great success in the early 1970s.
- The paper Jackie "wrote" is on French painter Théodore Géricault (1791–1824), a pioneer of the Romantic movement who had a penchant for painting severed limbs.
- Spencer calls the dolls A gives them "Chucky," referring to the horror movie series where a super sinister doll goes on a murdering rampage (and later gets married).
- Alison tells Emily that she can't tell her who A is because two can only keep a secret if one of them is dead, which is the Ben Franklin quote that was used as the epigraph for Sara

Shepard's first book and which is in the lyrics of the show's theme song, "Secret" by The Pierces.

- In her light-blue dress, looking rather Dorothy Gale, Emily wakes up from a beautiful dream to find her three worried friends leaning over her, just like in *The Wizard of Oz*.

- The geographic coordinates A gives the girls is for a forested area near Perkasie, in Pennsylvania, not too far from Allentown (where Maya now lives) — now we know where Rosewood is ... if only it were real.

- The Tory Burch boots that are buried in the dirt are the pair that the Gloved Wonder ordered online in "Never Letting Go," which, from surveillance tapes, A knew Hanna would recognize, having heard her make a comment about them in the therapy session in "It's Alive."

BACK TO THE BOOKS The inspiration for the *PLL* dolls came from the book covers, where each character is depicted as a Barbie-style doll. Emily gets a threatening dolly from A in *Unbelievable*: it's floating facedown in a hot tub with "Tell and die" written across its face.

SLIP UPS Why did Tom and Isabel have their wedding in Rosewood if they live in Baltimore? Why is A suddenly using cut-out letters for the notes when s/he's used handwriting before? Why was Emily using her GPS to drive to the local church? Why would the police send a helicopter and multiple officers to respond to an anonymous tip that four local girls are in the woods with a shovel? Unless the police had already examined the shovel, they couldn't know whether it was used to hit Ali, or was just a garden-variety shovel. And from the cops' perspective, why would the girls be using that shovel — a murder weapon — to unearth a mannequin head and some boots? If possession of the shovel is all the evidence the cops have to arrest the girls, then how did Detective Wilden get reinstated as lead on the murder case before the girls were found with it — a discovery based on an anonymous tip? The Rosewood PD are a bumbling lot, but this detective work makes less sense than usual.

PLL IRL In the poster for season 2, the girls are dressed up and covered in dirt, and there's a shovel resting beneath the table; Marlene King was worried it would be a dead giveaway to the weapon used to attack Ali, but they got away with it. The girls loved filming the scene where they were frantically digging

YANI GELLMAN AS GARRET REYNOLDS

Born to globe-trotting parents on September 2, 1985, Yani Gellman has lived in Spain, Australia, and the United States, but was raised primarily in Toronto, Canada. He began his career as a teenager in the kids shows *Animorphs* and *Goosebumps*, and continued to land guest spots until he found steady work as a lead on Arthurian time-travel tale *Guinevere Jones*. He'll be most familiar to young people as European pop star Paolo in *The Lizzie McGuire Movie* (2003). He also nabbed a recurring role on Canadian action series *Monster Warriors* and did a three-episode stint on *Greek*.

Yani's most significant role to date is playing lawyer Rafe Torres on *The Young and the Restless*, the historic soap's first gay role. The actor had no hesitation about playing a gay character, and commented that "it's about time" the soap had a gay story line. Filming on *Pretty Little Liars* has a much slower pace, which the actor likes because "we get the opportunity to dig that much deeper into the characters." Asked how he likes his regular gig in Rosewood, the actor was enthusiastic: "We're all huge fans of the show so there's always this buzz of excitement on set. It's a blast. Everyone's epic."

up what they thought was Dr. Sullivan; said Ashley, "That [was] one of the best nights. It was probably three in the morning, and digging in the mud was awesome."

Qs & A How did Emily get out of the barn? Who does Garrett think shouldn't have shown up at the police station? Garrett hands Jenna the only copy of page five of Ali's autopsy report, detailing the trace evidence found on her body, and tells her to destroy it. Was he the "corpse" in the morgue in "Save the Date"? What are Garrett and Jenna covering up? Was he referring to the Rosewood PD's storage room or a storage locker like the one Ali's memory key was found in? Why did Jenna and Garrett leave Jason the "I know what you did" note after Ali disappeared? If Jenna and Garrett wrote the note to Jason, did they also write Ian's suicide note? What did Peter Hastings admit to Jason that his wife doesn't know about, and what did Jason find in the DiLaurentis house? How long had Dr. Sullivan been following A's commands? What was in the envelope she got from A? The waitress calls A "pretty eyes," the second reference to A's eyes and a maddening clue because everyone on this show has pretty eyes!

2.13 THE FIRST SECRET

(AIRED OCTOBER 29, 2011 | WRITTEN BY I. MARLENE KING | DIRECTED BY DANA W. GONZALES)

Alison: "It's Halloween, Hanna. Don't you love a good scare?"

Halloween is all about masks and masking, but "The First Secret" is also about unmasking. New secrets are uncovered, but so are our liars, revealed from beneath the post-Ali identities the girls have crafted for themselves.

We go back in time to see our girls not yet hardened by tragedy and relentless cyberbullying (just predictable bestie bullying from

Alison). One of the most notable differences is in Spencer, hiding behind her giant frames. She is more tentative, not yet class prez, not yet driven by fierce competition with Melissa. Certainly, she's not the Spencer who would stand up to Ali. With Hanna's father just having left, her mother getting drunk in public (rather than sipping wine in the privacy of her own kitchen), and her weight still filling up her cupcake pajamas, Hanna seems meeker than ever: closer to the blonde who gets killed off at the beginning of the slasher flick than the one who fights through to the end. It's nice to see flashes of Emily's confidence and assertiveness from season 2 as she lets the rumors fly about her and Ben and spurs the girls to go back into the house to save Ali.

But the most interesting unmasking of all is that of Alison, whose perspective we get for the first time. She's still flippantly cruel to the girls, but in private we see how unnerved she is by the costume shop message, her anxiety as she hides the voodoo doll, and later, as she almost confides in Spencer, how thrown she is by Jenna's rejection of her help as Queen Bee Maker. Alison's always been all about control, and she is denied it here. No doubt it's this rejection and subsequent feelings of powerlessness that inspire The Jenna Thing, because playing with Ali is like playing with fire . . . she'll burn you right back.

"The First Secret" took terrifying to a whole new level, but as with any good ghost story or scary movie, it's not the things revealed that are scary, it's the suggestion of what else might still be lurking in the darkness.

HIGHLIGHT Though the haunted house had our hearts racing, nothing was a bigger game changer than Alison getting a text from A.

EXTRA CREDIT
- Two black–nail polished thumbs up to the Halloween'd credits. Stylish and spooky, just like show.
- The car in front of Rosewood's very own house of horrors (no,

not the Cavanaugh house) is from the Radley Sanitarium, the surname a reference to the creepiest house on the block in *To Kill a Mockingbird.*

- Melissa and Ian are dressing up as Bonnie and Clyde, a famous bankrobbing couple in the early 1930s who left numerous civilians and police officers dead in their wake and who were made more infamous by Faye Dunaway and Warren Beatty's portrayal of them in the 1967 Oscar–winning film *Bonnie and Clyde.*

- Lounging in Byron's office, Meredith is reading a book about or by James Joyce, the same Irish writer Ezra professes to love in "Surface Tension."

- Ali warns Emily that she wouldn't want to live like Juno, the pregnant teen title character of the Academy Award–winning 2007 film starring Ellen Page.

- Alison and Jenna are both dressing up as singer, songwriter, and envelope pusher Lady Gaga. It's a good costume for two confident trendsetters. Jenna's look is borrowed from Lady G's appearance on *MTV TRL* on August 12, 2008. Alison's studded jacket is actually closest to Gaga's look in her video for "Telephone," which wasn't released until 2010. Jenna did outdo her, but that's what Alison gets for wearing pants.

- Hanna dressed as Britney Spears from her ". . . Baby One More Time" video. Ali suggested she go as "Bald Britney," referring to the singer's heavily publicized head shave in 2007. It's a nice choice for Hanna, who still has the innocent eagerness of Brit Brit's early days.

- Spencer dresses as Mary, Queen of Scots, the 16th century ruler of Scotland, who knew something about family rivalry as she was considered by many Catholics to be the rightful ruler of England over Elizabeth I, who had her cousin beheaded.

- Giant Drag, an L.A.-based alternative rock band, is on stage at Noel's party playing "Firestorm."

- Ali asks Emily if she wants to taste Jenna's cherry Chapstick, referring to Katy Perry's June 2008 breakthrough single "I Kissed a Girl."

- The haunted house is at 313 Mockingbird, another reference to *To Kill a Mockingbird*, but also to Addams family-esque 1960s sitcom *The Munsters*, about a family of monsters who lived at 1313 Mockingbird Lane.
- This is an episode that really belongs to the dolls: we have the dolls the twins were fighting over in Ali's scary story (four dolls, four liars), the voodoo doll sent to Ali, the doll Ali keeps in her wooden box (which she uses as a creepy safe), and of course, that evil babydoll costume. Dolls are always a nice nod to the books, but the way the girls battle over the dolls in the beginning is also an illustration of how Ali controls them, and a nod to the dolls in "Over My Dead Body."

SLIPS UPS In "Save the Date," Hanna says that Garrett and Jenna grew up across the street from each other, but Jenna moves to town in this flashback, not even one year before Ali goes missing. Was Ali so drunk she couldn't recognize Mona in that Catwoman costume? If we could, she could.

BACK TO THE BOOKS In Sara Shepard's world, Spencer doesn't win her presidential bid. The Radley Sanitarium is featured heavily in *Killer*.

PLL IRL The show's broadcast schedule never coincides with Halloween, but Marlene King revealed why they decided to make an exception: "The producers and the network all agreed that it would be so organic to *Pretty Little Liars* to do a spooky Halloween episode. We decided to; it's sort of our thank-you to the fans. It's candy, the whole episode." Marlene's son Atticus is the boy Hanna's babysitting at the beginning of the episode. His mother says he had fun but was "most impressed with the size of the chocolate donut craft services gave him." Sasha Pieterse hinted that there are secrets in plain sight in the set design of Ali's room. *PLL* fans who have read to the eighth book may be able to pick them out, but for anyone else, they could be major spoilers! On set they called the creepy baby in burlap costumes, "zombie babydoll stalker" (an appropriate name in a season where someone has seemingly come back from the dead). The costume, like the others, was the brainchild of Mandi Line. The Halloween episode was the directorial debut of Dana Gonzales, the show's cinematographer. Though Shay generally loves action-packed scenes, her favorite part of the Halloween episode was the costumes: "Anytime we get to dress up, it's so much fun!"

Qs & A What was a vehicle from the sanitarium doing at the haunted house? Alison says she has a doctor who can get Emily birth control without involving her mom: who is the doctor? Also, is Ali having sex or planning to? With whom? In "Touched by an 'A'-ngel," Jason says he found the box in the floorboards, but Ali hides it in the air vent in this episode. When and why did Ali move it? Did she hide something else inside the doll that Aria has yet to find? Ali got an A message before they blinded Jenna, which takes away Jenna's primary known motive to retaliate against Ali, but Jenna's arrival is timed with the start of the bullying. Hmm. Was it A fighting Ali inside the haunted house? Does Lucas really have it in him to be a killer (or a haunted house tormenter)? Did we witness the beginning of an alliance between Jenna and Mona? What was Wilden talking to Jenna about? The threatening texts and messages to Ali aren't signed "A" until the last one: are they all from the same person? After Ali gets her A text, Ian and Melissa are seen in the bottom left of the overhead shot just before the Gloved Wonder closes his/her cell phone, ruling them out for this particular A-crime. Lucas and Noel are seen in the babydoll costume, making them suspects, and Jenna and Mona are suspiciously missing from that last group shot.

2.14 THROUGH MANY DANGERS, TOILS AND SNARES

(AIRED JANUARY 2, 2012 | WRITTEN BY JOSEPH DOUGHERTY | DIRECTED BY NORMAN BUCKLEY)

Emily: "The weakest link wants payback."

Always premiering with a bang — or a girl-on-girl garbage fight — *Pretty Little Liars* returned from its season 2 winter hiatus with an episode in which tension runs high and the tables are turned on A. Picking up a month after the girls were arrested for possession of a shovel, "Through Many Dangers, Toils and Snares" explores what happens when the girls try to wrench back control of their lives from A by using A's very strategy of dealing in secrets.

Like a round of two truths and a lie, the girls play on how they are perceived — liars, schemers, with Emily as the weak link and Spencer as the resented taskmaster — in order to trick A into thinking their disagreement is real, and that Emily would really go behind the others' backs to make a deal. But to fool the anonymous A, they have to trick everyone around them — and, for a time, they fool the audience too. This power move is not without a price, and Spencer seems to get the worst of it, with her estranged BF Toby accusing her of acting just like Alison.

But A has driven the girls to desperation, and they believe the ends will justify the means. The It Girls of Rosewood have been reduced to garbage-picking town pariahs, with boyfriends lost, parents betrayed, and their futures at risk — particularly Emily whose place on the swim team looks tenuous. The game they play with A is dangerous, and it ultimately backfires on both sides. A realizes s/he's been tricked, gets hit by Hanna's car (payback!), and loses a cell phone in the process. But in "Through Many Dangers, Toils and Snares," the girls are left without the answer they were looking for: who is A? Will A's phone be the key to finally discovering the truth?

With the notable exception of A, Byron's comment to Fitz rings true: nobody starts out to hurt people. Once Fitz learns why Aria ditched him after "Over My Dead Body" — that dastardly Jackie Molina and her blackmailing ways — he decides it's time for honesty, that their secret relationship should finally be made public. This much-anticipated moment has been a long time coming, and the scene does not disappoint. In the tensest, most awkward scene yet on *Pretty Little Liars*, Aria and Ezra are faced with the truth: they have been dreaming in Technicolor to expect her parents to react in any way other than total shock and horror. Aria only realizes how "dangerous" her relationship with Fitz is after seeing her parents' stunned disappointment and quiet fury (and Mike steps in with the punch to prevent Byron from swinging at Fitz).

The girls are desperate for payback and for freedom from the secrets and lies, but, as they realize, gaining control of their lives won't come without hardship. As Spence says, they will just have to slay one dragon at a time.

HIGHLIGHT Emily being a total badass, meeting alone with A in that derelict greenhouse.

EXTRA CREDIT
- This episode's title comes from the third stanza of "Amazing Grace": "Through many dangers, toils, and snares / I have already come. / T'was Grace that brought me safe thus far / and Grace will lead me home."
- In "The Jenna Thing," Hanna told Wilden she was willing to "pick up trash on the highway" if he'd leave her mother alone. He took her up on the offer! Luckily for Han, the "demented Creamsicle" ensemble works; as she told Sean in "Reality Bites Me," "Hideous looks good on me."
- The notes on Mrs. Montgomery's blackboard about isolation in *The Heart Is a Lonely Hunter* play into the faux fight among the PLLs: Emily separates herself from the other girls in

order to seem like easy prey for A.

- Spencer's extra credit paper for Mrs. Montgomery is on 20th-century writer Kurt Vonnegut, while Byron and Fitz — before their budding bromance is over — bond over 19th-century writer Henry James.
- When Ella and Byron are discussing the Ezria situation, on the wall behind Byron are photos of Aria as a child — a subtle reminder that he still thinks of his mature teenager as his little girl. These photos, as well as those of young Aria in her bedroom, are Lucy Hale's actual childhood snapshots used as set decoration.

SLIP UPS The girls started studying *The Heart Is a Lonely Hunter* way back in "The Devil You Know," and after the "one month later" jump, they're *still* studying it. Mrs. Montgomery needs to pick up the pace! How much older than Jenna is Garrett? It seems odd that their relationship garners no raised eyebrows when the age difference is about the same as that between Aria and Ezra.

BACK TO THE BOOKS In *Wicked*, Hanna not only has to deal with Kate and Isobel moving to Rosewood, but she has to live with them.

PLL IRL This episode, the winter premiere of season 2 (or "2B," as it's referred to) was the highest rated since "It's Alive." Marlene teased the second half of the season by telling TheInsider.com, "2B is a freight train driving full steam ahead with no breaks and this neverending series of 'oh my god' moments." Shay Mitchell took advantage of Emily's encounter with A in the greenhouse to live out her action-movie dreams. As she told AfterEllen.com, "We had stunt people on set doing the choreography, and I was like, 'Um, I'd really rather just do it myself.' They're always like, 'Shay, please don't jump over that table.' And I'm like, 'Yeah, no worries, I won't.' And then when the cameras start, I run full throttle and throw myself at it. My knees were so bruised up after that, but it was totally worth it." It's her favorite A moment, and the actress found it scary even though she knew the greenhouse was just a set and she was surrounded by the crew.

Qs & A Emily indicates her answer to A by circling "yes" on the blackboard: does that mean A is in her English class, or just spying on her there? Has A actually slipped up — is that why s/he was so keen on making a deal with Emily? What does A think is in the box? What secrets lurk on A's phone?!

2.15 A HOT PIECE OF "A"

(AIRED JANUARY 9, 2012 | WRITTEN BY OLIVER GOLDSTICK | DIRECTED BY MICHAEL GROSSMAN)

Ella: "Before we pick up our torches and pitchforks,
let's take a moment and figure it out."

After the harrowing near-A experience of the last episode, our girls emerge from the greenhouse of horrors largely unscathed and with a powerful new piece of evidence: A's phone. But what seems like it could be the key to A's identity turns out to be complicated and corrupted just like the mysterious bully. In any case it doesn't take heavy phone security or a shadowy hood to stop us from seeing someone clearly, and in "A Hot Piece of 'A,'" people struggle to see others as they are, rather than the way they want them to be.

Nowhere is that difficulty more evident than in Ella and Byron, who can't help but see their daughter in a new, unflattering light, a transition nicely illustrated by Byron's sudden objection to Aria's sexy school wear. During his man-to-man chat with Ezra, with one look at the rumpled bed, we see Byron drop his attempt at empathy (and given his past this shouldn't be a stretch) and jump straight to villainizing Ezra as child-seducer

and threatening to call the police. Making Ezra the baddie allows Byron to mentally preserve some of Aria's innocence, but Ella steps in to remind him that things aren't so black and white. She sees the potential fallout for her daughter and recognizes that the pre- and post-Fitz Aria are the same, noting, "We raised her to be independent and open-minded, and we don't get to be shocked that that is now who she is." No one's really seeing clearly in the Montgomery household though: Aria's addled enough to think that her mom's coming around and she doesn't get the message when Ezra tells her not to call.

Hanna is also willfully blind. Just like when Lucas made his crush for her clear, she won't see him as anything other than a harmless and dependable pal. Although Lucas had moved on to yearbook girl Danielle in "Blind Dates," his awkwardness when he sees Hanna with Caleb, his distraction, and his sweaty stammering suggests he might have rekindled his flame, but Han is too absorbed by party planning to notice. After their helpline intel, Spencer and Emily see it differently and insist Lucas is up to no good, but Hanna won't even consider it. Unfortunately it takes a confessional cruise on the lake and an unplanned swim to wash away the image of Lucas she's painted for herself, and perhaps the real Lucas too.

Toby's calm (and satisfyingly smug) conversation with Garrett about Jenna reveals that Garrett's vision is clouded by love. With Jenna headed to Boston with hopes of restoring her sight, it's the guy left behind who needs a fresh pair of eyes to see her as she is — not as a victim but as a victimizer.

"A Hot Piece of 'A'" is an episode of surprises, and not just for the birthday boy. Even though Lucas looks a little guilty at the end of this one, the other story lines remind us it's not time to grab the pitchforks just yet.

HIGHLIGHT Spencer's reaction to Em spilling about Hanna and Caleb's party for two; she'll never see her Nana's couch the same way either.

EXTRA CREDIT
- Hanna tells Spencer they're not her winged monkeys, another reference to *The Wizard of Oz*. Continuing with the theme, during class Hanna draws pictures of Spencer as the winged monkey–owning Wicked Witch of the West.
- Nana's couch saw its Haleb action when Hanna took him there to escape his mysterious stalker in "Save the Date."
- In English, the class is finishing their unit on *The Heart Is a Lonely Hunter*. The notes on the board say, "The Human Condition. Violence: Individuals frustrated with the world in which they live." Just another day under A.

SLIP UPS If Byron had called the police, what would he present as evidence and what would the charge be? Aria and Ezra have been careful to keep their relationship on the right side of legal, and both could deny everything. Why doesn't Hanna answer Emily and Spencer after she knocks Lucas out of the boat? She should be able to hear them calling: she's getting closer to shore, not farther from it.

PLL IRL Tyler Blackburn picked the scene with Hanna and Lucas in the rowboat as a fave. Part of the reason? Spencer's lakehouse (and the lake itself) were created on the Warner Brothers back lot! Of the episode Marlene noted, "I'm waiting for Poor Lucas to be a trending topic on Twitter," and she praises Brendan Robinson saying, "He's brought a lot to that character." Troian loves when the girls seize the opportunity to turn the tables on A: "Those moments where we're setting the web for A, those are the moments I like."

Qs & A Someone else is involved in Garrett and Jenna's alliance — and he's not doing what he's told. Also, Jenna left town and Garrett is frantic; does that mean their relationship is weakening? The dolls were in the attic of Spencer's lakehouse at some point, and, presumably, so was A (or one of A's minions). Were the soaked Mona and Noel up to something more scandalous than skinny-dipping? Why was the Gloved Wonder fishing Lucas's shoe out of the lake, and was s/he at the party, or did s/he just follow the group there?

2.16 LET THE WATER HOLD ME DOWN

(AIRED JANUARY 16, 2012 | WRITTEN BY BRYAN M. HOLDMAN | DIRECTED BY CHRIS GRISMER)

Hanna: "Emily, just because we want to throw up every time our phone rings doesn't mean everyone else is living in fear."

In the context of a show like *Pretty Little Liars*, so full of twists and high-stakes turns, the reveal of Lucas's big bad secret — he's addicted to online gambling! — fell flat, but thankfully, before that bean was spilled, "Let the Water Hold Me Down" provided lots of heartfelt moments and new connections.

The PLLs have long been drowning in secrets, which is par for the course in Rosewood. In this town, so many lies are told and secrets kept out of fear: Lucas acts irrationally and runs away from home because he's scared that Caleb and Hanna will be disappointed in him; Maya worries about Emily's reaction to the identity of her mystery caller, a boy she hooked up with at True North; and Hanna is terrified of what could happen to those she cares about if the truth surfaced.

Singled out by A with the lakewater incident and the bathroom prank, Hanna spends most of "Let the Water Hold Me Down" dodging people's questions and trying not to cry. Hanna and Lucas's friendship has navigated tricky waters before, but Hanna has always supported Lucas — she got Mona to stop being so cruel to him back in "The Perfect Storm," and she has kept the secret of his destroying Ali's memorial since "Moments Later." She knows she should have trusted her gut about him and not whacked him with the oar, throwing him into the lake, and that makes her judgment of him at the end of the episode feel forced and uncharacteristic. As Emily told Lucas at the lakehouse, Hanna is a forgiving friend — so why does she turn away from Lucas when he's clearly repentant and trying to make things right?

SHANE COFFEY AS HOLDEN STRAUSS

Holden Strauss is brought to life by Shane Coffey (sometimes credited with the last name Zwiner or Zwiener). While he's new to the show, he's no stranger to one of the PLLs: he and Troian Bellisario studied theater together at USC, graduating in 2009. Along with Troian, he's a founding member of the Casitas Group, a theater and film collective. Troian acted in a short film that he made, *Before the Cabin Burned Down*, and he's a part of her short film project *Exiles*. "We were in the same BFA acting program," Shane said. "I met her when I was 18, and the rest is history. . . . Troian and I actually have a two-piece band together called Family. It's underground. There are only video recordings of it, and some Garage Band audio files." Always busy with his own artistic endeavors, Shane has also appeared in some TV projects: pre-USC, he appeared in 2004's *Summerland* and post, in 2010's *The Whole Truth*. But the *PLL* audience knows him best as Jimmy Nash in *The Secret Life of the American Teenager*. Showrunner Marlene King is excited about Holden, the character she calls the first male pretty little liar: "He comes in with a big lie that's really fun." But Shane is starting to understand the seriousness with which some fans take their *PLL* relationships: "I, uh, read the comments [on a YouTube video featuring Holden and Aria]. I wish I hadn't, but I read the comments and it was like, 'Who is he? Who is he? Is he taking Ezra away?! What is this?!'"

Fortunately, the rest of her plotline is *PLL* epitomized. She feels trapped as the girlfriend who knows too much: if she told Caleb what he wants to know, she'd betray others' confidences and put a bull's-eye on his back for A to take aim at. Still, Caleb knows she's hiding things. Her friendship with Mona is also derailed by secrets: she can't tell Mona why she's so distracted, and Mona's rightly hurt because her BFF doesn't give an eff about her fizzling romance with Noel Kahn. After retail therapy fails to solve Mona's emotional problems, she has a serendipitous encounter with Spencer, who wisely advises her not to let a boy determine her self-worth.

Just as Mona's desperate attempt to hold on to Noel Kahn failed, Aria's hail-Mary pass for Ezra doesn't play out as she imagined it would. The stars seem aligned for Aria's bold, romantic move — a classic rainy, slo-mo Ezria moment — but instead of seizing the moment, Fitz feigns sickness and sneaks away. Will Aria give up too, or will Holden provide just the opportunity she and Fitz need?

HIGHLIGHT Though it's not fun to see Han so distraught, Ashley Benson put in a wonderful performance in this Hanna-centric episode.

EXTRA CREDIT
- The title for this episode comes from the Talking Heads' 1981 song "Once in a Lifetime." From the album *Remain in Light*, the lyrics reflect on the passage of time, the failure to live up to expectations, the feeling of being trapped, and on inevitability as the narrator questions how things got to be as they are. In the video, lead singer David Byrne dances like a marionette without strings.
- In A's text to Hanna, accompanying the creepy boat-in-the-sink prank, s/he quotes the last line of "Row, Row, Row Your Boat": "Life is but a dream."
- Aria takes Holden to see Arthur Miller's 1955–56 play *A*

View From the Bridge, which tells the story of Eddie who becomes obsessed with his niece, Catherine, and he goes to extremes to prevent her marriage to Rodolpho.

- Ezra's substitute date for the play is Mrs. Welch, who always seems to show up with Fitz. She popped into Fitz's classroom when Aria and Fitz were talking in "To Kill a Mocking Girl," she took over for Aria at the beanbag toss in "There's No Place Like Homecoming," and in "The New Normal," she was with Fitz and Ella in the cafeteria when they all planned to go to a reading.
- Emily and Maya go to a bar in Camden, New Jersey, which is right across the Delaware River from Philadelphia.
- Maya's hook-up with a guy at True North isn't her first hetero experience; in the pilot, Maya had a picture of a boy, Justin, on her dresser, who Emily inferred was her boyfriend left behind in California.
- Just as the girls' collective paranoia led Emily to go against her instincts about Toby in "There's No Place Like Homecoming," the girls make Hanna doubt her own instincts about Lucas, which turned out to be correct, just like Em's.
- In "Through Many Dangers, Toils and Snares," Lucas hid the website he was looking at as Hanna approached; it was a sports gambling site. He also mentions to Hanna in "A Hot Piece of 'A'" that he is totally broke.
- Aria contemplated using a fake boyfriend to cover up her relationship with Fitz in "Someone to Watch Over Me," but Emily discouraged her from leading someone on. Here Aria doesn't hesitate to go out with Holden despite her lack of romantic interest — and it works out. He seems to need his own cover story . . .

SLIP UPS In "The Homecoming Hangover," Lucas helps Hanna sell her handbags online, just like he does with his action figures. Why didn't Lucas start selling his comics online as soon as Caleb returned to earn back the money, instead of freaking out and running away? Why doesn't Caleb have his own bank account?

BACK TO THE BOOKS In *Unbelievable*, Mona and Spencer connect somewhat unexpectedly, after years of only knowing each other through Hanna.

PLL IRL The writers named the Kristen August School for the Blind after Sara Shepard's son because they "enjoy paying homage to Sara as much as possible." Sam, the student at the school, is played by Alexander Nifong, a Tisch graduate who's had guest roles on *Glee* and *Law & Order: SVU*.

Qs & A Has A been using the Hastings' lakehouse as an evil lair? Where were Jenna and Garrett the night Ali died? Was it a coincidence that Mona was on the same train as Spencer or was she following her? Does A have a special connection to that Chinese takeout place? S/he messed with the girls' fortune cookies in "There's No Place Like Homecoming" and here replaces the PLLs' food with live worms and dirt.

2.17 THE BLONDE LEADING THE BLIND

(AIRED JANUARY 23, 2012 | WRITTEN BY CHARLIE CRAIG | DIRECTED BY ARLENE SANFORD)

Aria: "You're protecting someone that you love. It's kind of romantic."
Hanna: "It's safe. It's what we all need to be."

Despite all the broken hearts and broken bones in this episode, everyone is trying to protect the people they love — whether through police-state parenting, breaking things off, or keeping someone in the dark. "The Blonde Leading the Blind" explores the ways in which we try to protect the people we love, but when it comes to fate (or the machinations of a faceless, omniscient bully), is making choices for someone else just a case of the blind leading the blind?

With Caleb now a satellite member of the Scooby Gang, the girls must decide how much to tell him. After the girls watch Ian's secret camera footage, Hanna is more convinced than ever that Caleb needs to be kept in the dark, declaring him to be out of the phone hacking biz — something she tries to guarantee with a USB key smoothie later in the episode. She wants to keep Caleb out of A's web, even if that means spinning a few lies of her own, and in her heart-to-heart with Ashley, her mother confirms that sometimes a lie can be the most humane option. Of course Hanna doesn't know that Caleb is thinking along the same lines. He insists he'll keep working on the video, hoping to unmask the Big Bad and save his damsel in distress. But protecting people by lying to them hasn't worked out too well for the liars thus far, and despite noble intentions, Hanna and Caleb could be playing right into A's hands.

After Toby's tumble and some harsh-but-true words from Jenna, Spencer realizes that keeping her distance was the right thing to do. But she can't risk another impulsive truck makeout, so she has to employ a few lies of her own (or at least deploy Emily on her behalf). She not only breaks up with him but, by implying she'd cheated on him with Wren, discourages Toby from continuing to pursue her.

Fitz is no stranger to this kind of sacrifice, as he's been ignoring Aria since his unfortunate confrontation with Byron in "A Hot Piece of 'A.'" Aria won't let herself be cut out though, and with a nudge from his hopelessly romantic student, Ezra realizes that what he thinks is best may not be. After their rain-soaked reunion, he is sure to note, "I want you to be safe, to be happy," but it turns out that being together, and not apart, is what can give that to Aria. It's a stark contrast from Spencer's choice; for Ezria, romance triumphs over realism. Perhaps love itself is the mighty force that has come to their aid.

And perhaps our hopeful couple has it right. For even though the photos of the lovers are cut apart and set aflame by their anonymous enemy, we're reminded that staying united could be the best way to burn A right back.

HIGHLIGHT Between the romantic downpour and the haunting refrain of the Rescues' "My Heart With You," Aria and Ezra's (literally) traffic stopping kiss proved nobody does an epic smooch like Ezria.

EXTRA CREDIT
- Aria puts her money on "Officer Garrett in the greenhouse with the cell phone," a reference to the classic board game Clue, which was already playfully referenced in the concluding scene of "Je Suis une Amie."
- When they discover the note in the doll's head, the girls are clued in to what we learned in "The First Secret": A harassed Ali first.

Rosewood in transition: Lucky Leon's is part hair salon for another shoot on the WB back lot. The door to Dr. Anne's office is the visible on the right.

- "Be bold and mighty forces will come to your aid" is a quote attributed to Basil King, a Canadian-born clergyman and writer.

SLIP UPS In Hanna's kitchen confrontation with Caleb, watch the bowl of strawberries: depending on the camera angle it alternates from being partially covered in plastic wrap to being uncovered.

BACK TO THE BOOKS Rive Gauche is a frequent hangout for Hanna and Mona in Sara Shepard's Rosewood, though the restaurant is located at the King James Mall, rather than downtown. (There seem to be more in-town dining options in the book-based Rosewood.) In the flashback, Ali says, "Back alleys and backyards have always been the best way to my house" and in the second cycle of *PLL* books (*Wicked* to *Wanted*) the crucial flashback that opens each of the books has our liars hiding in Ali's backyard.

PLL IRL Marlene tweeted that this episode had "romance up the wazoo" and noted that what happened is "better than sex." Hopefully Ezra and Aria see it that way too! Philadelphia is a lot closer to Rosewood than you'd think: the Philly street scenes are shot on the WB back lot also. The urban street set has been used to re-create many cities, including New York City for shows like *Friends*.

Qs & A The NAT club was in Ali's room the night she was murdered. Jason's story about being passed out and not remembering the night of Ali's murder is confirmed by Garrett. What's on the videos that the NAT club wants back from Alison, or were they looking for the key Ali gave Emily the day she was killed? What did Garrett find in Ali's wooden box? Why did Garrett try to leave the club? In what way did Ian go too far — by secretly filming them?

2.18 A KISS BEFORE LYING

(AIRED JANUARY 30, 2012 | WRITTEN BY MAYA GOLDSMITH | DIRECTED BY WENDEY STANZLER)

Aria: "There are just certain situations where you have to lie to your friends, even if you hate doing it."

The split among the girls that they play-acted in "Through Many Dangers, Toils and Snares" has come true with Hanna. Her friends hide from her the fact that Caleb is still working on decoding A's phone, leaving Hanna on the outs. Though the opening scene was hilarious — Spencer standing close enough to Caleb for him to guess correctly what she had for lunch, and the consecutive ignored calls from Han — it also perfectly set up the tension for the rest of "A Kiss Before Lying."

Spencer isn't Hanna's best friend among the four girls — she's the "low man on the totem pole" — but she is still fiercely loyal, protective, and loving of her. She agonizes over their decision to lie to Hanna, feeling like the ringleader, and goes out of her way to protect Hanna from "ugly on the inside" Kate. In her apology to Hanna, Spencer distinguishes between an act of betrayal and one of desperation but, as Hanna points out, there's no real distinction. Spencer is heartbroken over pushing away Toby with a lie — a desperate act that is also a betrayal of the trust between them — and fears being further isolated and alone without Hanna.

It wasn't so long ago that Hanna was the desperate one who betrayed a friend — giving Ella the art show ticket at A's bidding. She understands others' missteps because she makes her own, and she proves that here, with both Spencer and Caleb, also showing how forgiving she can be. Instead of pushing Caleb away for breaking her trust again, she opens up to him even more — to help him understand *why* it was so important to her that he leave A's phone alone. In more ways than just being nice to Kate on her first days of school, Hanna takes the high road in this episode. But no matter how hard she tries to be good, a snake always lies in her path — which is why the mass text sent from Hanna's phone packs such a punch at the end.

Hanna's reconciliations with Caleb and with Spencer aren't the only ones in "A Kiss Before Lying": Emily and Maya's relationship hits another bump when dinner with Mrs. Fields is almost as awkward as the family meal in "Moments Later." This time it's Maya who's "torpedoing" dinner, antagonizing Pam, while Emily watches in disbelief. But both girls want to move past that über-awkwardness, and their apologies the next morning — where both admit their insecurities and unresolved feelings about the past — lead to one of the most romantic and intimate scenes of the series.

While those two connect, Aria and Ezra's relationship has devolved to illicit car hook-ups and missed dates, but Aria's dad has a surefire plan to get Mr. Fitz out of his daughter's life — a promotion that would take him a thousand miles away to Hollis's satellite school in New Orleans. In a nice contrast to the clandestine Ezria scenes, Aria has an easy, carefree accidental date with Holden: sipping soda, playing air hockey, and laughing with a boy she's known her whole life and who remembers just how she likes her pizza. But even her uncomplicated time with Holden takes a turn: Aria spots his nasty bruise and is reminded that secrets and lies are part of Holden's life too.

Though she is long dead, the queen of the liars continues to string along the girls as more pieces of the Alison DiLaurentis puzzle are revealed. After all this time, the foursome is still retracing Ali's final steps — was she hiding under that dark wig, or using the disguise to track down her cyberbully? It's chilling to think of Ali going through A's torment all alone — despite her tough exterior, she was a 15-year-old, targeted and terrorized and ultimately killed. And that's one advantage A lacks against the girls, who know that their greatest strength lies in their bonds with each other.

HIGHLIGHT Emily and Maya's "I love you" exchange in the beautifully romantic underwater world Maya created for Emily in her bedroom.

EXTRA CREDIT

- This episode's title is a play on *A Kiss Before Dying*, a 1953 novel by Ira Levin which has twice been adapted for the silver screen (once in 1956 and again in 1991). The story follows a seemingly charming, normal man who hides his dark, murderous nature as he seduces, lies, and kills in the hopes of gaining the riches he grew up without.
- Pam Fields had a poster of late great jazz musician Miles Davis in her room at college; the trumpeter, bandleader, and composer influenced 20th-century music well outside his genre, and his album *Kind of Blue* is the bestselling jazz record in history.
- Hanna compares Kate to a fangblenny, a fish that mimics the behavior and appearance of wrasse, a "cleaner" fish that helpfully removes parasites and unwanted matter from other reef dwellers; the fangblenny's "aggressive mimicry" allows it to viciously attack unsuspecting, trusting victims, and it drops its disguise as soon as the coast is clear.
- Ali's dark-haired alter ego is Vivian Darkbloom, which as Spencer learns, is an anagram of Vladimir Nabokov, author of *Lolita* — the book that Hanna stole from Ali after seeing her with it all the time in the weeks before she disappeared. Vivian Darkbloom is also a minor character in Nabokov's 1955 novel about middle-aged Humbert Humbert and his sexual obsession with 12-year-old "Lolita" Dolores Haze.

SLIP UPS Ezra must be an expert driver: he makes out with Aria without crashing the car. Eyes on the road, Fitz! The song playing at the salon where Hanna bumps into "Vivian" is "Get Some" by Lykke Li, which came out in October 2010 — a full year after Ali went missing.

BIANCA LAWSON AS MAYA ST. GERMAIN

Strange as it may seem, Bianca Lawson has been playing teen-agers for longer than most teens have been alive! Filming the pilot of *PLL* she was 30 going on 16 yet again. Asked how she stays looking so young, the actress brushes it off, saying, "I think it's genetics. I'm not a super-healthy person! I am kind of lazy, I eat tons of junk food . . . I feel really blessed that I get to play all these great characters even though they might be a lot younger . . . But as I get older I feel like I'm regressing a bit, like Maya is a lot more mature than I am."

Born March 20, 1979, in Los Angeles, California, the actress of African American, Italian, Blackfoot, Portuguese, and Creole descent felt safer expressing herself in a fictional world than in a real one. She explained, "I was shy and a loner. I had all this stuff inside of me that I wanted to express, but couldn't, for some reason, in my regular life. There was something really magical to me about the movies and the actors in them. I wanted to be there. They felt almost more real to me than real life. I was a voracious movie watcher. Still am. I was a hugely imaginative child and very creative. My parents are artists as well, which probably influenced me to some degree, although not consciously." Her first gig was one a lot of young girls would dream of: she starred in a Barbie commercial.

Bianca played her first teenager when she was only 13. She was picked to play Megan Jones on *Saved by the Bell: The New Class*, a major part that she kept for the first two seasons. Reflecting on her early days in the biz, Bianca noted, "I loved being 13 and going off to work every morning. I felt so productive and adult! I just loved the whole structure of a set and how close you become [with everyone on set]. Also, making my own money at that age gave me a lot of self-esteem and a feeling of independence."

After her *Saved by the Bell* stint, roles started rolling in, and the young actress appeared on *Sister, Sister, Goode Behavior, Dawson's Creek*, and, in one of her most memorable guest spots, as "Kendra da vampire slayer" on *Buffy the Vampire Slayer*. She made her film debut in *Primary Colors* (1998) and went on to another role for which she still gets recognized, Derek's feisty ex-girlfriend Nikki in the dance flick *Save the Last Dance* (2001). The common thread between her most enduring roles? They're tough, mean girls. "Every time I meet people," said Bianca, "they're like, 'Oh my god — I thought you were going to be such a bitch.'"

Though most people would have to give up teen roles at this point, Bianca experienced another teen renaissance in 2009 when she nabbed recurring roles in three prime teen series: *The Secret Life of the American Teenager* as Shawna, *The Vampire Diaries* as Emily Bennett from olde-timey Mystic Falls, and, of course, in *Pretty Little Liars* as Maya St. Germain.

Bianca didn't audition for the cool alterna-girl Maya initially. Along with Sasha Pieterse and Ashley Benson, she was gunning for sassy It Girl Hanna. The producers offered her Maya instead. "I didn't know anything about Maya up until that point," said Bianca. "I hadn't read the books and I hadn't read any of [Sara Shepard's] stuff, so I said, "Oh, okay," and then I read it and I said, 'Oh my god, this is a kickass part!' It's unusual, it's something I've never played before. I immediately connected with her."

What does she like so much about playing Maya? "She's very, very confident, and very self-assured. She's probably a lot more mature than I am, and a lot more confident. She's such a free spirit and she doesn't care what anyone thinks. You always want to be that person that doesn't care and says exactly what you want to say at the exact moment, but you still have that filter because you don't want to hurt feelings and you're conscious of how you're coming off and want to be liked. She honestly doesn't care, and she so lives in her truth. I just feel like how free that would be, to be so secure and to not care what people think that you are constantly living in your absolute truth all the time. I can work out my stuff through Maya."

Some actors might be hesitant to play a role with a same-sex love interest, but Maya was unconcerned. She'd actually played a lesbian once before, in 2002 on TV drama *For the People*. Even with that experience under her belt, Bianca approached Maya the way she would any character. She told After Ellen, "I just dove right in because I never look at her like 'she's a lesbian character.' She's a person and this is what she's gone through and these are her characteristics. This is the person that I love; not this is the girl that I love." And it's just that kind of empathy and understanding that make us hope Bianca Lawson has a few more teen years ahead of her.

BACK TO THE BOOKS In *Wicked*, Hanna attempts to be friendly with Kate when she starts at Rosewood Day, but she's certain Kate is secretly plotting against her.

PLL IRL Director Wendey Stanzler returned to the helm for this episode. She had previously directed "Reality Bites Me," and in the time between her *PLL* gigs worked on its sister show *The Lying Game* as well as other excellent TV series like *The Vampire Diaries* and *Parks and Recreation*.

Qs & A Why did Ali create an alternate self, and is her choice of Vivian Darkbloom as her pseudonym a clue? Garrett tells Caleb that Jenna found someone else for his "old job" of spying on the

girls; does he mean himself or Noel Kahn? Did Noel somehow mess with Maya's phone? How did the Gloved Wonder get into the Hastings' house and what is s/he planning to do with Peter's gun?!

2.19 THE NAKED TRUTH

(AIRED FEBRUARY 6, 2012 | WRITTEN BY OLIVER GOLDSTICK & FRANCESCA ROLLINS | DIRECTED BY ELODIE KEENE)

Caleb: "We are telling the whole truth today, right? Not just the part we want to remember?"

When Rosewood High schedules a Truth Up day, people are encouraged to lay themselves bare — not so literally as Kate does — but to "break barriers, form new connections, and own up to bad behavior." In a show that's a virtual tapestry of lies, this seems like an opportunity for a big reveal, but instead the writers show us how closely everyone is woven together, how all these different colored threads are cut from the same cloth.

Though the Truth Up activities are unforgivably awkward, some of them actually do illustrate the students' common ground pretty well. In Ashley's step-forward exercise, after a few prompts, it's practically a line dance in there. And the scribbled notes on the wall reveal that no one is as put together as they seem. Of course, most of the interesting revelations happen outside of the cue-carded activities. Watching Mona's face as Emily apologizes for not standing up to Ali showcases a gorgeous moment of vulnerability in Mona before she snaps back to her carefree public persona. And she's not an innocent, bruised babe either, and we see Mona's usual confidence in a scenario that, for once, isn't socializing or shoplifting: raiding, hacking, and blackmailing on Emily's behalf. With these A-like extracurriculars, and her telling Emily, "Honey, you can't be a shark if you're toothless," Mona gets a lot more interesting, and menacing, in this episode.

In another great scheme that proves that, as Noel Kahn says, "Bad boys got nothing on mean girls," Kate's plan to bring down Hanna and make herself look good proves she's a shark with teeth. But perfect-and-polished Kate's plan ultimately backfires, because behind her Photoshopped self-image hides a girl so desperate to fit in, so horrified by her past, that she'd stage an elaborate prank (and make a few physical adjustments) just to protect herself from a threat she's only imagined, to cover flaws no one else can see. And how does Hanna drag it out of her? By sharing her own insecurities.

But in terms of the mystery arc, the most interesting and unexpected tie is the literal one, as Spencer discovers that she and Jason are bonded by blood. Suddenly Spencer is forced to look at her family in a whole new light, and with all the lies, betrayal, and cheating, she's not even sure she can call the Hastings manse home. In this case finding out what she has in common with someone actually sets Spencer apart, forcing her to question the family relationships she took for granted. But now her father's a cheater, her parents are both liars, and her sister is still in the dark. Seems like Jason will fit right in.

HIGHLIGHT Hanna bringing down Kate with her savvy sting operation. Nice to see Han and the girls victorious over at least one bully, and the fact that the revenge comes in a bathroom is a nice nod back to the fallout zone of Kate's vodka sabotage. Second place goes to Caleb's fearless honesty and defense of Hanna as he refuses to let Jenna play the victim.

EXTRA CREDIT
- Mona calls Vice Principal Tamborelli "Toad of Toad Hall," a reference to Kenneth Grahame's 1908 children's novel *The Wind in the Willows*. It's also the title of the 1929 stage adaptation of the novel penned by Grahame's fellow kid-lit contemporary A.A. Milne (creator of Winnie-the-Pooh).

- Ali's story of the German classified ad cannibal is based on a true story. The killer was Armin Meiwes, a 42-year-old computer expert, who in 2001 advertised online for someone he could kill and eat, and found a willing dinner date in 43-year-old engineer Bernd Brandes. Meiwes was eventually caught and sentenced to life imprisonment. Although Ali's takeaway was that every woman thinks that she can change a guy, in fact, Meiwes was looking exclusively for men.
- Ali hints that a relationship between Melissa and Jason would be "a match frowned upon by the gods," referring to the fact that incest is considered one of the oldest and most universal human taboos.
- Caleb's snarky line to Jenna was a deliberate echo of Hanna's post-slap line from "Someone to Watch Over Me," meaning Hanna gave her BF a blow-by-blow of the bathroom showdown.

SLIP UPS Jenna takes out a piece of gum twice, but only puts one in her mouth.

BACK TO THE BOOKS In *Wicked*, it's Hanna who takes the social offensive, not Kate, spreading a rumor that her stepsister has an STD. Spencer discovers family ties with the DiLaurentis family in *Heartless*, but Veronica Hastings is as shocked as Spencer is to discover the connection.

PLL IRL Marlene's fave line in the episode is Hanna's "Where the hell am I?" when she is woken up by the others in the middle of the Truth Up sleepover.

Qs & A Mona is capable of disguising her voice and seems to have significant tech savvy and access to a lot of the school's information. One of the black-light secrets was "I know who killed Alison DiLaurentis," so someone at Truth Up day (and maybe even someone in Aria, Caleb, and Jenna's group) knows what went down. What were Jenna and Noel doing in the black-light room? If Jason is Mr. Hastings' son, is Ali related to the Hastings clan too? Is this Noel Kahn's first time donning a hood for shady business? What is A planning to do with Caleb's laptop?

2.20 CTRL: A

(AIRED FEBRUARY 13, 2012 | WRITTEN BY JOSEPH DOUGHERTY &
LIJAH J. BARASZ | DIRECTED BY RON LAGOMARSINO)

*Holden: "Sometimes what people believe is
best for you is not what's actually best for you."*

"Now it's Caleb's turn," warns A, and this episode sees Rosewood's resident hacker in the hot seat as the cops try to infiltrate Caleb's secret-filled laptop. This second half of season 2 has been about the girls trying to wrest control back from A, and "CTRL: A" sees their anonymous enemy trying to fight back with the planted "Hefty" evidence. Though they are very much still in A's clutches, the girls are victorious in this rematch — kicking down A just like Holden does to his fearsome Tang Soo Do opponent.

Though the secrets they keep couldn't be more different, Aria has found a kindred spirit in Holden. Both struggle for self-determination and independence from their parents who believe their hearts' desires are actually harmful to them. For Holden, his parents fear he's literally endangering his life by getting kicked repeatedly, instead of staying home for quiet nights of Apples to Apples (and, really, that game *is* fun even when it is played with parentals). In a fortuitous move, Aria chooses to watch Holden compete in an attempt to understand why he does what he does, and in doing so avoids having her father, led by A's note, catch her and Fitz canoodling over French vegan food.

The parental strategy debate continues between Ella and Byron: is it time to give Aria more freedom since she's been so good (Ha! If only Ella knew) or is Byron right to keep a tight leash on his wayward daughter? He is clearly still suspicious — and rightfully so, since Ezra and Aria *are* sneaking around together — and Ella, though nobler, seems a little naive in her trust, since we know it's being violated. In a parallel plot, Ashley is once again exasperated with her daughter, knowing that she's not getting the whole truth from her about the candy-striper-costumed morgue "prank." Her ability to tell when Hanna is lying no longer seems to get her close to the real story.

Following the big reveal of the last episode, Spencer's dealing with a double-whammy: tracking the Vivian Darkbloom clues while coming to terms with her redefined relationship with Jason DiLaurentis, her half-sibling, who for his part is highly suspicious of their father. With each answer Spencer gets, she finds more questions: where did Ali get the $15,000? Would she blackmail Peter Hastings? Did he have anything to do with Ali's murder? What information did Jonah uncover for Alison? As the season finale approaches, the plot thickens: the cops have a photo of the girls outside the morgue, they know about the missing page five, and Maya's back to smoking weed and thinking about running away.

Though the war against A and his/her allies is yet to be fought, Hanna is happy to celebrate a battle won. When she realizes that Caleb's complicated password ends not in four random numbers but in numbers that represent an exclamation-point memory for him, Hanna feels even more secure and loved. Their smooch-athon outside the Rosewood police station not only throws their win in Garrett's face but reminds us what the girls are fighting so hard to hold on to.

HIGHLIGHT The hilarious and incredibly tense hacking scene with Spencer yelling, "Ctrl A!" at Hanna, and Hanna totally not getting it.

EXTRA CREDIT
- Caleb makes a Beatles reference with his "I am the wifi — goo-goo-g'joob," playing on the Fab Four's 1967 psychedelic "I Am the Walrus."
- Spencer is having an extended sleepover at the Montgomerys, something she hoped for back in "To Kill a Mocking Girl,"

when she half-jokingly asked Aria, "Any chance your family wants to adopt me?"

- Holden has been keeping two big secrets. He hides from his parents that he practices Tang Soo Do, a Korean martial art related to taekwondo and karate, which was popularized in North America by action star Chuck Norris. And from Aria, he hides that he has an abdominal aortic aneurysm, meaning his blood vessel feeding the lower half of his body is engorged. While treatable surgically if it is of a certain size, a ruptured aneurysm is indeed life threatening.
- Spencer quotes Ali, telling Jason she used to say, "When I hide things, they stay hid," which we heard Ali tell the girls in "The Goodbye Look."

SLIP UPS Establishing the exact date that Hanna and Caleb slept together — November 5, 2010 — makes the already sketchy *PLL* timeline even less realistic. Since the homecoming dance took place on October 16, that leaves just 20 days for the events from "The Homecoming Hangover" to "A Person of Interest," which includes Hanna's broken leg healing. In "Je Suis une Amie," Caleb rhymed off a slightly different list of previous residences before Rosewood: Seattle, Salt Lake, Denver, and Chicago.

PLL IRL Reflecting on the big episode for Caleb, Tyler Blackburn wasn't too worried about his character going against the Rosewood PD: "Caleb is a tough dude, you know? He has a lot of street smarts, and he can keep up pretty well." As for Caleb's romance with Hanna, he believes their strength lies in their common ground: "They're both similar in the sense that they put out this tougher exterior, but they have a lot of sensitivity inside. So I think when they're together, it's kind of a platform for them to be able to open up and really feel something. You know what I mean? I think that that makes them feel safe together, and I think that feeling safety with a significant other is just really important." Bianca Lawson told HollywoodLife.com that there was supposed to be a showdown between Emily's exes in this episode. "It was so deliciously written, and I was so excited to meet and work with Lindsey," said Bianca. But a scheduling conflict meant the scenes couldn't be filmed in time, and instead of both girls congratulating Emily after the swim meet, it was just Maya. Bianca told AfterEllen.com, in the scene on the stairs at Hanna's, "There was a conversation that was so beautifully written, but we only got to see a portion of it."

Qs & A How did Caleb's IP address get linked to the school records' break-in? Was Garrett after Caleb's laptop, or did Mona do it, given that we saw her access the confidential files in "The Naked Truth"? Why were Jason and Maya talking by the fruit stand? Did Ali get the $15,000 in cash from Peter Hastings? Did Ali actually find out who A is from Jonah's illegal intel? Who tipped off Wilden with the photo of the girls lurking outside the morgue? Who was watching Emily from outside the window?

2.21 BREAKING THE CODE

(AIRED FEBRUARY 20, 2012 | WRITTEN BY JONELL LENNON| DIRECTED BY ROGER KUMBLE)

Emily: "A knows we're getting closer."

Marlene King called the second half of season 2 "the season of no more victims," and in this episode it's especially true of our ladies, who in one way or another all decide to stand up for themselves, whether to faceless cyberbullies or the people they love.

Take Mona, who's faced with a new lunch table, a checked-out BFF, and some mysterious texts. A lot for anyone to handle, but Mona takes all these challenges in stride. She shows flashes of insecurity when she's faced with the imposing posse of Ali's former gang, but unlike her bestie in season 1, Mona doesn't even contemplate chucking a friend under the bus. She bravely turns herself in, risking a police record and, worse, a hairnet. Mona's been bullied before (as she doesn't fail to remind Hanna), and she's unwilling to let anyone get the upper hand again.

With her punked-out trench coat and Katniss Everdeen braid, Spencer is stellar at the sketchy park rendezvous, standing up (literally and repeatedly) to the sketchy Jonah and his inferior intel. Later, she fights an even harder battle, standing up to her friends when the new video footage has them ready to deliver Melissa to the Rosewood PD.

Whereas Spencer's courage manifests itself in her aggression, for Ella courage lies in avoiding the warpath. Her motherly instincts are certainly battling it out though. Her initial urge is to protect her daughter from being victimized; upon seeing Aria's total heartbreak, she decides to take the time to listen and try to understand the situation before passing judgment. But Ella's strategy differs from Byron's antagonistic (and scheming) approach — apparently they haven't revisited their parenting repertoire since their troubles with Mike. Individually, Byron and Ella have ventured to Ezra's apartment to talk it out with significantly different results. Neither visit is comfortable, but for all of Byron's bluster and bravado, Ella's awkward tea party is the braver move any day.

With Ashley taking her exhibit A down to the station, Ella connecting her two A notes, and Mona initiated into the A crowd, more and more people have A on their radar. And with this tough and determined crew out for blood, there may be one victim left in Rosewood after all: A.

HIGHLIGHT The Ingrid Michaelson cover of "Can't Help Falling in Love with You" was the perfect theme song for Aria as her unstoppable love came up against Fitz's loss of faith. Her final choking sobs are heartbreak distilled.

EXTRA CREDIT
• A "burner" phone is one bought cheaply and replaced

frequently, often used for illegal activities, because the vendor requires very little personal information and no contract.

- When Paige tells Emily, "You handled coming out so well it made it possible for me to do it too," it's a nice acknowledgment of what many grateful fans felt watching Emily's coming out story.
- This is the second time Paige has chosen the wrong moment to kiss Emily: the first time was her sudden car smooch in "The New Normal."
- A warned Emily that s/he'd be targeting Mona: in "The Naked Truth," A texts Emily saying that Emily's "new pal" Mona will be "hurt." Emily doesn't tell the girls that Mona helped her get back on the swim team, or that A threatened retaliation.
- Both Hanna and Aria spill their big secrets — that Ashley hooked up with Wilden, and that Aria's still seeing Fitz — but Spencer doesn't reveal hers. She keeps her promise to Melissa and doesn't tell the girls about Jason being her half-bro.
- Spencer teases Wren about Aristotle being in the wrong place on his bookshelf. The influential Greek philosopher's work influenced many fields, including medicine.

SLIP UPS Why didn't Spencer and Aria just google the address as soon as they got it from Jonah? They would have found out right away that it was a law firm and Spencer would know that Melissa interned there. Officer Barry says, "Emily Fields?" as if he doesn't already know her; he questioned Emily in the aftermath of homecoming.

BACK TO THE BOOKS In *Perfect*, Hanna gets a warning from A that Mona isn't her friend. Mona tells Spencer she's been getting texts from A in *Unbelievable*. In the same book, Melissa starts looking like a possible murder suspect when she has a conversation with Spencer about Ali while she pops the head off a

Barbie and creepily says, "It takes a very unique person to kill."

PLL IRL Emily's scene with Paige outside the Grill is one of Marlene's faves.

Qs & A The text to Ali's phone came from the law office where Melissa interned. How was Melissa involved the night of Ali's murder? Why is Melissa hanging out with Garrett? What does Melissa want to tell Spencer? What happened to Maya? The Gloved Wonder has excellent aim — could that be a clue that it's someone who's had a lot of target practice, like Garrett?

2.22 FATHER KNOWS BEST

(AIRED FEBRUARY 27, 2012 | WRITTEN BY CHARLIE CRAIG &
BRYAN M. HOLDMAN | DIRECTED BY CHAD LOWE)

Aria: "I'm A — A for anonymous, A for Aria, A for . . ."
Ashley: "I get it."

Another jam-packed episode, "Father Knows Best" centers on the Rosewood High father-daughter dance, an annual event that, this year, only serves to highlight the dysfunction when it comes to the PLLs' dads, and the tension that exists between parent and child because of secrets kept.

For the girls, there are two kinds of dads: absentee, and over-compensaters. Hanna's dad bails entirely on the dance, citing a prior commitment (at least he didn't show up with Kate on his arm), while Emily's dad reveals in a touching scene that this weekend spent together will be their last for a while, as he will head back to Afghanistan for a six-month stint. Wayne Fields may not be around much for his Emmy, but it's clear that he cherishes each moment he spends with his daughter — even if it's spent tramping through bus stations to find Maya. Ashley valiantly tries to step up and fill Tom's empty dancing shoes for Hanna, arguing that it's more lame to miss the dance than to show up with your mom, but the A-related tension between the Marin women ruins their night. Hanna ends up at the dance sans dad, dress, and phone — and her wistfulness is unmistakable as she watches Em dance with her military dad.

Melissa declares that Father Hastings is overcompensating — big time — for his past lies and the breach of trust, and while Melissa herself seems rather untrustworthy, she's dead right about Peter's behavior. He lays it on thick: buying Spence a diamond necklace, taking her to her favorite restaurant, asking her

to play tennis with him, and sucking up to her by telling her they make such a great "team." Spence is justifiably wary: it's heartbreaking that the love and attention she wants from her father only arrives when he's trying to repair a potentially disastrous situation for himself. While Spencer opts for honesty in the face of her dad's OTT attempt to win her back, she's less forthcoming with Melissa, unsure of how much she can trust her big sis. Has Melissa now told her the whole truth about her harassment campaign against Alison? Why was she in Ali's room with the NAT club on the night Ali died? Thanks to those secrets Spence doesn't feel she can share even with her best friends, she's left carrying the weight of the Hastings family alone.

While Aria felt she gained an ally in her mother in the previous episode, her hope is put on pause in "Father Knows Best," as Ella asks her to keep mum about her "trying to understand" process. Byron is also on hold: he prefers living in the past to confronting the reality of his current relationship with his daughter. No longer his little girl, Aria has a hard time "embracing the irony" of the situation and playing along. Byron is incredibly sentimental — poor Mike shaves for the first time when his dad's out of town to avoid it being a *thing* — and his nostalgia for the sweet, uncomplicated way things were with his daughter is pretty tragic. That relationship has been gone for a long time now, ever since Aria saw him with Meredith. But Byron is just coming to terms with that and with the fact that Aria's grown up and no longer fits in with the cutesy, childish candy theme of the dance.

In a hilarious moment Mona (whose attention from A has earned her a tentative spot in the gang) asks the girls who is the best at lying to loved ones, and Aria is the unanimous winner. So it's fitting that she's the one mistaken for Ali's alter ego, Vivian, when she puts on the red coat in Brookhaven. The hunt to find out what Vivian knew is heating up, just as the meeting of the moms signals more parental investigation into the series' biggest question: who is A?

While the story lines race to the end-of-season conclusion, it's little bro Mike who asks the most philosophical of questions, and gives his father pause. Mike points out that Byron never asked Aria *why* she lied — and it's an important question with telling answers for all of the liars in Rosewood. It's the heart of the story: what makes these characters do what they know isn't right? For Aria, her skill at compromising the truth (and her willingness to do it) stems from her unwavering commitment to the fight for love — no matter how impossible and messy it may be.

HIGHLIGHT No one does defiant, pouty teenager better than Ashley Benson: Hanna tosses her phone in the water-filled sink and struts out of that kitchen like a boss — and in the same moment it's clear how conflicted she is about keeping the truth from her mother.

EXTRA CREDIT
- *Father Knows Best* was first a radio program and then a TV series that ran from 1949 to 1960 about the Andersons, a "typical" Midwest family — cheery entertainment with a moral in each episode. But even on that series, as on today's *PLL*, father didn't always know best.
- Mona compares community service to the ninth circle of hell, the area reserved for those guilty of treachery in Dante Alighieri's 14th-century poem *The Divine Comedy*. Given that she chose that circle in particular, is this a hint that the ninth circle is where Mona thinks she belongs?
- Mike and his DJ friend, Gavin, are playing to the crowd: instead of the usual tunes heard at a Rosewood High dance, they play Tears for Fears' 1985 hit "Everybody Wants to Rule the World," which will appeal to the dad demographic.
- In Peter Hastings' cringe-inducing attempts to be a cool dad, he references 1989 hits "Pump Up the Jam" by Technotronic and "Bust a Move" by Young MC.
- The revelation that Peter Hastings was worried that Melissa may have been involved in Ali's disappearance puts his decision to burn the field hockey stick Toby unearthed in "Surface Tension" in a new light. He may have been protecting his daughter, not covering his own bloody tracks.
- On a tip from Jonah, the girls go to Brookhaven, a real town in Delaware County, Pennsylvania (which is the same county that fictional Rosewood is in).

SLIP UPS Wilden and Ashley need a lesson in clandestine meetings: you don't sit in a parked car on a busy street if you want to go unnoticed. In "A Kiss Before Lying," the Gloved Wonder appeared to pick the lock of Peter's desk; wouldn't Peter have had to relock the drawer for it to be locked when Spencer tried to open it? Why hadn't he already noticed the missing gun?

BACK TO THE BOOKS Emily thinks Maya ran away, but in *Unbelievable* it's Emily who plays runaway, escaping her über-religious aunt and uncle in Iowa.

PLL IRL Was it Toby driving past the school on his motorbike? Marlene coyly suggested on Twitter that that's what Spencer believes, and she believes that too. Fittingly, this dad-centric episode was directed by Chad "Byron Montgomery" Lowe, who described Rachel Kamerman's confectionary design for the school dance a "beautiful sweet world to act and direct in." The location was referred to as "Candyburg," and Chad joked that it looked like Katy Perry's bedroom.

Qs & A Who is the guy who mistook Aria for Vivian? The newspaper with Maya on the front page is eerily similar to Ali's Missing Girl front page — is Maya in serious trouble? The car A returned to in "Through Many Dangers, Toils and Snares" was dark colored — is it A's car that the bus station attendant saw? Can Spencer trust her sister or her father? What did her father's P.I. turn up? What will A do now that the Mom Brigade is on the warpath?

2.23 EYE OF THE BEHOLDER

(AIRED MARCH 5, 2012 | WRITTEN BY JOSEPH DOUGHERTY | DIRECTED BY MELANIE MAYRON)

Spencer: "We each know little chunks of
the truth and we have to share what we know
or else this is all going to come apart."

"Eye of the Beholder" plays on the old adage that "Beauty is in
the eye of the beholder." It's the perfect title for an episode in
which perspective affects both the mystery and the relationships
between characters, introducing new tensions in some cases and
offering possible resolution in others.

Jenna returns to Rosewood after having surgery to return her
sight in one eye (which, if successful, would leave her with poor
depth perception, another interesting perspective). But what's
more intriguing is Toby's sudden shift back to being Jenna's
loyal seeing eye dog. In an awkward hallway conversation with
Spencer, Toby refrains from using an "I" response, always link-
ing himself with Jenna in a rather cringe-inducing "we." Is his
new loyalty to his stepsister just a way to get back at Spencer?
Running back to an abuser seems like an extreme reaction to a
broken heart, and Toby makes it clear to Hanna that he hasn't
forgotten any part of Jenna's roles as victimizer or victim.

In Ezria-land, different perspectives on reality lead to conflict,
in this case a power struggle between the two English profes-
sors. (You'd think this would involve some angry slam poetry or
roaring recitations of Shakespeare, but alas.) Interestingly, while
Ezra maintains that Ella's opinion is important to him, he won't
let Byron's manipulations influence his path or his self-image.
He tells Byron, "You think I'm the kind of man who would take
this way out, and I know I'm not." Even Ella and Byron see
the situation, and Byron's tactics, in different ways: she calls setting up Fitz with the position in New Orleans "strong-arming"

whereas he calls it "a dream job with housing." In a nice reflection of the episode's big picture, Aria's parents fail to share their strategies and insights with one another, but fight independent battles and ultimately leave Fitz with mixed signals.

Emotional isolation and mixed signals are a way of life at the Hastings household, with each family member shouldering his or her own burdens and secrets. And this secrecy is fueled by more than just pride. Take the situation with Jason ("that boy," according to Veronica, or "my brother," according to Spencer). While Veronica certainly wouldn't want the scandal to get out, it's about more than reputation: she believes the DiLaurentis family has always tried to "blow things up," to shake the foundations that the Hastings have built. Veronica's trying to keep things "uncomplicated," and, in a way, her attempt mirrors the foursome's in season 1 as they kept secrets even from the people they should trust. But there's a new order of openness among the liars. Spencer has seen how much better her friends work when they share their secrets, and she wants to do the same for her family. Her frustrated plea — "Do you see? Do you see how this all just spins and feeds on itself?" — shows she has learned what happens when lies and secrets cloud the truth, and thankfully it's enough to move her mother to open up.

The writers also offer some new perspectives on the mystery. Aria gets to see Rosewood from a new angle (literally) and gets Duncan's insight into Ali's state of mind and final days. The girls sort through Ali's stuff and discover that one person's trash is another person's treasure: the newspapers point the way to A. As Ali suggested in Hanna's hospital dream, discovering the truth may just be a matter of combining what they already know. Hanna realizes, "We're the key"; now they need to unlock the case.

HIGHLIGHT Hastings vs. Hastings matchups are always the stuff of title fights: you could practically see sparks in the air as Spencer and her mother had a highly charged (and very necessary) showdown.

EXTRA CREDIT

- The episode takes its title from the old saying "Beauty is in the eye of the beholder," and from a 1961 episode of *The Twilight Zone*, in which a beautiful woman undergoes 11 surgeries so she can fit in with her society, in which most people have, from our perspective, deformed, gruesome faces.
- The date on the *Rosewood Observer* is July 14, 2009. Ali first received a message from A the previous October ("The First Secret").

SLIP UPS As we saw with Hanna's leg, it seems broken bones are no problem in Rosewood: Toby broke his wrist just six episodes ago in "The Blonde Leading the Blind," and he already has his cast off; in real life, it would remain on for six to eight weeks.

BACK TO THE BOOKS It's the girls, not Jenna, who get caught in two near-deadly blazes: one in the forest in *Killer*, and one at the Hastings' cottage in *Wanted*.

PLL IRL Lachlan Buchanan, who plays Duncan, noted that the red coat is a major clue. He also revealed that his flight scene with Aria was filmed in a plane that the crew members shook to simulate turbulence. He said, "It's hot and it's cramped but we're having fun. We're pretending it's a freezing cold night and it's like 90 degrees in that thing." While many fans were disappointed to see Toby run back to Jenna, Keegan Allen told Wetpaint, "I think at this point Toby is smarter than anybody really gets. He understands a lot. He really does know when he's being manipulated and sometimes he'll go along with it to avoid confrontation. But recently, I think he has worked really hard to find more of himself. So that's why he left. He realizes the toxicity of both of these friendships and relationships. He's a lot more wary now than he ever was before."

Qs & A Why is Maya blocking her ID on her texts and emails to Emily? Why was Garrett peeling away from Jenna's place? Who lured Jenna to the fire and why? What did Ali figure out while she was in Hilton Head? Why did Ali save those newspapers? Who was Ali meeting at the Labor Day festivities? The Gloved Wonder put a Rosewood PD badge by Jason's burnt porch; why is s/he trying to implicate Garrett in the fire?

2.24 IF THESE DOLLS COULD TALK

(AIRED MARCH 12, 2012 | WRITTEN BY OLIVER GOLDSTICK
& MAYA GOLDSMITH | DIRECTED BY RON LAGOMARSINO)

Alison: "This isn't Yahtzee, sweetie. This is some seriously messed-up stuff. But here's the good news: you're getting warmer."

"Follow me, end up like me," repeats the disembodied voice of the Ali doll. But the Ali who visits Spencer has a much different message: don't stop chasing the truth. Alison spent her last days tracking down A, and the girls can't rest until they know what became of their friend, and who A is. As they struggle to parse the clues that Alison left behind, they are unable to tell for sure who is bluffing, nor is it clear whether they really *know* anything or if they're still just guessing. But the four little liars aren't the only ones pushed to extremes.

After someone tried to kill Jenna in a fiery blaze at Jason DiLaurentis's house, the master manipulator has taken up a new strategy: alliance building. Her huge lie — that her surgery failed and she is still, and always will be, blind — coupled with her tearful plea for peace makes her appear to be a changed girl. She tells the liars that she's seeing clearly, "just not with my eyes," that people can grow, and she wants to move past her hatred and her grudge against them. Though the girls are wary of Jenna's about-face, we find out by episode's end that not only has

Jenna turned over page five to the cops and had Garrett arrested, but she *has* regained her sight. In a perfect *PLL* moment, Jenna, who's been playing the sweet and repentant girl who wouldn't hurt a fly, kills one with alarming precision and force before gleefully admiring her reflection. Garrett made a huge mistake in trusting Jenna, asking her to destroy page five in "Over My Dead Body," and he may be making the same mistake with his new secret girlfriend, Melissa. She tells him to trust in her, convinced that Spence won't hand over the NAT club video to the police, when her little sis is preparing to do just that.

Though the relationship between the Hastings girls has been far from idyllic, Spencer struggles with the decision to cast her sister as A. Family matters to Spence, and she isn't willing to betray Melissa. But like Ali says in her nighttime visit to Spencer, "You deserve a decent sister." Neither Ali (keeping her pseudosister status a secret) nor Melissa have stepped up for Spencer the way Emily, Aria, and Hanna have with unconditional support, no matter if they might disagree about how to handle the A of it all. Melissa doesn't hesitate to blackmail Spencer and her friends with a threat of revealing incriminating videos to the police. With the reveal that Melissa and Garrett are more than friends (ew!), it's clear she still holds power among the remaining NAT club members.

Ella has been warning Byron about pushing Aria into a corner, fearing she'd run away or elope, but she never expected Aria to turn on her family. In a desperate moment, faced with being "exiled to Siberia" (a.k.a. Vermont), Aria blackmails her mother by threatening to rat out her dad's affair to the dean. It's a dark moment for Aria, who decides to adopt a bully's tactic in order to get her way. But as Ezra says to her when she gets riled up over the news that he's been fired, destroying her family to save their relationship is *not* a choice. With Fitz on his way out of Rosewood, the couple realizes this phase of their relationship is over, and they decide to take it to the next one: off the couch and onto the bed.

Determined to trap A with their very own bluff, Hanna orchestrates a Mona-Caleb smooch (which beats out Melissa-Garrett for cringe-inducing kiss of the season) perfectly timed for Melissa to see. A takes the bait, but the more revealing aspect of this charade is Mona's speech to Caleb in the car. Just as Jenna opens up to the girls in the courtyard, exposing her own vulnerability, Mona reveals a softer side to the guy who hates her. Instead of her usual self-centered snark, Mona explains how much she loves Hanna, what her friendship means to her, and that she's been jealous of Hanna's relationship with Caleb while she's been chasing superficial trysts with superficial guys. The A trap is a bizarre trust-building exercise for Hanna, Caleb, and Mona, but Hanna is still keeping secrets from Mona — about their Melissa suspicions, about Brookhaven, and about Alison's final weekend.

With only one episode left in the season of "no more victims," the girls all have that fierce look in their eyes that Ali so admires. They are determined to know the answer: who is A?!

HIGHLIGHT The Brookhaven Doll Hospital is the creepiest place on earth, thanks to a haunting set with disembodied heads, upside down dolls hanging from the ceiling, the eeriest sun-deprived child, and a gruesome Ali-doll tableau warning the girls against following in their dead best friend's footsteps. As Hanna would say, *terrifying*.

EXTRA CREDIT
- This episode takes its title from another Marlene King project, *If These Walls Could Talk*. Marlene wrote the "1996" segment of the HBO television movie about three generations of women and their experiences with abortion. It also happens to be the name of a chapter in Sara Shepard's sixth PLL novel, *Killer*.
- Spencer's encounter with Alison makes her the third liar to talk to Ali post-mortem: Emily was rescued by Alison

from the barn and then talked to her in "Over My Dead Body," while Hanna got a visit from her in "Moments Later." In "Eye of the Beholder," Hanna refers to that conversation as if it was real, saying, "Ali said we know more about

that summer than we think we do." Hanna may think it's ludicrous to consult Seth and his sideshow ability, but she believes in her friend communicating from beyond the grave.

- The girls walk by a sign outside the Brookhaven bookshop that advertises *Joanne Fluke's Lake Eden Cookbook*, a collection of recipes and stories in the Hannah Swensen murder mystery series.
- The "folksy, burlappy," "terrifying" voodoo doll that was among Ali's things was given to her by A in "The First Secret" along with a note that read, "It's my turn to torture you."
- For Caleb, kissing Mona is as frightening a prospect as eating bugs or performing a daredevil stunt, the kinds of challenges contestants face on *Fear Factor*, the NBC game show that came back from the dead in 2011.
- Aria and Fitz have their own music cue in Michael Suby's score, and they also have their own signature song style. In a choice similar to the cover of "Can't Help Falling in Love" that played in "Breaking the Code," music supervisor Chris Mollere plays Gemma Hayes' haunting cover of Chris Isaak's "Wicked Game" for the moment Ezria fans have been waiting for.
- Spoon bending is a popular display of psychic paranormal phenomena. But just like in a magician's show, Seth's apparent "second sight" is a trick. He's been fed his lines as part of his mother's deal with A.
- In another great music moment, Billie Holiday's version of jazz standard "Them There Eyes" kicks in for the reveal of Jenna's big secret. Will her eyes get her in a whole lot of trouble like the song warns?

BACK TO THE BOOKS In Sara Shepard's world, the girls often think they see Ali, hear her giggling, or dream about her, and in *Wicked*, Ali says, "The truth is right in front of you." In *Perfect*, Aria and Ezra spend the night together.

PLL IRL Seth, the creepy doll boy, is played by Maxwell Huckabee, a.k.a. Bobby Draper in season 1 of *Mad Men* and traumatized toddler and serial-killer-to-be Dexter in flashbacks of *Dexter*. About Jenna's post-operation story line, Tammin Sursok told TheInsider.com, "She wants to get back at those people [who blinded her], and I think there's a lot of anger, and there's a lot of sadness. I think anger masks sadness and depression, so definitely you'll see a side of that, that will make audiences maybe feel something for her, whether it's good or not. . . . I think everything with Jenna comes with manipulation, and getting what she wants. . . . Everything she does, she does with motive." Though the scene where Ezra and Aria cross into illegal territory could have had viewers up in arms, Marlene noted that the showrunners received "an overwhelmingly positive response to those characters finally doing more than order Chinese takeout."

Qs & A When did Melissa and Garrett start getting smoochy? What happened when Alison went to meet A in Brookhaven at 235 Spruce Street? Did Alison ever go to the doll hospital? Why did Jenna decide to turn over her evidence against Garrett, leading to his arrest for Ali's murder? Did Melissa send the text to Hanna about the Mona-Caleb kiss or did someone else? Was Melissa bluffing about the incriminating videos, or could the girls go down for The Jenna Thing? What did Alison want from the bag? Though Jenna was lying about still being blind, was she telling the truth about not being the person the girls "really need to fear"? If Seth's "psychic" information actually came from A, what man and brown-haired woman did A want the girls to believe killed Ali? Where is Maya?

2.25 UNMASKED

(AIRED MARCH 19, 2012 | WRITTEN BY I. MARLENE KING | DIRECTED BY LESLI LINKA GLATTER)

Mona: "It's easier to forgive an enemy than it is to forgive a friend."

Faced with the big reveal after two long seasons of hide-and-seek, fans, cast, and crew were as hyped up on A-Day as over-caffeinated Spencer. And we got our A, but because this is *PLL* we also got so much more: a masked ball, lovers reunited, a seriously sinister motel, team Sparia, another murder, and a new mysterious mastermind. As Marlene said, "Red is the new black."

Fans and PLLs alike may be dying for answers (Spencer almost literally), but this episode was never going to be about tidying up all the loose ends. In some ways it circles back to the very beginning of the show. The final moments have the girls reliving the discovery of Ali's body through the discovery of Maya's body, and the echo is unmistakable, from the crowded residential street and the police cars right down to playing the same song, "Suggestions" by Orelia Has Orchestra. *Pretty Little Liars'* central mystery has always been about the past, and the past keeps the girls ensnared in its secrets. Lately the girls have been retracing Ali's steps, first to Brookhaven, and now to the Lost Woods Resort, where the *Psycho* homage and creepy desk clerk offer a warning against indulging an obsession, especially an obsession with things long gone.

Mona's relationship with the past proves to be an interesting one, for while she has claimed many times to be "over" what happened with Ali, she just can't let go of Hanna's abandonment of her. These two issues are connected more deeply than Mona's willing to admit, of course. She tells Spencer that she spent years without any friends during Ali's reign of terror, and it's that experience of being totally alone that made Hanna's distance cut so deep. Twisted as it is, being A and constantly watching the girls, texting them and tormenting them, playing games with them, was a way of interacting, of forcing them to care about her, even if they didn't know who she was. It was a connection she could control. And as a member of the A-team, Mona became part of something powerful, a group that can never abandon each other because of their criminal connection.

Being alone in the *PLL* world is more frightening than even the terrible A. Fear of isolation is why the girls protect their loved ones so fiercely, even if it means lying. It's why team Sparia was so touching, and so necessary, when it comes to raiding spooky motel offices under the gaze of taxidermied birds, and why Spencer's "You're little, but you're big" comment to Aria was pitch-perfect. It's why Ezra was willing to take such a huge risk by unmasking himself and Aria at the ball — because that love, that connection, is worth risking everything he has left. Amid all the horror and suspense, the writers offer a few peaceful pauses courtesy of our couples, who share a slow dance to a romantic tune, or, in Emily's case, reconnect with an old flame, even if only as friends. Poor Spencer gets left out of this love fest at the ball, but she has her own romantic unmasking at the end. Toby reveals that he is still the one person who can be trusted in Rosewood, and that steadfastness includes his love for the youngest Hastings.

Season 2 ends much like season 1 did, with the discovery of a body and the whole town gathered around. And while the loss of a friend and lover packs a more powerful emotional punch than Ian's death did, the image of the girls coming together, supporting Emily and each other, symbolizes how much stronger they are after all they've been through this season. They have learned not to lie or betray one another, they have shared their secrets, they have chased the mystery rather than letting it chase them. Frightened, devastated, and shocked by Maya's death, the friends hold tight to one another. If they can handle Mona and this heartbreaking turn, they can handle whatever the Red Coat will throw at them, and they'll do it together.

HIGHLIGHT While this episode had no shortage of big reveals and romantic moments, Shay Mitchell stole the show with Emily's raw, unbridled grief when Maya's body is discovered.

EXTRA CREDIT

- Among the tip-offs that Mona was A: the "Previously on *Pretty Little Liars*" intro was voiced by Janel Parrish, and in Mona's first scene in the episode, she's wearing a red jacket and speaks French, like A was learning in "Je Suis une Amie."
- Spencer insists that the Hastings sisters have comparable IQs if you consider the Lexile Measure, a tool for assessing reading ability, and the Flynn effect, the sustained increase in IQ scores all over the world.
- Mr. Fitz has a thing for doomed romance, indeed. Tristan and Isolde are two lovers of a pre-Arthurian medieval tale about the tragic love between Tristan, a knight, and Isolde, the wife of his king. Héloïse d'Argenteuil was a medieval French scholar who was seduced by Peter Abélard, another scholar, in a relationship frowned upon by Héloïse's uncle. Things didn't end well here, either: he was castrated and she was sent to a convent, but the two continued to correspond for many years afterward.
- The Black Swan costume is a reference to the 2010 psychological thriller *Black Swan*, starring Natalie Portman. The film follows a ballerina cast in the lead role in Tchaikovsky's *Swan Lake* who is driven to madness by her obsession with trying to play both the pure, good white swan and the sensual, conniving black swan. As with the *Psycho* homage, the *Black Swan* reference reinforces the notion of the separation of self and warns of the dangers of obsession. We know two-faced Mona's not the Black Swan, but in this case she sure acted like it.
- According to the registration book, guests who have stayed at the Lost Woods Resort include *Pretty Little Liars*' co-producer and writer Bryan Holdman and writer Francesca Rollins.

- Things you may have noticed in A's lair: the clown mask ("Monsters in the End"), the zombie babydoll getup ("The First Secret"), posters for the fashion show ("Never Letting Go"), a camera, multiple phones, tripods, a map marked with pushpins, a dollhouse that contains the girls as Bratz dolls (a nice nod to Janel Parrish's role in the Bratz movie), the carpet we saw in the A scene at the end of "The Blonde Leading the Blind," and a blond wig. And fittingly for a girl who admires Spencer, Mona has the most pictures of Spencer up on the walls of her evil lair, second only to Alison.
- The diary entries that Spencer flips through are from October 2008; in them, Alison wrote about shopping, meeting Jenna, the Halloween party, Mr. Montgomery's affair, and delighting in making other people jealous.
- Cinderella references make their way into the fairytale ball: the girls have to hand over what A wants by midnight, and the mysterious Black Swan leaves a feather behind, just like Cinderella's glass slipper.
- *The A-Team* was a 1980s action-adventure show about former U.S. Army Special Forces personnel who were branded as war criminals but were actually out to do good.
- Hanna manages to hit the brakes before running down Mona, but in "Through Many Dangers, Toils, and Snares" Hanna's behind-the-wheel reflexes weren't so quick.
- Dr. Anne says Mona is living in a hyperreality, a state in which an individual gets satisfaction from simulating reality, rather than engaging with it.

SLIP UPS The Rosewood Junior Society forgot to add a date to their masked ball invites . . . unless that's all part of the mysterious allure. At the DiLaurentis house, why is Toby moving the charred refuse from one spot to another two feet away? How did Toby know how to find Dr. Anne? When A is watching the girls through the peephole, there are no clippings or photos around it, but when Spencer enters A's lair later, the photos go almost up to the framed bird painting. Did A have time to redecorate? When Spencer calls Aria from the car, the girls can hear Mona, but Mona doesn't hear any noise (the party or the girls talking) coming from the phone.

BACK TO THE BOOKS In *Unbelievable*, Mona tells Spencer, "Truthfully I was stunned when Hanna wanted to be friends with me in the eighth grade. She was part of Ali's clique, and you guys were legend. I always thought our friendship was too good to be true. Maybe I still kind of feel that way from time to time." In Sara Shepard's version, Spencer has the run-in with A, but it's Hanna who figures out A's identity when she recovers a repressed memory. A is unmasked and tries to form an alliance with Spencer, but doesn't survive the showdown with Spence. In *Heartless*, Hanna is the one carted off to a sanitarium. Chewing gum is also a key clue in the books, but it's a distinct banana gum rather than TV Mona's go-to spearmint.

PLL IRL The all-seeing portrait on the wall of the Lost Woods Resort lobby is actually of Marlene's mom. Marlene says she let Janel know about her role as A midway through season 2, but the rest of the cast found out together at the table read of the finale. It was a big shift for Janel's character, and she explained, "I kind of just had to go to that place and get a little dark with it. I've never had to play a role like that before, and it's obviously such a different persona from Mona . . . the normal Mona. I had to completely let go of the character that I've been playing for the past two years and find a new one." Marlene explained that Mona was the "most logical and also the most satisfying" person to be A. Like others, she was tormented by Alison, but it's the post-Ali era that really did the damage. Explained Marlene, "This fear of losing Hanna again inspired Mona to start tormenting these girls in the way that they tormented her, and then it kind of backfires. She ends up bringing them closer together than ever, so then she's even more pissed than ever in season 2."

The producers have noted that there are two A tricks that Mona couldn't have pulled off solo (like Emily's creeptastic massage in "Touched by an 'A'-ngel," when Mona was at the stables with Hanna), so Mona must have had some help from the A-team. The writers picked a costume ball theme as a backdrop to A's unmasking, and Marlene noted that production designer Rachel Kamerman's design is "magical but at the same time it exudes a haunting, fairytale feel . . . it has more of a Grimm's fairytale vibe." Of the final scene with the girls finding out about Maya's death, Marlene told *EW*, "That scene has me on my knees every time I watch it." Shay Mitchell confided, "I was speechless when I found out. I was completely shocked. For me, it was one of my favorite and my most heartbreaking scenes. I didn't think they were going to get rid of Emily's only stable relationship, you know?" The A-day hype paid off, and "unmAsked" took in series high ratings and made history by generating more social media buzz than any TV show had to date, with 645,000 tweets over the hour, peaking at 32,000 tweets per minute.

Qs & A Melissa suggests to the girls that Garrett killed Alison in an act of revenge for Ali blinding Jenna. Is she right? Jenna meets someone in the park that she hasn't seen in a long time and wasn't sure she would see again. Who was it and what did she give him/her? Why is Jenna lying about being blind? How can she drive if only one eye sees? Who is the Black Swan? Why does Lucas talk with Jenna and the Black Swan? Who killed Maya? How long has she been dead, and were any of messages to Emily really from her? Who else is on the A-team? Is there a reason Mona mentions the color of her lipstick, Toffee Tango, or any connection to Melissa thinking the fro yo was toffee flavored? The red coat is a symbol of Ali's other identity, Vivian; why is that color connected to the mysterious figure who visits Mona at the asylum? Is the red coat the new black hoodie?

PSYCHO AND
THE "MASTER OF SUSPENSE"

For *Pretty Little Liars'* season 2 finale extravaganza, the writers turned once again to the filmmaker from whom they've drawn inspiration since the beginning by recreating scenes from one of Alfred Hitchcock's best known pictures, *Psycho*. And fittingly the 1960 movie that spawned the slasher genre was itself filmed by a TV crew; Hitchcock borrowed the *Alfred Hitchcock Presents* crew to deliver big scares on a small budget.

The iconic Bates Motel is reborn as the Lost Woods Resort, and besides the absence of the looming Bates house beside it, the set in "unmAsked" captures all the creep of that original location from the shape of the building to the décor of the motel keeper's office and parlor — complete with taxidermied creatures, eyes watching — to the motel rooms themselves. The motel keeper snacks on candies from a little bag, imitating Anthony Perkins' quirk for Norman Bates. In *Psycho*, the psychopathic character stares through a hidden peephole, watching his would-be victim — just as A does, watching from room 2.

"unmAsked" reorders and repurposes famous scenes from *Psycho* with blonde Hanna taking on the most famous one when she decides to wash off that mud. Marion Crane (Janet Leigh) takes a shower at the Bates Motel and comes to a bloody end when her attacker sneaks into the bathroom with a knife. Hitchcock composed his scene in an innovative (and often-imitated) way, conveying the violence of the attack through the violence of the editing. Cuts jump through the whole lexicon of framing as Marion is stabbed, and the famous strings-only score accentuates the action. (That score was imitated in "The First Secret" when Ali fought the masked attacker.) In "unmAsked," A doesn't go in for the kill, but the episode's director gives a nod to Hitch with shots of the showerhead, as well as the suspenseful moment of seeing the attacker approach through the white shower curtain.

The registration book plays a key part in *Psycho* just as it does in the girls' investigation of Ali's time at the Lost Woods Resort.

Like Marion Crane before her, Spencer uses a fake name to register and, like Marion's sister who investigates her disappearance, Spencer needs to see the names of past guests logged in that book. Though Marion snacks on sandwiches with Norman Bates having no ulterior motive, Spencer sits in this motel keeper's parlor with A on her mind. In *Psycho*'s famous "We all go a little mad sometimes" parlor scene between Norman and Marion, Norman's insight into their situations also applies to Mona's psychological state and to the girls', whose past still directs their present. He says, "I think that we're all in our private traps, clamped in them, and none of us can ever get out. We scratch and we claw, but only at the air, only at each other, and for all of it, we never budge an inch."

Finally, the conclusion of "unmAsked" recreates *Psycho*'s denouement: a psychiatrist provides a somewhat convoluted and nonsensical explanation of the psychology, while an imprisoned Mona sits stock-still, staring ahead, and we get a glimpse inside her head, hearing her twisted thoughts in voiceover. Like Hitchcock's titular psycho, Mona has taken her love for Hanna to the extremes of obsession and hatred, trying to destroy anything that threatens her relationship and hurting the object of her psychosis in the process.

Hitchcock thought of mystery as being intellectual, and of suspense as emotional; he wanted to engage both things in the viewer's mind, just as the creators of *Pretty Little Liars* do. The goal of Hitch's moviemaking was creating suspense, to have his audience fear for a character despite the rational knowledge that a lead actor won't be killed off (at least not in the first act). A classic trick is letting the audience know more than the character does in order to create suspense. For example, when a character (say Marion Crane in *Psycho* or Hanna in "unmAsked") is in the shower, naked and vulnerable, with the noise of the running water muffling other sounds, she's unaware that someone is creeping into the room with her, but we, the audience, can see the attacker and we fear for her safety. Another technique Hitchcock relied on was communicating through film's two levels of information: the aural and visual, which complement each other. So instead of showing a person delivering their lines, Hitch opts to show the listener's reaction. In "If These Dolls Could Talk," there's a wonderfully effective example of this, where we hear Seth's unsettling voice but see the girls' reactions to his seemingly psychic insight.

Often the narrative of a Hitchcock film is structured around a "lure" that, though it could be an object, is frequently a person, dead or missing (*Rebecca*, *The Lady Vanishes*, *Psycho*, and *Vertigo*). *Pretty Little Liars*' narrative begins with and revolves around the "lure" of Alison DiLaurentis. Hitch was fond of showing an ordinary character experiencing a "moment of madness" like when *Psycho*'s Marion Crane steals $40,000 from her boss, or Ashley Marin nicks old Mrs. Potter's money, or Spencer takes her sister's engagement ring. Thanks to a character's distrust of the police's ability to deliver justice in complex situations, the "double chase" also figures repeatedly in Hitchcock's films — where the cops chase an innocent party, and that innocent person chases the real murderer — and *Pretty Little Liars* follows that structure too, with the girls chasing the killer as either A or the police or both are close on their tail. Feeding off this conundrum is the age-old problem of dueling motivations: a conflict that prevents the truth from being told. If a character — in one of Hitchcock's films or in *Pretty Little Liars* — revealed what he or she knew, it would incriminate either the character or a loved one, someone who is guilty of another, lesser crime. A character's inability to be completely honest neatly makes that character somewhat complicit in the villain's misdeed — think, for instance, of the girls letting Toby go to juvie instead of telling the police that it was Alison who threw the stink bomb and blinded Jenna. Through willful silence, the guilt is shared, blurring the distinction between bad guys and good. Perhaps most famously, Hitchcock had his "MacGuffins" — a term for the thing that everyone in the story wants, that's important to the characters but not to the audience, which drives the action. In *Pretty Little Liars*, things like memory keys, laptops, or NAT club videos function as MacGuffins. Instead of happy endings, Hitchcock preferred to leave an audience slightly off-kilter with "momentary optimism" in a story's resolution, like the four girls in "unmAsked" thinking that their battle with Mona is finally done, only to find death on their doorstep.

Other preoccupations in Hitchcock's films resurface in *Pretty Little Liars*, such as: falling and extreme heights, which *PLL* has used for climactic moments in both season finales; the use of point-of-view shots and framing devices that position the audience as voyeur, which *PLL* uses most frequently for A's perspective;

recurring visual symbols like keys or a ring, which, in Rosewood, translates to objects like the girls' friendship bracelets; doppelgangers or doubles; self-destructive characters; and the trope of unmasking a character's false face by the end of the story.

Even the criticism that Hitchcock sometimes received — notably that he would build up a tricky situation for a scare, for its effect on the audience, only to drop it at the expense of plot logic — could be leveled at *Pretty Little Liars*, which has been known to ditch a story line or reveal an unrealistic twist. But just as an audience member at the movies to see the new Hitchcock film had certain expectations, the *Pretty Little Liars* viewer at home has vicarious thrills and scares at the top of the must-list. *Pretty Little Liars* achieves what Hitch hoped for when he said, with his imitable black humor, "With the help of television, murder should be brought into the home where it rightly belongs."